The American POOR

The American POOR

Edited by **John A. Schiller**

AUGSBURG Publishing House • Minneapolis

THE AMERICAN POOR

Copyright © 1982 Augsburg Publishing House

Library of Congress Catalog Card No. 81-052271

International Standard Book No. 0-8066-1903-1

Scripture quotations unless otherwise noted are from the Revised Standard Version of the Bible, copyright 1946, 1952, and 1971 by the Division of Christian Education of the National Council of Churches.

MANUFACTURED IN THE UNITED STATES OF AMERICA

CONTENTS

CONTRIBUTORS

ARTURO BIBLARZ. Associate Professor of Sociology; Director, Off-Campus Graduate Programs. B.A., M.A., Ph.D. in Sociology, University of California, Los Angeles, 1955, 1960, 1968.

KATHARINE H. BRIAR. Associate Professor of Social Work. B.A. from Connecticut College for Women, 1966; Master's Degree in Social Work, Columbia University, 1968; D.S.W. in Social Work, University of California, Berkeley, 1976.

STANLEY L. BRUE. Associate Professor of Economics. B.A. in Economics, Augustana College, 1967; Ph.D. in Economics, University of Nebraska, 1971.

WALTER E. PILGRIM. Associate Professor of Religion and Director of Lutheran Institute of Theological Education. B.A. in Sociology, Wartburg College, 1956; B.D., Wartburg Theological Seminary, 1960; Th.M., Ph.D. in New Testament, Princeton Theological Seminary, 1966, 1971.

JOHN A. SCHILLER. Professor of Sociology and Social Work; Director of Graduate Programs, Division of Social Sciences. B.A. in History, Capital University, 1945; Cand. Theo., Evangelical Lutheran Theological Seminary, 1947; M.A. in Sociology, University of Missouri, Kansas City, 1959; Ph.D. in Sociology, University of Washington, 1967.

WALLACE H. SPENCER. Assistant Professor of Political Science. B.A. and M.A. in Political Science, University of Arizona, 1963, 1968; Ph.D. in Political Science, University of Washington, 1977.

ROBERT L. STIVERS. Associate Professor of Religion. B.A. in Economics, Yale University, 1962; M. Div., Union Theological Seminary, New York, 1969; Ph.D. in Religion and Society, Columbia University, 1973.

PREFACE

During the 1960s America became more aware of poverty at home and abroad. The "war on poverty" was short-lived however. The Vietnam War and internal dissension at home over the war quickly overshadowed the "war on poverty." Presently, inflation, energy shortages, and increased military spending have endangered efforts at reducing poverty and its consequences. Some would argue that Reagan's supply economics indicate a lack of concern for persons living in poverty. Some may wonder if our society has lost the will and vision to end poverty.

Concerns about poverty and efforts to alleviate it are not restricted to the United States. Every contemporary society is struggling for solutions. Various political-economic systems—capitalism, the welfare state, and socialism—are being tried. Feelings run high about the desirability and feasibility of these systems, or aspects of these systems, in seeking a solution to poverty.

Concerns about the seeming persistence of poverty prompt this multidisciplinary analysis of poverty. Inequities in the distribution of wealth and income grow out of complex economic, political, and social processes and structures. When seeking solutions to these inequities, we cannot ignore the ethical dimension. The structures a society creates for the distribution of resources and rewards emanate from a particular value system. Once created, those structures affect the values that influence the choices made in distributing resources and in creating policies and programs that regulate the distribution of resources and rewards.

Structures, policies, and programs that have developed in America affecting the incidence of poverty, as well as efforts to alleviate poverty, have been influenced by a multiplicity of forces. America's Jewish-Christian heritage, the western scientific and industrial revolution, and the conviction that growth and progress would solve problems have all contributed to America's perception of the causes of poverty and its solution. Though these perspectives had their origin in Europe and England, the United States has given each of these perspectives its own unique dimension. The United States developed its own brand of rugged individualism. Its frontier history influenced attitudes toward poverty. It has developed its own brand of Puritanistic ethic.

This book seeks to gain a better understanding of the causes of poverty, the consequences of poverty, the economic, political, and social structures that contribute to the creation and alleviation of poverty, and value questions that enlighten and direct solutions to poverty. Though scholars representing almost every discipline have addressed this issue, seldom have scholars from six different disciplines, simultaneously and cooperatively, directed their individual and disciplinary attention to an examination of poverty. That makes this book unique. The resources and perceptions of economics, ethics, political science, social work, sociology, and theology are brought together to examine the causes of poverty and to explore solutions.

This collective effort places the discussion of poverty into the context of tension between the analyses and solutions supported by the social sciences and the insights and implications provided by ethics and theology. For this no apologies are offered. Rather, it is the intentional effort of an independent church-related university, where all the writers are teaching, to foster that tension and dialog. In seeking solutions to poverty both in their own communities and through the policies and programs of their respective states and national government, citizens, policy planners, and elected officials cannot avoid that tension.

Chapter 1 draws a profile of poverty and examines changes in the distribution of income and wealth in the United States. From that data John Schiller draws conclusions about factors that contribute to the incidence, pattern, and persistence of poverty.

Katharine Briar examines the consequences of poverty in Chapters 2 and 3. Through vignettes of three persons you could well meet in your own community, the social dimensions of poverty are discussed. Assumptions about poverty, the persistence of poverty, and the consequences of unemployment are presented. Chapter 3 discusses the impacts of poverty upon family interaction and relationships of the family to other social structures of society. The author concludes that poverty has a deteriorating effect upon family functioning.

A crucial structure in understanding poverty is the economic system. In Chapter 4 Stanley Brue analyzes the forces that operate in our economic system and how they relate to poverty. Central to that analysis is the question of trade-offs that must be made in seeking a more just and equitable system. The author illustrates the complexity of the issue and the solutions related to poverty.

The problem becomes still more complex when looking at the political process. Chapter 5 describes the pluralistic and fragmented political structure and its relationship to economic policy and social programs. Wallace Spencer shows how social legislation passes through a tangled web of power groups and complex decision making. He concludes that the American democratic system inevitably results in a gradual process of change in seeking solutions to poverty.

Underpinning economic and political structures, programs, and policies is the American value system. How should that value system be evaluated and shaped? Chapters 6 and 7 provide a possible answer. Against the backdrop of Old Testament social ethics, Chapter 6 examines what the New Testament has to say about poverty and wealth. Using the Gospel tradition, the new community of the book of Acts, and the letters of Paul, Walter Pilgrim challenges American values and provides a vision from which to seek different solutions to poverty. The application of those values and that vision is addressed in Chapter 7. Using the data and analyses of the previous chapters, the paradox of vision and reality is considered. By raising questions of justice and equity, freedom and coercion, and by looking at values and the normative order, Robert Stivers concludes that America must devise means to narrow the gap between the rich and the poor, without resort to violent revolution, while retaining a reward system that maintains incentive.

In Chapter 8 Arturo Biblarz and John Schiller discuss political-economic programs in the People's Republic of China, the Union of Soviet Socialist Republics, Tanzania, Sweden, the United Kingdom, and the United States. These countries provide examples of economic and political systems that stretch from economic democracy to a free-market economy. This brief examination provides an opportunity to see the implications and the consequences of diverse structures, policies, and programs utilized in distributing the economic resources and rewards of a country. It also provides clarifications about capitalism, socialism, the welfare state, and communism in relationship to economic and political systems.

This study, like others on poverty, is always limited by recent and comparable data. Analytic data from the 1980 census of the United States has not yet become available to us. Countries like China and the Soviet Union have been very slow to gather or to share recent information about unemployment, poverty, or their class structures. Too often we had to rely on data that was 15 years old.

This book is offered as a resource that citizens may use to facilitate and enlighten the search for solutions to poverty. At the same time, the book is demanding enough to be used in freshman and sophomore college courses.

The contributors have written with the firm conviction that poverty is one of the most disturbing, destructive, and challenging problems facing American society and the world. It demands immediate and forthright attention.

As editor of this volume, I wish to express appreciation to my colleagues at Pacific Lutheran University for their collegial spirit, scholarly integrity, and commitment to the objectives of this effort. All of them were forthright in expressing their viewpoints. We thank Augsburg Publishing House for being willing to give us this opportunity. David Yagow deserves our heartfelt thanks for reading the manuscript and providing suggestions for clarity. Where we have failed to express ourselves clearly, the reader will have to fault the authors.

JOHN A. SCHILLER

1

Poverty, Income, and Wealth-Distribution Trends

John A. Schiller

This chapter provides information about the incidence of poverty and the distribution of both income and wealth. It concludes with a discussion of the challenges confronting the United States if a more equitable distribution of income is to be achieved and the incidence of poverty is to be reduced.

Any examination of the unequal distribution of economic reward should distinguish between the distribution of *income* and the distribution of *wealth*. *Income* refers to wages and salaries, and both the Census Bureau and the Department of Commerce have regularly gathered data regarding all segments of the population over a long period of time. *Wealth*, on the other hand, refers to economic assets. Data on the distribution of wealth are incomplete and have been gathered neither systematically over a period of time nor across all segments of society, although some information is available from the Federal Reserve System.

DEFINITION OF POVERTY

Economists usually define poverty in either *absolute* terms or *relative* terms.

The absolute definition specifies the dollar cost of the minimal goods and services essential to a family's welfare. In its least humanitarian form, such a definition prescribes what minimal caloric intake and what minimal form of shelter are required to sustain life and then estimates their cost in dollars. As a result, agencies and organizations differ in their establishment of the poverty level. For example, in 1973, for a family of four, the State of Mississippi set $600 as the level of poverty, the federal government set it at $4540, and the National Welfare Rights Organization established it at $7200.[1]

In contrast, a definition of poverty in *relative* terms calculates the poverty level at a certain percentage *below* the average income of the population. Definitions of poverty, therefore, vary according to the deviations from the average that are regarded as acceptable. Such definitions perpetuate poverty in a statistical sense and do not indicate anything at all about how well or how poorly people at the bottom of the income distribution actually live. Using relative terms, Victor Fuchs has argued that the poverty line should be set at 50% of median income.[2] For 1977 the median income in the U.S. was $16,009, and therefore, Fuchs would argue, the poverty line or poverty threshold would be $8004. In absolute terms the federal government established the poverty threshold at a little less than $7400 for 1979.

In 1963 the President's Council of Economic Advisors reviewed the Department of Agriculture's analysis of a basic food budget and stated that $2.73 per day was the amount necessary to buy food for a minimal caloric intake. They also observed that poor families spend about two times their food budget on other essentials. As a result, the poverty threshold for 1963 for a family of four was established at $2989.35 (3 × $2.73 × 365). The Social Security Administration under the leadership of Mollie Orshansky made adjustments to that figure, based on differences in family need resulting from family size or place of residence. Using the variables of family size, family location (farm/nonfarm), and family head (male/female), the Administration created 124 types of families and set different poverty levels for each family type. A nonfarm family consisting of a father, a mother, and two children was determined to need a minimum income of $3130 to reach the poverty threshold.

Since 1963, adjustments to the poverty line have been made by increasing the 1963 amount each year by the annual cost-of-living increase.

Increasing this absolute index of poverty by the annual rate of inflation results in a growing disparity between the status of the poor and the rest of the population. Furthermore, such an automatic increase in the poverty threshold each year tends to diminish critical examination of the real needs of those who are poor. The official index of poverty says that living up to that standard means no more than having a sanitary dwelling and sufficient food and clothing to keep one's body in working order.

The poverty level established by the federal government differs widely from what American citizens think a minimum income ought to be. In 1975 the Gallup Poll asked a cross section of Americans, "What is the smallest amount of money that a family of four needs each week to get along in the community in which you live?" Responses averaged $161 a week, or $8372 a year. That amount was almost twice as much as the poverty index for 1975 and over a thousand dollars more than the poverty index for the U.S. in 1979, which was just under $7400.[3]

It has been argued that the poverty line should be determined after adding governmental in-kind income transfers provided to lower income families, for example, food stamps. However, since all family incomes in the United States are affected indirectly by governmental taxing policies, all family incomes would have to be adjusted upward. But no one has ever attempted that when calculating the number of persons living in poverty. Some authors have called this indirect influence upon all family incomes through taxing policies "wealthfare payments." Surrey has calculated that wealthfare payments in 1972 ranged from an average yearly payment of $1500 to families with incomes under $3000 to wealthfare payments of $5896 to families with incomes between $50,000 and $100,000.[4] In this chapter, however, in-kind contributions have not been included in any income figures.

There are other nonstatistical approaches to a definition of poverty. One may talk about a way of life or define it in terms of spiritual and material deprivation. It may be described as a state of mind. Tolstoy said, "Poverty is not the lack of things; it is the fear and dread of want." Whatever definition one may wish to employ, when governmental policy or government program guidelines are established, it is persons in the upper income-levels who determine the definition of poverty. (In Chapter 5 reference is made to the issue of the poor speaking for themselves in creating change in poverty policies.)

STATISTICS ON POVERTY IN THE U.S.

Out of 213,867,000 individual Americans in 1977, 11.6% lived in poverty. Out of 57,215,000 families in the U.S., 9.3% lived in poverty. Among those families living in poverty, families in which the head of the household was a female predominated. Black families had the highest poverty rate. (See Table I.)

Table I reveals that since 1959 families with male household heads have been steadily declining, but families in which there is a female head have been increasing. Although there has been an increase in the number of households headed by females, the poverty rate for all families has been decreasing.

Table II narrows the data to the number of households. The first three columns of Table II indicate the number of families of various types living in poverty for each of three years: 1959, 1969, and 1977. The number of male-headed households living in poverty has been decreasing since 1959, while the number of poverty-level households headed by females and unrelated individuals has been increasing. But it is also true that the poverty rate for each group has actually decreased since 1959. (Poverty rates are computed by dividing the number of families in poverty in each category by the total number of families in that category.) It is evident that blacks have a higher rate of poverty than whites and that households headed by females or unrelated individuals have a higher rate than males. Households headed by black females have the highest rate of all. Examining the rows in the last three columns, one can see that the poverty rates for black females are declining less rapidly than those for any other family types of unrelated individuals. In fact, 71% of all black households living in poverty are headed by a female.

Daniel Patrick Moynihan notes an alarming trend about children, female-headed households and poverty. He notes that 7% of all children born in 1940 were likely to live in female-headed households receiving Aid to Families with Dependent Children, but in 1979 that had increased to 38 percent. He quotes the 1980 report to the president of the National Advisory Council on Economic Opportunity, which states: "All other things being equal, if the proportion of the poor who are female-headed families were to increase at the same rate as it did from 1967 to 1977, the poverty population would be composed solely of women and their children by the year 2000." [5]

Table I

**Persons Below Poverty Level, Persons Below 125 Percent of Poverty
Level, and Persons Living in Families Below Poverty Level
According to Various Characteristics for
1977, 1967, and 1959**

	Number in Thousands			*Poverty Rate*		
	1977	1967	1959	1977	1967	1959
A. *Persons Below Poverty Level*						
All Races	24,720	27,769	39,490	11.6	14.2	22.4
White	16,416	18,983	39,490	8.9	11.0	18.1
Black	7,726	8,486	N.A.	31.3	39.3	N.A.
Spanish	2,700	2,414°	N.A.	22.4	22.8°	N.A.
Persons 65 and over	3,177	5,388	5,481	14.1	29.5	35.2
All Families	5,311	5,667	8,320	9.3	11.4	18.5
Families—						
Male Head	2,701	3,893	6,404	5.5	8.7	15.8
Families—						
Female Head	2,690	1,774	1,916	31.7	33.3	42.6
B. *Persons Below 125 Percent of Poverty Level*						
All Races	35,659	39,206	54,942	16.7	20.0	27.7
White Persons	24,636	28,005	41,849	13.3	16.3	26.7
Black Persons	10,135	10,701	N.A.	41.0	49.5	N.A.
Spanish Persons	3,686	3,359°	N.A.	30.6	31.1°	N.A.
C. *Persons in Families Below Poverty Level*						
All Races—						
Male Head	10,300	15,873	27,548	6.2	9.6	18.2
All Races—						
Female Head	9,205	6,898	10,390	36.2	38.6	49.4
White—Male Head	7,890	11,398	20,211	5.3	7.7	15.2
White—Female Head	4,474	3,453	4,232	26.2	28.5	40.2
Black—Male Head	2,072	4,315	N.A.	15.3	29.7	N.A.
Black—Female Head	4,595	3,362	N.A.	55.3	61.6	N.A.
Spanish—						
Male Head	1,386	1,519°	N.A.	14.8	17.4°	N.A.
Spanish—						
Female Head	1,077	733°	N.A.	56.7	53.5°	N.A.

° 1972 date. Earlier information not provided.

Source: Current Population Reports. Consumer Income. Characteristics of the Population Below the Poverty Level: 1977. U.S. Department of Commerce, Bureau of the Census. Series P-60, No. 119, Issued March, 1979. Adapted from Tables 1, 2, 3, 5.

Table II

Number of Households Living in Poverty Where Females are Heads of Households with No Husband Present Compared to All Other Households for 1977, 1969, 1959

	In Thousands No. Below Poverty Level			Poverty Rate		
	1977	1969	1959	1977	1969	1959
Female-Headed Household						
All Races	2,610	1,827	1,916	31.7	32.7	42.6
White	1,400	1,069	1,233	24.0	25.7	34.8
Black	1,162	737	551	51.0	53.3	65.4
Male-Headed Household						
All Races	2,701	3,181	6,404	6.2	7.4	18.2
White	2,140	2,595	4,952	5.3	6.3	13.3
Black	475	629	1,309	13.5	17.9	43.3
Unrelated Individuals						
All Races						
Male	1,796	1,439	1,552	18.0	26.2	36.8
Female	3,419	3,532	3,376	26.1	38.7	52.1
White						
Male	1,305	1,083	1,158	15.7	24.1	33.8
Female	2,747	2,953	2,883	23.7	36.6	50.3
Black						
Male	423	308	325	28.8	36.5	46.4
Female	636	541	490	45.8	55.5	67.1

Source: Current Population Reports. Consumer Income. Characteristics of the Population Below the Poverty Level: 1977. U.S. Department of Commerce, Bureau of the Census. Series P-60, No. 119, Issued March, 1979. Adapted from Table 1.

In the judgment of some writers, the federal government's method of defining property is unrealistic. The number of people considered to be living in poverty changes if one uses a base that is 125% of the poverty threshold, a figure regarded by many government and nongovernment specialists as more realistic. This point is illustrated in Table I, Section B. By this calculation, in 1977 the United States had 35,659,000 people living in poverty instead of 24,720,000, and the poverty rate was 16.7% instead of 11.6%. At that threshold 41% of all black people were considered to be living in poverty.

Levels of educational attainment are also related to poverty. Table III shows that as education increases, mean income also increases. At least one of the contributing factors is that education is related to full-time employment, which assures a greater income. However it is also evident that persons with less education working full-time often have incomes that leave them in poverty. The data also reveal, however, that there is almost a $10,000 difference between the mean income of males and females and that females suffer the most from partial employment.

Table IV sheds further light on the relationship of poverty to education. As education increases, poverty decreases. However, rates of poverty are greater for blacks than for whites at all educational levels and are most severe for black women. Even though black women have attained a college education, they still experience a 13.6% poverty rate.

On the basis of Tables III and IV, which show that the mean income for men is twice as great as it is for women, that women have a higher poverty rate than males, and that blacks suffer a higher poverty rate than whites at all educational levels, one can conclude differential wage scales, discriminatory employment practices, and unequal educational opportunities affect poverty. The educational system has not been as successful in helping women and racial minorities to achieve rewards comparable to that of white males in the job market. Furthermore, the poverty status of minority nonwhites has been influenced by discriminatory practices and unequal opportunities in education and employment.

Table III

Education as Related to Mean Income and Full-Time Employment of Head of Household, 1977

Education		Mean Years Completed	Mean Income	Head of Household Working Full-Time
Total		11.7	$18,791	61.0
Elementary:	Less than 8 yrs.	4.9	10,856	31.7
	8 years	8.0	13,082	36.6
High School:	1 to 3 years	10.0	14,683	50.1
	4 years	12.0	18,401	67.0
College:	1 to 3 years	13.8	20,844	71.5
	4 years or more	16.8	28,562	79.3
Male Head		11.9	19,686	65.0
Female Head		10.8	9,811	33.1

Source: Current Population Reports. Consumer Income. Money Income in 1977 of Families and Persons in the United States. U.S. Department of Commerce. Bureau of the Census. Series P-60, No. 118. Issued March, 1979. Adapted from Table 2.

Table IV

**Educational Attainment: Persons 14 Years Old and Over
by Poverty Status in 1977 by Sex and Race**

		All	*Percent White*	*Black*
Both Sexes				
Years of School Completed		27.1	23.0	39.1
Elementary:	1 to 5 years	29.6	25.6	41.2
	6 to 7 years	22.0	18.8	38.2
	8 years	15.6	12.9	36.9
High School:	1 to 3 years	13.7	10.1	33.6
	4 years	6.7	5.6	18.3
College:	1 year or more	4.6	4.1	10.9
Male				
Years of School Completed		23.6	20.4	29.9
Elementary:	1 to 5 years	24.0	21.7	30.6
	6 to 7 years	17.9	15.4	30.6
	8 years	12.1	10.0	28.9
High School:	1 to 3 years	10.8	8.0	26.7
	4 years	5.0	4.2	11.8
College:	1 year or more	3.9	3.5	7.7
Female				
Years of School Completed		30.7	25.3	56.2
Elementary:	1 to 5 years	35.2	29.6	52.8
	6 to 7 years	26.2	22.3	45.7
	8 years	18.8	15.7	43.1
High School:	1 to 3 years	16.4	12.0	38.9
	4 years	8.0	6.6	23.2
College:	1 year or more	5.5	4.7	13.6

Source: Current Population Reports. Consumer Income. Characteristics of the Population Below the Poverty Level: 1977. U.S. Department of Commerce, Bureau of the Census. Series P-60, No. 119, Issued March, 1979. Adapted from Table 3.2.

A factor closely related to educational opportunities and employment opportunities is the geographical distribution of families living in poverty. Poor people are not distributed equally throughout the United States. Although the percentage of the population of the

United States living in the South has not changed much since 1959, and although the percentage of the population living in poverty in the South has declined since 1959, the South still has more than its share of poverty. Although only 32% of U.S. citizens live in the South, 41% of the poverty-level population lives in the South. Even though the poverty rate in the South dropped from 26.8% in 1959 to 14.8% in 1977, the South still has the highest poverty rate of any region of the United States. However, the poverty rate has not dropped very much for the North and the West since 1959 either. In fact, the percentage of the poverty-level population that lives in the North and West has increased from 51% to 59%.

This increase in poverty in the North and the West is related to the development of metropolitan areas. The proportion of U.S. population in metropolitan areas has increased since 1959, but the proportion living in central cities has declined from 32% to 28%. Poverty in metropolitan areas has increased by 16% since 1959. A comparison of the statistics for the central part of the city with those of the population living outside central cities indicates that more of the poverty-stricken population resides *in* central cities. Living in the central city creates several problems for poor people. They do not have the opportunity to supplement their meager income with gardens. They are more vulnerable to fluctuations in the job market, in terms of both numbers of jobs and skills required for jobs. They find it hard to get to work sites since more and more industries and warehouses have moved outside of the central city. Transportation to work places outside of the central city is inadequate. And educational opportunities within central city schools are not as numerous. Location of residence, therefore, has a negative influence on income and job opportunities, either producing poverty or making it more difficult to climb out of poverty.

Tables V, VI, VII, and VIII provide further information about the relationship between work and poverty. Table V suggests that the proportion of poor-family householders who work has decreased from 1959 to 1977. This holds true for households headed by either males or females. The table also implies that females find it more difficult both to work and to carry out parental obligations. The decline in the proportion of poor-family households who work is the result of two factors. There has been some increase in wages for less skilled work since 1959, as a result of which some one-parent families have moved out of poverty. But the unemployment picture is also affected by a reduction in the number of less skilled jobs, which has a direct negative effect on employment opportunities for those who have not finished high school.

How many people who live in poverty are in fact working? Table VI shows that 48.6% of family householders below the poverty level worked year-round or at least part of the year. Another 43.8% did not work because they had parental obligations at home which prevented them from working, or because they were ill or disabled, or retired. Furthermore, 15.2% experienced poverty because they could not find work, although 11.3% of those were able to work on a part-time basis.

Table V

Proportion of Poor-Family Householders Who Worked by Sex of Householder: 1959, 1969 and 1977

	1959 Percent	1969 Percent	1977 Percent
Female Householders	43	43	36
All Other Householders	77	62	61

Source: Current Population Reports. Consumer Income. Characteristics of the Population Below the Poverty Level: 1977. U.S. Department of Commerce, Bureau of the Census. Series P-60, No. 119, Issued March, 1979. Adapted from Figure 4.

Table VI

Work Experience and Reasons for Not Working of Civilian Family Householders Below the Poverty Level in 1977 in Thousands

	Number in Thousands	Percent
Worked Year Round	1,068	20.2
Full-Time	912	17.2
Part-Time	156	3.0
Worked Part of Year	1,500	28.4
Unable to Find Work	599	11.3
Keeping House	428	8.1
Ill or Disabled	202	3.9
Other	271	5.1
Did Not Work	2,722	51.5
Keeping House	1,149	21.7
Ill or Disabled	759	14.4
Retired	409	7.7
Unable to Find Work	207	3.9
Going to School	114	2.2
Other	84	1.6

Source: Current Population Reports. Consumer Income. Characteristics of the Population Below the Poverty Level: 1977. U.S. Department of Commerce, Bureau of the Census. Series P-60, No. 119, Issued March, 1979. Adapted from Figure 5.

Often people who are unemployed, on welfare, or living in poverty are labeled as lazy. It is said that anybody who wants to work can find a job or that those on welfare could work if they wanted. Available data appears to refute such claims, however. The one category of people in Table VI which might include those who just do not care to work is the category titled *Other*, which represents 355,000 households (271,000 + 84,000). That constitutes 6.7% of the families in poverty, .6% of all families in the United States, and .5% of all people in the United States.° Since it is inconceivable that all people who fall into the category of *Other* are too lazy to work, it would appear that many Americans have developed a false perception of people living in poverty and of what causes their poverty.

Table VII indicates a significant pattern of change for female householders. Since 1959 the number of female-headed households which live in poverty has steadily increased. In contrast, during the same period the poverty rate for all other households has decreased. Poverty-level households headed by females have doubled since 1959. Clearly, women suffer the most from financial hardships in American society, whether they work or not.

Various arguments have been advanced to account for people living in poverty. Some argue, out of a Protestant work-ethic value system, that a flawed character accounts for persons living in poverty. Others argue that environmental forces beyond the control of the individual result in restricted opportunities, and thus persons fall into poverty. Data in this paper sheds some light on the validity of such arguments.

° Percentages were derived as illustrated in the following formulas: 355,000 households in the category "Other" divided by 5,290,000 poverty households in the U.S. equals 6.7% (.067); 355,000 households divided by 57,215,000 families in the U.S. equals .6 of 1% (.006); 1,065,000 persons in poverty families in the category "Other" divided by 213,867,000 people in the U.S. in 1977 equals .5 of 1% (.005).

Table VII

Work Experience of Civilian Family Householders by Poverty Status: 1959, 1969 and 1977

Work Experience	Percent Distribution		
	1977	*1969*	*1959*
Below Poverty Level			
Total	100.0	100.0	100.0
Female Householder	49.3	36.9	23.5
All Other Householders	50.6	63.1	76.5
Worked	58.5	54.8	68.9
Female Householder	17.7	15.7	10.1
All Other Householders	30.8	39.1	58.8
Full-Time	17.2	21.6	32.1
50 to 52 Weeks	20.2	26.2	37.3
Less Than 50 Weeks	28.4	28.6	31.6
Did Not Work	51.5	45.2	31.1
Female Householder	31.6	21.2	13.4
All Other Householders	19.8	24.0	17.7

Source: Current Population Reports. Consumer Income. Characteristics of the Population Below the Poverty Level: 1977. U.S. Department of Commerce, Bureau of the Census. Series P-60, No. 119, Issued March, 1979. Adapted from Table E.

FACTORS AFFECTING THE INCIDENCE OF POVERTY

In an issue so complex as poverty it may be misleading to talk about its *causes*. Many factors affect poverty. Until the effect of each factor or variable can be measured precisely, it may be presumptuous to talk about causes. Nonetheless, several factors influence the incidence of poverty.

Discrimination is one factor that influences poverty. Black males have a greater poverty and unemployment rate than white males. Black females have a greater poverty rate and unemployment rate than white females. Black youth under 20 have a 35% unemployment rate in comparison to a 16% unemployment rate for white youth. As long as blacks are not given an equal chance to succeed in the employment market or as long as they suffer discrimination, they will continue to live in poverty in greater numbers, either because they receive low wages when employed or because they are at the bottom of the ladder of employment or because they are victims of preferential employment practices which leave them unemployed or underemployed.

Another factor contributing to poverty is a deficiency in the skills and abilities gained through education. There is a direct relationship between education and employment, and the amount of one's income is directly related to education. The dropout rate for minorities and low-income people during high school is quite high. In some parts of the U.S., especially in central cities, it runs as high as 35 to 40%. As a result, a portion of each new generation of adults is destined for unemployment and poverty. The educational system is affected by the value placed on high-school curricula and the economic resources expended for them. Noncollege-preparatory courses and programs are perceived to be for second-class citizens and hence receive second-class status when budgets are constructed. As a result, high schools do not provide sufficient skills that are directly applicable to job seeking, employment, and human problem solving.

Crises in life arising from illness, layoffs, divorce, or accident leave families in poverty because they lose their source of income and because societal support systems do not provide enough resources to keep them out of poverty or to get their members back into the labor market. It is interesting to note that most people who lose their jobs find another one through sources other than those provided by social structures created to help people locate jobs. And it is also significant that the longer one is unemployed or on welfare, the less likely it is that he or she will ever get a job or move off the welfare roles. Rein and Rainwater's research indicates that after people have been on welfare for one year, there is a 57% probability they will be on welfare a second year; after a second year on welfare, there is a 70% probability they will be on welfare a third year; after a third year on welfare, there is a 75% probability they will stay on welfare. After a fourth year the probability reaches 80% and remains there.[6]

Most people in American society want to work and do in fact work if they are able and can find a job. In 1977 90% of all family heads aged 25 to 60 participated in the labor force. Only about .5% of the population is in poverty because they lack the desire to work.

Many people over 65 live in poverty because their retirement benefits are not adequate. People who have lived in poverty all their lives naturally will live in poverty in old age. People who work but do not earn enough to stay above the poverty level retire into poverty. Benefits provided by society for retired people guarantee a poverty-level existence. In fact, research shows that illness and malnutrition among older people is directly related to inadequate financial resources.

Unemployment

Certainly one of the major causes of poverty is unemployment. There are four types of unemployment: frictional, seasonal, aggregate, and structural. Frictional unemployment occurs when people move from one job to another within a short interval of time. Reentry into the labor market is high for such people. More than 50% of them reenter the labor market when unemployed for less than five weeks. Among the frictionally unemployed there is a 400% turnover rate within a year's time.

Seasonal unemployment also contributes to poverty. Poverty increases in direct proportion to the number of weeks a person does not work. Because of the structure of the American economic system, there is a demand for seasonal employment, which in turn results in seasonal *un*employment. Until a better way of managing the economy is developed, seasonal demands for labor as well as seasonal unemployment will continue to contribute its share of people living in poverty. (See Table VII for the effects of seasonal unemployment on poverty.)

Aggregate or cyclical unemployment results when there is less demand for labor in the economy than there is labor available. In such a situation, discrimination becomes operative and causes its greatest hurt when the demand for labor decreases. For example, in 1969 the unemployment rate was under 4%, and in 1977 it was nearly twice that high. The unemployment rate for minorities, especially youth ages 18 to 24, almost quadruples in comparison to the rest of society. What kept the rate lower was the fact that the employing sector reached further down the ladder of the least skilled and the minorities when hiring.

Table VIII

Poverty Rate for Families Below the Poverty Level According to Work Experience and Occupation of Head of Household: 1977

	Poverty Rate
Work Experience of Head	
Head Worked	5.6
Worked 50 to 52 Weeks	3.0

Worked Full Time	**2.7**
Worked 1 to 49 Weeks	14.8
Worked 27 to 49 Weeks	8.0
Worked 1 to 26 Weeks	26.9
Head Did Not Work	24.8

Occupation of Longest Job of Head

Professional and Managerial Workers	2.2
Clerical and Sales Workers	4.8
Craft and Kindred Workers	3.5
Operatives, incl. Transport Workers	6.0
Service Workers, incl. Pvt. Household	14.1
Laborers, Except Farm	9.1
Farmers and Farm Laborers	23.8

Source: Current Population Reports. Consumer Income. Characteristics of the Population Below the Poverty Level: 1977. U.S. Department of Commerce, Bureau of the Census. Series P-60, No. 119, Issued March 1979. Adapted from Table 5.

Unemployment also affects the more skilled and professional populations. This occurs because of structural aspects of unemployment and poverty. Certain occupations and certain parts of the country are affected at different times in the nation's economic history. Table VIII shows that poverty moves across the total occupational ladder. Previous analysis of regional differences in poverty and the increased concentration of poverty in central cities provide additional support for the contention that structural unemployment contributes to poverty. When industries are relocated or when plants and railroad centers are closed, individuals and families are left without adequate opportunities for reemployment. Sometimes career changes are required for which people are not prepared or for which they find it impossible to learn the requisite skills and competencies.

Inadequate Wages

A second major factor influencing poverty is the amount of wages paid to people working at unskilled or semiskilled jobs. This is compounded by the discriminatory practice of paying women a lesser wage than men. Fundamental to this issue, however, is the larger issue of income distribution in the United States. The Lorenz Curve, developed by an economist, helps us to examine income distribution. It plots the cumulative percent of units on one axis (the abscissa) against the cumulative percent of aggregate income on the other axis (the ordinate) as accounted for by those units. (See Figure 1.) Aggregate income is obtained by multiplying the frequency in each income class interval by an assumed mean for that income class interval.

If income were distributed so that every 10% of the population received 10% of the income, a straight regression line would occur. As inequality in the distribution of income becomes greater, so also the area between the diagonal (regression) line and the actual Lorenz curve becomes greater. Figure 1 illustrates that income distribution in the United States was quite constant from 1910 to 1964.

The Index of Income Concentration for families in the U.S. from 1949 to 1977 was between .39 and .41. If the Index of Income Concentration were 0.00, the Lorenz Curve would be a straight line represented by the Line of Absolute Equality shown in Figure 1.

Figure 1

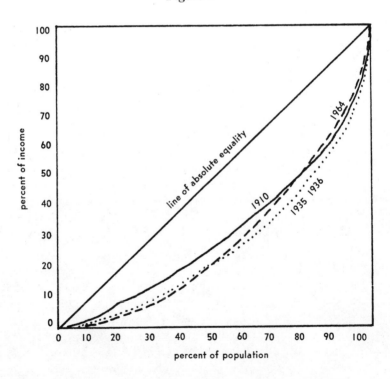

Source: Lorenz Curves of Income Distribution, 1910, 1935-1936, 1964 from *A Primer on the Economics of Poverty* by David Hamilton. New York: Random House, 1968, page 20.[7]

In other words, if each 10% of the population received an equal proportion of the income produced, a straight diagonal line would emerge. But an unequal distribution pattern has remained quite constant since 1947. In fact, the pattern since 1910 has remained quite constant. Table IX illustrates this in another way by listing the percentage distribution of aggregate income in the United States for each fifth of the population and for the top 5% of the earning units in the United States. No real changes in income distribution have occurred. The bottom 20% of American families still receive 5% of the earned income in the U.S., and the top 20% of American families receive 42% of the earned income.

Table IX

Income at Selected Positions and Percentage Share of Aggregate Income in 1949 to 1977 Received by Each Fifth and Top 5 Percent of Families

Percent Distribution of Aggregate Income

Year	Lowest Fifth	Second Fifth	Middle Fifth	Fourth Fifth	Highest Fifth	Top 5 Percent	Mean Income Cols.
1977	5.2	11.6	17.5	24.2	41.5	15.7	18,264
1972	5.4	11.9	17.5	23.9	41.4	15.9	12,625
1967	5.5	12.4	17.9	23.9	40.4	15.2	8,801
1962	5.0	12.1	17.6	24.0	41.3	15.7	6,670
1957	5.1	12.7	18.1	23.8	40.4	15.6	5,443
1952	4.9	12.3	17.4	23.4	41.9	17.4	4,457
1947	5.0	11.9	17.0	23.1	43.1	17.5	3,546

Source: Current Population Reports. Consumer Income. Money Income in 1977 of Families and Persons in the United States. U.S. Department of Commerce. Bureau of the Census. Series P-60, No. 118, Issued March, 1979. Adapted from Table 13.

Another way to examine the income distribution of families in America is to calculate the ratio of the mean income of each fifth of families to the mean income of all families. In 1947 the ratio of the mean income of the lowest fifth of families to the mean income of all families was .25, and the ratio of the mean income of the top 5% of families to the mean income of all families was 3.50. By 1971 the ratio for the lowest fifth of families was .28, and the ratio of the top 5% was 3.24.[8] It is clear that lower income families have not received a larger share of the nation's aggregate income.

Table X summarizes information provided by the Census Bureau about changes in income distribution from 1950 to 1977 in current dollars and constant dollars. The upper half of the table uses current dollar income figures. Adjustments for inflation can be made by referring to the bottom half of the table, which provides a more realistic assessment of actual purchasing power over the years.

Table X

Total Money Income for Families in 1950, 1955, 1960, 1965, 1970, 1975, 1977 in Current Dollars and in Constant Dollars

Current Dollars	1950	1955	1960	1965	1970	1975	1977
Under $1000	11.5	7.7	5.0	2.9	1.6	2.2	2.0
$1000 to $1999	13.2	9.8	8.0	6.0	3.0		
$2000 to $2999	17.8	11.0	8.7	7.2	4.3	2.4	1.6
$3000 to $3999	20.7	14.5	9.8	7.7	5.0	3.4	2.7
$4000 to $4999	13.6	15.5	10.5	7.9	5.3	4.1	3.1
$5000 to $5999	9.0	12.7	12.9	9.3	5.8	4.1	3.5
$6000 to $6999	5.2	9.5	10.8	9.5	6.0	4.2	3.7
$7000 to $7999	2.9	6.6	8.7	9.7	6.3	4.3	3.7
$8000 to $9999	2.9	6.3	11.3	14.6	13.6	8.6	7.2
$10,000 to $14,999		4.8	10.6	17.7	26.8	22.3	18.4
$15,000 to $24,999	3.2	0.9	2.8	6.2	17.7	30.3	31.7
$25,000 and over		0.5	0.9	1.4	4.6	14.1	22.4
Constant Dollars							
Under $3000	14.3	11.2	8.6	6.1	4.3	3.9	3.6
$3000 to $4999	10.3	8.9	8.5	7.1	5.7	6.0	5.7
$5000 to $6999	14.4	10.1	8.8	7.9	6.7	7.2	7.2
$7000 to $9999	23.8	20.0	15.0	12.7	11.0	11.5	10.9
$10,000 to $11,999		15.3	14.8	9.8	7.9	7.7	7.2
$12,000 to $14,999		12.5	13.2	15.0	13.0	12.1	11.3
$15,000 to $24,999	37.3	17.8	23.6	29.6	33.3	32.2	31.7
$25,000 and over		4.3	7.4	11.8	18.2	19.4	22.4

Source: Current Population Reports. Consumer Income. Money Income in 1977 of Families and Persons in the United States. U.S. Department of Commerce. Bureau of the Census. Series P-60, No. 118, Issued March, 1979. Adapted from Table 3.

In 1950 42.5% of all American families received under $3000 income (in current dollars). By 1977 that number had dropped to 3.6%. The greatest drop occurred from 1950 to 1955, but since then the drop has been much slower. When the figures for actual buying power during those years are used, the change is much less. In constant dollars, 14.3% of all families in 1950 had incomes under $3000, and that percentage dropped to 3.6% in 1977.

Therefore, it is possible to conclude that American family incomes have improved somewhat over the past thirty years. Some families have moved out of poverty. However, most of the upward movement in incomes occurred before 1960. Since 1960 there has been little movement in terms of constant dollars, except for families whose incomes are above $25,000.

One other factor must be added to any discussion about income distribution when one considers economic well-being: What effect do taxes have on income? Income taxes tend to affect most people in the same manner. But certain taxes are considered regressive because they affect some income groups more severely than others, for example, sales taxes. Sales taxes take a larger percentage of the income of families who have lower incomes. This is particularly true of families living in poverty or just above the poverty threshold.

Table XI provides additional information about families whose income places them into poverty. Even some families whose head worked full-time in 1977 had median incomes well below the poverty threshold. Those who were working full-time but were still considered below the poverty level had a median income of $4104. That means that half of those working full-time had an income below $4104.

Table XI

Median Total Money Income of Families: Families Below Poverty Level in 1977 by Presence of Related Children Under 18 Years Old by Race and Spanish Origin of Head

	All Races	White	Black	Spanish Origin*
All Families	$3401	$3364	$3480	$4116
Head Worked Year-Round and Full-Time	$4104	$3491	$5591	$5777
Families Without Related Children Under 18	$2956	$2908	$3072	N.A.
Families with 1 or More Children Under 18	3762	$3786	$3741	$4404
Head 60 to 64 Years Old	$3010	$2882	$3160	N.A.
Head 65 Years Old and Over	$3108	$3075	$3238	N.A.

*Spanish Origin May Be of Any Race

Source: Current Population Reports. Consumer Income. Characteristics of the Population Below the Poverty Level: 1977. U.S. Department of Commerce. Bureau of the Census. Series P-60, No. 119, Issued March, 1979. Adapted from Table 34.

In 1979 the poverty threshold was approximately $7000. The minimum wage for 1979 was $2.80 an hour, as set by the federal government. A person working 40 hours a week for 52 weeks a year would earn a maximum of $5824. To get above the poverty level a person had to earn over $3.36 an hour in 1979. In part, inequitable distribution of income and inadequate wages arise from the value that society attaches to products produced or tasks performed, thus reflecting collective social decisions.

An example from the past illustrates this point. During the 1940s wage rates and incomes at the bottom of the occupational ladder rose faster than those at the top of the occupational ladder because of an upsurge in demand for unskilled and semiskilled laborers to produce war material. The structure of demand since the 1940s, however, has benefited primarily workers with higher education and more technical expertise.

In 1977 the Federal Government sponsored 182 different programs of income transfer to help correct the unequal distribution of income in the U.S. Through those programs $250 billion dollars, or 69 cents out of every tax dollar, were distributed to American citizens. And yet the index of income distribution for families in the U.S. was not altered from what it had been in 1910. One could conclude, therefore, that the private enterprise system and governmental programs of income transfer have not been very effective in altering poverty rates or patterns of income distribution.

THE DISTRIBUTION OF WEALTH

Since colonial days America has had a concentration of wealth in the hands of a small percentage of its families. Earliest records show that in cities like Baltimore, Boston, Brooklyn, and New Orleans over half of the wealth was held by 8-10% of the population. Such an unequal distribution of capital resources was perhaps inevitable, especially since wealthy families from England were the recipients of colonial grants.[9]

Although many poor people gradually attained a small parcel of land or a job through indenture to the favored upper class, political power was often intimately connected with wealth in the United States. Diverse advantages have accrued to that segment of American society fortunate enough to inherit wealth or to accumulate great economic resources.

An analysis by the Federal Reserve System in 1966 indicated that the wealth of Americans at the lower end of the pyramid consisted of owning an automobile and that the wealth of the next group, the middle classes, consisted of owning a car and a house and of having a little money in the bank. Those considered to be wealthy had the major portion of their assets in professional and business investments.

Using a variety of sources, Turner and Starnes provided a historical pattern of the percentage of wealth held by 1% of American society from 1810 to 1969.[10] Over a century and a half, that segment of society held from 21% of the wealth in 1810 to 24.9% in 1969. Such a pattern of concentration of wealth further supports the conclusion that economic resources have not been redistributed more equitably.

The distribution of wealth is an important factor in accounting for the constant pattern of the index of economic concentration.[11] Wealth is closely related to the exercise of political and economic power. (See Figure 2.) Political power assures the enactment of legislation and economic policy favorable to the increase of wealth and to its retention. Tax laws and inheritance laws are primary examples. Economic resources provide significant advantages in the arenas of education and business. It should also be noted, however, that economic growth in a capitalistic system is dependent on the accumulation of wealth to promote the structures that create increased economic opporunity for everyone. Succeeding chapters will address the issue of how much unequal distribution of wealth and income is necessary or appropriate.

Although the unequal distribution of wealth and the unequal distribution of income are related and although increased wealth helps to assure a greater income, one ought to ask whether a more equitable distribution of *wealth* would automatically produce a greater distribution of *income*. Alan S. Blinder has noted that income and wealth are affected by the total life cycle.[12] Examination of just one point in a person's economic history is not adequate. Therefore, Blinder has analyzed the effect over the life cycle that various factors (wealth, wages, the tax system, sex, and race, among others) have upon income inequality. Different wage rates contribute almost 40% of the inequality of lifetime income; life-cycle factors contribute almost 30%; unequal distributions of inherited wealth account for only 2%.

Since the relationship between economic power and political influence is strong, it seems logical to argue that the segment of society which holds the greatest wealth has an opportunity to influence economic policy, social policy, and legislation which could effect a more equitable distribution of income through wages and salaries.

Figure 2

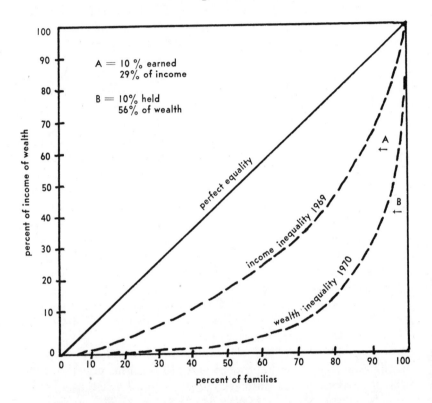

Source: Jonathan H. Turner & Charles E. Starnes. Inequality: Privilege & Poverty in America. Pacific Palisades, California, Goodyear Publishing Company, Inc., 1976, page 54.

THE CHALLENGE

In his perceptive book, *The Cultural Contradictions of Capitalism*, Daniel Bell has observed that the challenge of society today is to develop a comprehensive theory of the public household. He notes that in feudal times the domestic household was concerned more with human beings than property and more interested in conditions under which people were living than in the condition of their property.[13]

As industrial society emerged, a market economy was created in which the value of goods and services was measured by the relative prices registered in the exchange of money. This process was bolstered by the development of individual rights and freedom. And as Max Weber observed in *The Protestant Ethic and Spirit of Capitalism,* Protestant ideology, as epitomized in the preaching of Cotton Mather, provided the spark for industrial capitalism.[14] But Bell correctly notes that as wants replaced needs in bourgeois society, capitalism was motivated by individualistic hedonism. Bourgeois society was characterized by class power, and only one class, the wealthy upper class, held the power. Gradually, however, as other groups gained greater economic and political power, hedonism expressed itself in group conflict. Rights and entitlements became the center of the struggle among groups in a pluralistic society who sought their advantage in the economic system.

Bell argues that the challenge today is to develop a theory of public household in which the government manages distribution of justice based on the centrality of the concept of the public household. American society has a long way to go in seeking such a theory of government management within the concept of public household.

In his book *The Broken Covenant,* Robert Bellah maintains that the founding fathers fashioned the new America on the foundation of two basic principles: individual freedom and covenant community.[15] Covenant community manifests itself when every individual is responsible for and to every other individual. Such a community exists when people covenant together for the common good. Bellah argues that today's accent on individual rights has led to the loss of the notion of a covenant community. Bell argues that the present 20th-century public household is not a community but an arena—an arena in which the individualistic hedonism of the 19th century has become the hedonism of group interest and struggles.

Succeeding chapters will develop other perspectives—economic, political, social, theological—on the subject of poverty. We hope they will enable the reader to come to terms with poverty and ultimately to become actively involved in resolving the problems of those who suffer it.

NOTES

1. Schiller, Bradley R. *The Economics of Poverty and Discrimination,* Second Edition. New Jersey: Prentice Hall, Inc., 1976, Chapter 1.
2. Schiller, Bradley R. *The Economics of Poverty and Discrimination,* Third Edition. New Jersey: Prentice Hall, Inc., 1980, Chapter 1.
3. *Ibid.*
4. Turner, Jonathan H., and Charles E. Starnes. *Inequality: Privilege and Poverty in America.* Pacific Palisades: Goodyear Publishing Company, Inc., 1976, Chapter 6.
5. Moynihan, Daniel Patrick. "Children and Welfare Reform" in *The Journal of The Institute for Socioeconomic Studies.* Vol. VI, No. 1, Spring, 1981, pp. 8-10.
6. Rein, Martin, and Lee Rainwater. *Patterns of Welfare Use.* Working Paper No. 47. Joint Center for Urban Studies of MIT and Harvard University. November, 1977.
7. Hamilton, David. *A Primer on the Economics of Poverty.* New York: Random House, 1968, page 20.
8. U.S. Bureau of Census, *Social Indicators,* 1973. Washington, D.C.: Government Printing Office, 1973, p. 179.
9. Turner, Jonathan H., and Charles E. Starnes, pp. 12-14.
10. *Ibid.,* Chapter 2.
11. *Ibid.,* p. 54.
12. Blinder, Alan S. *Toward an Economic Theory of Income Distribution.* Cambridge: MIT Press, 1974. Chapter 4.
13. Bell, Daniel. *The Cultural Contradictions of Capitalism.* New York: Basic Books, Inc., 1976. Bell also notes that the Greek word *oikos* (household) is the root word for "economics."
14. Weber, Max. *The Protestant Ethic and the Spirit of Capitalism.* New York: Charles Scribner's Sons, 1958.
15. Bellah, Robert Neelly. *The Broken Covenant: American Civil Religion in a Time of Trial.* New York: Seabury Press, 1975.

SUGGESTED READINGS

Galbraith, John Kenneth. *The Nature of Mass Poverty.* Cambridge: Harvard University Press. 1979. A reputable American economist provides a reasoned examination, in readable fashion, of the cause of mass poverty. His book grows out of experiences in trying to solve poverty in India and careful reflection upon those efforts.

Lampman, Robert J. *Ends and Means of Reducing Income Poverty.* Chicago: Markham Publishing Company, 1971. Provides an analysis of the strategies used in the U.S. to overcome poverty. It places solutions to poverty within larger social, economic, and political questions.

Lawrence, William J. and Stephen Leeds. *An Inventory of Federal Income Transfer Programs.* White Plains, New York: The Institute for Socioeconomic Studies, 1978. A good source that describes the 182 federal income transfor programs of the U.S. It includes the dollars involved and major services provided in each of those programs.

Lawrence, William J., and Stephen Leeds. *An Inventory of State and Local Income Transfer Programs, Fiscal Year 1977.* White Plains, New York: The Institute for Socioeconomic Studies, 1980. The authors identify and describe 633 income transfer programs operating at state and local levels of government; includes a detailed analysis of those programs in 25 states; and provides an appreciation for the large number and diversity of state and local income transfer programs.

Rodgers, Harrel R. Jr. *Poverty and Plenty: A Political and Economic Analysis.* Reading, Massachusetts: Addison-Wesley Publishing Company, 1979. While providing data on poverty, the book also presents four interesting chapters on programs employed by the federal government to lessen poverty.

Tevoedjre, Albert. *Poverty: Wealth of Mankind.* New York: Pergamon Press, 1978. This book causes one to rethink the definition of poverty. The author, a nonwesterner and director of the International Institute for Labour Studies at the Hague, looks at economic growth, wealth, and poverty in a refreshing light. The book provides insight into the role of values in choosing possible solutions to poverty.

Turner, Jonathan H., and Charles E. Starnes, eds. *Inequality: Privilege and Poverty in America.* Pacific Palisades, California: Goodyear Publishing Company, Inc., 1976. This is an excellent and concise analysis of the distribution of income and wealth in the U.S. It includes two chapters that discuss the relationship of "wealthfare" and welfare to inequality.

Waxman, Chaim I. *The Stigma of Poverty: A Critique of Poverty Theories and Policies.* New York: Pergamon Press, 1977. Waxman looks at several theories that attempt to explain why poverty exists. Then he includes some modest social policy recommendations to help address poverty.

STUDY QUESTIONS

1. Examine the data on the relationship of poverty to race, sex, full-time employment and part-time employment. Using that information, develop a plan of action that will help eliminate some of the poverty in America.

2. Assume you live in a metropolitan area of the United States with a population of 750,000 people. Among its basic industries are wood products, wearing apparel, recreational vehicles, airplanes, automobiles, and food products. Because of severe shortages of oil, one-half of the people employed in plants producing recreational vehicles, airplanes, and automobiles have been laid off with no hope of being rehired for the next several years. What kinds of action could be taken to help the unemployment situation and support the growing number of families and individuals who would be entering poverty?

3. If one assumes that education should enhance success in the world of work, what can be done to improve the educational experience, including the nature of the curriculum, to better prepare students and to reduce the dropout rate? As you develop your answer, consider what the educational process was like when the family was the primary source of education and had to provide both basic education and vocational education. Are there aspects of that educational process that may give us some clues about the way curriculum is developed and the educational process is implemented today? Go to your local school district and find out what kinds of educational programs exist to prevent student dropout and to prepare students for entering the work world?

4. What kind of a value system would produce an economic reward system in which the income differential for various tasks in society would be more equal? How would that affect the incidence of poverty in America?

5. How is the incidence of poverty affected when altering the definition of poverty from absolute poverty to relative poverty? Which of the two definitions do you think is most useful? Why? Can you find evidence to support your conclusion?

6. Since there is such an uneven distribution of rates of poverty from one part of the United States to another, what, if anything, does this tell us about the role of the federal government versus the role of local government in seeking solutions to poverty?

2

Social Dimensions of Poverty

Katharine H. Briar

A man we shall call Robert Peters stated these views:

What this nation needs is a return to the good old days of hard work, pride, and independence. Nowadays everyone's looking for a handout—welfare, unemployment benefits, food stamps, medicare, and housing assistance. That's what is ruining this country and the character of my so-called fellow Americans. Sure I'm bitter; it's my hard work they're living off. And being poor isn't so bad anymore. You got poor folks living good with TVs, a car, and lots of food and booze. It's easier to take a handout than to work for what you get. Some of us pay our dues—from hard-earned bucks. But why do our dues have to go to the lazy bums who refuse to work?

Robert Peters is not alone; he is joined by millions of Americans who believe that people are poor by choice because it is easier to take a "handout" than to work for one's livelihood. Robert cannot understand what happened to the values of rugged individualism and the ability to look after oneself, expecting help from no one.

Robert recalls that he was six when the great depression of the 1930s hit his family. He lived on a farm that enabled his family to be self-sufficient, so they were not seriously affected at first. But the following year the owner from whom they rented wanted to move back to his farm, and Robert and his family were forced to move to the city. "That didn't stop my father," Robert recalled, "he either found work or made work. He sold insurance; you can imagine how difficult that was during the Depression. He cut and hauled wood and went into the chicken business. I remember going with my father to buy chickens. We often had to catch them with a long wire hook."

Robert's story continues:

> At the age of eight, I became efficient at the chicken business. Then right in the middle of the Depression, my mother died, leaving my father with a family of ten, and lo and behold, no insurance. But he didn't go on welfare or accept charity. He took a part-time job as a grocery clerk and later went to work in the county clerk's office. My older brothers and sisters and I all worked part-time after school and weekends. We were poor, but we made it, and we didn't have to rip off anyone to do it. We worked hard, all sharing in the responsibility of providing.

TRAPPED IN POVERTY IN OLD AGE

Like Robert, Zella Grange never intended to live in poverty. Yet at age 86, she lives alone in a tiny, bleak apartment that looks out on rooftops littered with the trappings of slum life. All are constant reminders of the frustration and pain suffocating the young people in the neighborhood.

Zella cares about the people around her. Her caring brings her, in return, tokens of kindness from her neighbors. She has no one else to turn to; her husband died seven years ago. Even though she worked for many years as a cashier in the local grocery store, her sole income is the $120 social security that she receives monthly. She is not unlike the four million aged poor in the United States. She has worked diligently, expecting to remain financially independent. The few times she or her husband was laid off were hard on her family. Yet even the cold nights that her children were fed soup and stale crackers and sent to bed early to conserve heating oil were nowhere near as demanding as the living she is consigned to now that she is old, idle, alone, and poor.

Zella eats cold meals because she can't afford the gas bill and is afraid of fire. Her shaky hands have already spilled fat on the flaming burner. Zella's problems are more than financial. She is emotionally sapped, depressed by her neighborhood, and dreading the bleak years ahead. If her arthritis worsens, she will not be able to go out of her apartment, yet she refuses to go to a nursing home where she's sure she'll die.

ON SURVIVING WELFARE

Day after day, I worry for fear they'll take my kids away. And day after day I try to get ahead. I buy used clothes, and get free clothes. I go to school mornings to become a medical secretary. I always wanted to be a nurse but could never make it through high school. Guess I failed then, because when I dropped out I got married, got pregnant, and now I have nothing but worries. My husband left me after he was laid off; says I pushed him too much. I've been on and off welfare four times over the last 16 years. No matter what job I take, I can't seem to get ahead. The job ends or the pay isn't enough to live on so I slide back on welfare. This last time I felt really stuck. At times, I go into my bedroom, slam the door, and scream. My kids don't know how I hate this life. Sometimes, being on welfare makes me feel like I'm in a coffin with someone nailing down the lid. I can't feel sorry for myself long though, because the baby cries, and the girls are fighting, and it's time to put them down for the night. Wish they each could have their own beds. When the new apartments for low income folks are built, then I'll be able to afford more for them than we have now. I get $202 in welfare a month. $140 goes to rent.

Few people are as steretotyped, however, as welfare recipients. Mary O'Neill, who has been on welfare for a number of years, resents the accusations leveled against her and others in her situation. Moreover, her days are filled with fears, since, like most supplicants, she remains dependent on a system that provides less income than she needs to see her family through to better days.

The three vignettes of Robert Peters, Zella Grange, and Mary O'Neill blur the issue of who is to blame for their poverty and suggest that their plight may be attributable to situational factors rather than some moral or character defect.[1]

WHY ARE PEOPLE POOR?

Theories about the causes of poverty have existed as long as the poor have been around. Consequently, each attempt to respond to the poor and to alleviate their poverty is derived from assumptions about causation and culpability. If one believes, for example, that poverty is due to idleness and laziness, its solution might involve a program to encourage more socially productive and desirable behavior. On the other hand, a view that attributes poverty to an insufficient number of jobs available would compel increased employment opportunities. Because such assumptions shape the way society relates to the poor and attempts to alleviate their condition, it is important to examine the prevailing major assumptions about poverty and their implications for intervention.

Distinctions must be made between *attributes* of the poor person and the possible *causes* of his or her poverty. Considerable confusion has been prompted, for example, by research that generates a profile of characteristics about the poor (such as inadequate education or large family size) which in turn may be misconstrued as the *cause* of their impoverishment. Additional confusion occurs when ideas offered by some about the cause of poverty may be adopted by others as the definition or determinant of who is poor.

Whether conceptualized as the definition or as the cause of poverty, income insufficiency clearly leads to impoverishment. Income insufficiency, or the lack of resources sufficient to meet one's basic subsistence needs, has been adopted by the federal government as the official method for determining and defining who is poor.[2] Judiciously, but arbitrarily, designed as an instrument with pecuniary dimensions, the poverty index has significant political and economic implications. Politically, the best interests of elected officials are served when the fewest numbers of persons are counted as poor; thus, the government's criteria are pegged to count only those at a low level of subsistence.

Defining poverty as income insufficiency implies that poverty would be solved if more money were provided to the poor to make up the deficit in their resources. How much should be provided, on what basis, and to whom has been the subject of debate for centuries. In the last decade, proponents of welfare or income maintenance reform, for example, have offered alternative social-assistance programs as substitutes for the current welfare system. Meanwhile, other social welfare writers question whether the income insufficiency approach to poverty is an oversimplification of this complex phenomenon. They challenge the notion that income insufficiency is a satisfactory explanation for Mary or Zella's poverty. Furthermore, they wonder if adequate income provisions would ever eliminate Mary or Zella's poverty because even though they are recipients of aid, they will probably remain consigned to the bottom rung of the income ladder.

British scholar Richard Titmuss argued that poverty is caused by income *inequality* rather than income insufficiency.[3] Theorists who support this view insist that as long as inequities exist in the distribution of income, always leaving someone on the bottom, poverty will exist. Nothing short of a redistribution of income to effect equalization would eradicate poverty when defined in these broadened terms. Such inequalities, it is argued, are reinforced by a system that does not lack in resources but suffers from inequities in their distribution.

If one were to equalize the average amount of income per person from the population's total income, the average per capita income would be sufficient to lift the poor above the poverty line. According to Pamela Roby, in 1972 the average amount of income per person (before taxes) was $4478, which was somewhat above the 1972 poverty line designated for a family of four of $4334.[4] Such a redistribution would lift not only individuals but entire families above the poverty line.

Even now, such programs as welfare bring some of the 25.9 million persons whose incomes fall below the poverty line up a notch, yet 11 million welfare recipients continue to subsist below the poverty level. Many people in Mary and Zella's situation do not receive any aid at all; in fact, it is estimated about one-third of all the poor receive no assistance.[5]

According to Frances Fox Piven and Richard Cloward, promoting an increase or equalization of resources may not be the sole key to eradicating poverty. They argue that power is the critical resource needed by the poor; without it economic deprivation will persist.[6] Because of their powerlessness, the poor are unable to shape decisions that affect the distribution of societal goods and resources. Such a view of poverty suggests that collective action, for example, boycotts, will force improved political and economic responses to this disenfranchised group. In fact, the welfare rights movement, so prominent in the late 1960s, was spawned by the belief that an improved distribution of power must precede economic reform.

CULTURE OF POVERTY

Robert Peters, whose perspectives differed from Zella Grange and Mary O'Neill, is convinced that people are poor because they subscribe to values and attitudes different from those of the rest of society. He believes that the poor could get ahead if they really wanted to, but they are unmotivated, lazy, and shiftless.[7] Attempts to address the extent to which low-income persons exhibit attitudinal and behavioral patterns different from others have given rise to the notion of a "culture of poverty." Proponents of this cultural view hold that poverty involves a life-style substantially divergent from that exhibited by the nonpoor. Moreover, the norms, values, and behaviors that shape this deviant life-style are learned and transmitted through childrearing and socialization patterns from generation to generation.

Because of the higher incidence of social problems among the poor such as crime, out-of-wedlock children, and family disruption, some policy makers, such as Daniel P. Moynihan, have characterized such problems as a pathological consequence of the subculture among the poor.[8] Perceived as caught in a "tangle of pathology" promoting a cycle of poverty and disrepute, the poor are characterized as unable to control their impulses, to defer their need for immediate gratification, or to plan for the future. Once inducted into this subculture, many cannot extricate themselves.

Robert Peters claims that while there are some who are earnest and deserving, most are poor because of their attitude. "They don't want to work," he says. "They live from crisis to crisis. If you were to give them money, it would be spent tomorrow, but not on the right things like an education; instead it would be for booze, color TVs, or a fancy car." Roberts adds, "I've been in poor homes—a real eye-opener. Beer cans, wine bottles, people just lying around, beat-up cars in the driveway with grown kids who have never worked and who get pregnant just to get more welfare."

These stereotypical views of the poor are so pervasive that it would be hard to convince Robert Peters that he is overgeneralizing, as well as oversimplifying, the dynamics of the life of the poor. In fact, readily available data that contradict such views might still not penetrate Robert's bias. (See Chapter 1.) The blind, the disabled, and the aged—despite their earnestness and thrift—are also poor. Recipients of Aid to Families with Dependent Children (AFDC) are predominantly single-parent mothers with preschool children. Contrary to popular opinion, most children born out of wedlock do not receive aid, nor are most AFDC children born to unmarried mothers.[9] Stereotypical views of the poor regarding their race are also prevalent. Robert thinks that most of the poor are black, even though the majority are actually white.

Like some of the culture of poverty theorists, Robert has confused the *consequences* of poverty with its *cause*. As a result, the poor are held culpable for their plight. Culture of poverty theorists have been criticized for viewing deviant behaviorial patterns as by-products of culture rather than of the impoverished condition itself.

Some writers are sympathetic to the notion that there is a culture of poverty but are able to distinguish cultural factors from the consequences of poverty. They argue that the cultural components (behaviors, attitudes, and values) are, in fact, merely learned adaptive responses to economic deprivation and social degradation.[10] They explain that initial responses to an impoverished environment evolve into values, patterns, and habits that are transmitted to each succeeding generation.

The culture of poverty approach suggests clear directions for intervention, which tend to focus on changing the poor person. Casework, therapy, and other special help to alter specific behavioral patterns are all supported by this theoretical framework. Some have argued that, in order for them to break out of the vicious cycle of poverty, the children of the poor should be inculcated with middle-class values. Such reasoning might go so far as to support the removal of children from their families so that such an infusion of middle-class values can occur. Edward Banfield suggests that the children of the poor be sold off or provided "scholarships" to induce their parents to place them in year-round middle-class boarding schools.[11]

Clearly, the assumptions of those who view poverty from such a cultural perspective can lead to highly unethical interventions. On the other hand, many of the attitudes, actions, policies, and services directed toward the poor derive from this kind of victim-blaming ideology. Buttressed by ingrained socialization patterns and the assumption that the poor are lazy, the culture of poverty approach is in fact shaped by basic American values and is therefore most difficult to counter, even though evidence for alternative explanations of poverty is readily available.

CASE POVERTY

Complementing the culture of poverty approach is "case poverty," which refers to some affliction that causes people to slide into impoverishment. Mental illness, physical or mental disability, alcoholism, or drug addiction may precipitate a downward economic skid. Case poverty was first described by Galbraith, but social workers witness it daily as they counsel people whose handicaps may keep them from productive employment and leave them vulnerable to economic privation.[12]

Since the earliest times, those afflicted with disease or other conditions that prevent them from "pulling their own weight" have been a dominant concern of policymakers. Over the centuries people who are dependent on others have been taken care of by their family, the church, or the state. The provision of income alone will not alter the condition of such people, since their affliction shackles them in some way or another to the good will of others. They cannot be productive themselves. Because their misfortunes generate compassion, these people are often called the "worthy poor," while the remainder of the poor are cast as the "unworthy poor," since their poverty is thought to be of their own making.

Even though the casebook approach implies that therapy and personal services directed at an affliction constitute the primary interventions for treatment, recent trends have demonstrated that other approaches are also productive. In the last few years legislation to prevent discrimination against the handicapped has encouraged alterations in values. As a result, some of the "worthy poor" have actually risen from the ranks of the poor into the productive working world of the middle class. Instead of treating or eliminating afflictions, such programs focus on "mainstreaming" afflicted persons and call the public's attention to their capabilities rather than their afflictions. Thus, the case approach, which initially appears only to mandate therapy, actually encourages a range of socially innovative programs as well as legislation. Opportunities are provided for people to exchange their dependency role for that of a partially or fully productive, independent person.

In some ways Zella's situation might reflect a "casebook" concept of poverty. Because of her infirm condition and age, she is unable to work and is therefore dependent on whatever resources she is able to marshal. In her case her only resource is the social security benefits to which she is entitled.

INSULAR POVERTY

Sometimes the entrapment that promotes social and economic privation is environmental. The term *insular poverty* has been devised to describe this form of bondage that occurs in pockets of poverty. Ghettos, Indian reservations, areas devastated by plant closures, single-industry towns with insufficient jobs for all who need to work—all exhibit the insulating characteristics that tend to impel those who dwell in such areas into the ranks of the poor. Appalachia, Watts, and Harlem exemplify some of the characteristics associated with insular poverty. In these pockets of poverty victims are geographically landlocked because pathways to other areas appear blocked. Residents often cannot afford to move and fear they may be worse off elsewhere.

When geographically impoverished, the poor are victims of discrimination. Essential services such as fire, police, garbage, and maintenance are inadequately, if not negligently, provided. Zella complains that no matter how crime-infested the neighborhood, many residents have little police protection and inadequate police intervention compared to the services provided to residents in other parts of the city. She figures that because some ghetto residents are thought to be tax-eaters instead of taxpayers they have insufficient leverage to command services on a par with those delivered to less impoverished areas. Zella thinks that within these insulated areas, residents are exploited like caged animals. "Shopkeepers," she argues, "know that residents are stuck; thus prices are higher than in higher income areas. Price hikes occur routinely on days that welfare checks arrive." Rents are high for squalid, substandard housing; the same rent money outside Zella's area would be sufficient for a decent apartment. Not only is it difficult for victims of insular poverty to find work, but the employment opportunities that exist may be insufficient to meet basic needs. Many poor work full-time but may be geographically constrained from improving their condition. The corrosive effects of insular poverty can also be seen in the depression and anger that pervade the neighborhood where Zella lives.

Kathy Kahn's depiction of Sandra, an Appalachian woman, illustrates the plight of these geographically landlocked victims.[13] Sandra's husband died at a young age of black lung disease, and while government compensation was promised, she knew that it might take years for it to come. Meanwhile, she had to care for her small children. In her grief, she appealed for help to the "boss" of the mine where her husband had worked and was told that her children should eat the bark off the trees. Sandra ended up in a mill where she worked 12 hours a day as a "linthead." Her only break was to go to the bathroom. She would be fired if she did not keep up with the fastest worker. Several weeks later Sandra developed tremors, lost weight, and died.

In Appalachia machines are replacing these workers, and unemployment is becoming a way of life for some. Migration out of the area guarantees nothing more than joblessness elsewhere. Most Appalachians have lower educational attainments than others outside the area. The Appalachian, like many victims of insular poverty, is trapped. The sight of these Appalachian families' struggles to survive gave rise to John Kennedy's promise of aid in the early 1960s.

Attempts to eradicate insular poverty have included environmental development efforts such as model cities and other programs that try to upgrade inadequate facilities and services in insulated areas. Efforts to restore physical structures through urban-renewal programs have also evolved from concern about the way in which physical structures may shape aspirations and social functioning. Redevelopment activities that attempt to reduce the blight of urban ghettos and induce new services and businesses to renovated areas also help to dismantle insular poverty.

Current discussion about ways to relieve depressed areas, such as "inner cities" or those devastated by plant closures or those with a shaky economic base, centers on stimulating economic expansion, developing new jobs, or providing incentives for victims to relocate. Redevelopment programs have not proved successful, even though some available programs provide low-interest, high-risk loans to industry, as well as training to workers who live in the vicinity of relocated industries.[14]

SOCIAL POVERTY

Mary complains that the most trying aspect of poverty is being forced to ask for help. Some writers support Mary's protest. They argue that poverty is a state of being, derived not so much from sheer income privation as from the misery of having to seek assistance. George Simmel's important work on reciprocity maintains that the provision of aid fulfills social needs of the rich by assuaging their guilt over the disparity between their income and that of the poor.[15] Various forms of aid cast the poor in the role of supplicants who, because they are able to return the gift of assistance, are demeaned and forever obligated to the rest of society, especially the rich.

Simmel argues that what is given is not as important as the spirit in which it is provided. Thus, since seeking aid is a privilege and not a right, the poor are stigmatized and castigated when they seek assistance. Furthermore, since it appears that the poor cannot reciprocate, the rich are able to keep aid recipients obligated, dependent, and socially poor.

Simmel's work has led to research that demonstrates ways in which the poor contribute to society. Herbert Gans has suggested that the poor perform a number of positive functions for society.[16] For example, the poor work at the dangerous, dirty jobs that others are unwilling to do. The existence of poverty gives rise to bureaucracies which must administer programs and services. Richard Titmuss has shown that the poor contribute to the rest of society the most life-sustaining gift that could be offered: blood donations. His research on the receipt and distribution of blood documents the way in which donated blood flows from the poor to the rich, as well as to the rest of society.[17]

As a result of such studies, arguments that the poor neither contribute nor reciprocate can no longer be sustained. Even so, most people believe that the poor do not pay their way. Consequently, society does not guarantee a minimum income or offer assistance as a right. In addition to being economically poor, recipients are made to feel socially ostracized. Mary O'Neill describes what it was like the last time a welfare worker came to her house to investigate her compliance with welfare regulations:

> They call it quality control in our state. This is when an eligibility worker comes to the house to investigate and to make sure that nothing fraudulent has occurred. In my case, I have been careful to report everything to welfare—even crummy jewelry. They know that my last child was born out of wedlock. I was not, nor am I now, married to her father. But when this worker came, he made me burn inside. He kept asking me about Sonia's father: How could I be sure who the father was? Did Sonia live with me? Who could he call to verify that I was really caring for my child? The nerve of this man made me burn with hatred. I was so angry I was shaking. I love my daughter, and no one is going to ask questions about her father in front of her again. The welfare worker *acted like my welfare payment was his money from his pocket,* and he acted like he was better than I. Worst of all, he made it very clear that if I didn't comply by giving him all of the information he needed (some of which I couldn't—imagine him asking me why Sonia's father never put into writing that he was the father), my refusal would be interpreted as noncooperation and my benefits could be terminated. With that hanging over my head, along with the future survival of my family, I had to let him drill me with questions.

Mary recalls the humiliation of applying for aid, for that is when she really began to feel poor. Simmel would argue that she may have been economically poor, but she was not socially poor until actually placed in the position of having to ask for assistance. Thus, proponents of reforming income maintenance argue that one way to minimize the social stigma associated with receiving aid is to make assistance a right rather than a privilege.

POVERTY IN ENGLAND

Throughout history people have been the victims of misfortune. Some people have been afflicted by handicaps or made dependent through the loss of parents or a physical disability. Early accounts of the poor, the handicapped, the widowed, and the orphaned suggest that most societies devised some means to care for their dependents. For example, the church was central to society's caregiving functions until the Industrial Revolution. Sympathy for afflicted people was widespread since they were viewed as blameless victims and not as perpetrators of their dependency. By and large, poverty was not associated with able-bodied people, who were expected to care for themselves. It was not until around the 12th century that poverty among able-bodied people emerged.

Zella has been able to trace her origins back to ancestors who, generation after generation, lived off the land as tenant farmers on feudal estates in England. One set of her ancestors, the Groves, had been locked into a social and economic arrangement that assured security even though it rarely exceeded a subsistence level. In exchange for work performed for the feudal lord, including fighting his wars, her ancestors were provided with basic necessities for survival—shelter, food, and clothing.

In many ways, William and Sara Grove and their children were protected from the economic insecurities that pervade modern life. They worked hard, and the feudal nobility, Lord Sheffield, took care of them. They had their own share of the harvest and their own garden to keep them going during the year. When the enclosure movement forced Lord Sheffield to evacuate his tenant farmers from the land so that it could support the grazing of animals, the Groves were caught in both a curse and a blessing. Like thousands of other families, they were "freed" from their farming existence, yet were left unprepared for another way of life.[18]

Even though the dislocation of workers and their families from their servitude to the feudal state occurred over a period of several centuries, the social order became increasingly threatened by dislocated families like the Groves living day after day as transients. Like many other families, the Groves resorted to begging, looting, and stealing to feed their children and to survive. In their desperation, the Groves heard of a new place where jobs, shelter, and food were provided. It was called the workhouse and had just opened in the town of Sheffield. This workhouse emerged as part of a strategy by the British government to deal with the threat to the social order posed by the vagrant, begging, able-bodied unemployed. The so-called Poor Law held that poverty was due to inadequate employment opportunities.[19] In fact, its provisions for employment of the poor suggested that structural defects in the economic system, not the poor, were the source of the problem. In reality workhouses constituted haphazard relief programs rather than sources of public service jobs. Although wages were paid, they were deliberately maintained at a level well below what the lowest-paid independent worker might earn. Thus private work was made to appear more attractive than publicly sponsored workhouse programs.[20]

Initially the workhouse system was intended to pay for itself, but work programs were hazardous and poorly supervised. Because workers were given no training, in reality workhouses simply warehoused rather than productively employed the poor.

Later, "outdoor relief," the care of the poor in their own houses, was developed as another response to the indigent. Throughout these early Poor Law years, one policy issue that troubled the Poor Law guardians and persists even today in the United States, was the issue of "less eligibility." This principle mandated that the amount of relief should always be less than the wages of the lowest-paid worker. Yet, in England as elsewhere, many persons worked for menial wages and, despite their hard labor, were still poor.

EARLY AMERICAN POVERTY

Despite promises of an emerging classless society free of poverty, the American colonies were riddled with dependent poor people: widows, orphans, and sick persons who could not work and had no one to care for them. These early settlers, who had once railed against British society for the development of the Poor Law and the workhouse system, repeated the same solutions in America.

Poverty was viewed as a sign of sloth and of human failing and was a moral, not an employment issue. Work was critical to both social and physical survival. Prevailing Puritan ethics held that idleness and dependency, even if not a person's fault, were a form of blasphemy in the eyes of God. Moreover, people who did not work risked starvation and death because of the harsh conditions of life in the early New England colonies.

Yet the very presence of poverty was perceived as paradoxical. People had expected the New World to be unfettered by dependency and relief efforts. Consequently, reactions to the dependent poor were harsh and punitive. Some were branded with the letter P; others were treated as criminals.[21] Poverty was viewed as the work of the devil. Once one was labeled a pauper, work was difficult to acquire. Residency laws enabled communities to monitor newcomers during a probationary period to ensure that they would not become dependent. In the 1800s, Societies for the Prevention of Pauperism emerged to deal with the ever-growing population of destitute newcomers to the shores of the New World.

Despite the prevalence of the workhouse system, private charity organizations also emerged to aid poor people. Such organizations espoused the principle that aid should be meted out judiciously to build character and self-sufficiency. Reflecting the motto "not alms, but a friend," many people involved in charity work, some of whom were wealthy, assumed that aid would encourage dependency. Within the framework of "scientific philanthropy" they sought ways to instill in the poor social values that would lift them out of their destitution. On the assumption that improved morality would eliminate poverty, relief-giving was drastically reduced. For example, by 1905, the average annual assistance to a family on relief in Brooklyn was $1.05.[22]

DEPRESSION ERA

Despite the enactment of state programs like mothers' pensions, private charity continued to complement if not dominate public relief efforts in the early 1900s. But by 1928, the escalating cry for aid overtaxed the resources of private charities and became the harbinger of the economic crisis that soon engulfed the United States. In spite of the needs of homeless and penniless victims of the Depression, haphazard provisions persisted. Any governmental inclinations to respond to the growing masses of poor were muted by the belief that federal aid was immoral and unconstitutional. Ironically, loans to banks and businesses were acceptable and represented the primary form of governmental intervention until the New Deal. Ushered in by Franklin D. Roosevelt, the New Deal was a composite of employment and loan programs designed to uplift the economic conditions of people and businesses.

Robert Peters was a victim of the Depression who never expected that he and his family might require governmental assistance. It was not until the death of his father that Robert's family was forced to inquire about training programs and jobs.

The Social Security Act of 1935 was hailed by some as the most courageous legislation ever advanced in the United States. Would this new legislation bring economic security to someone like the Peters family? Actually it did not. The legislation promoted a contributory insurance-based program, and because they had not yet paid into it, they could not draw from it. The clause providing for public assistance, which was interpreted by many as nothing more than the dole, was not an answer to the Peters' problems. In fact, they so deeply believed that "you don't get something for nothing," no matter how deserving, that they would rather have starved than take a handout. Yet it was people like the Peters family to whom the public assistance clause was directed. Designed to provide emergency funds to those who had not been able to contribute to social security, public assistance was to function as an economic safety net. At the time of its passage the Social Security Act contained provisions for the unemployed and the aged. Since its inception additional coverage has been added for survivors, health care, and disability insurance (OASDHI).

Ironically, it was the public assistance provisions of Social Security that were expected to be redundant after the Social Security system became fully operable. Public relief provisions did not "wither away" but steadily climbed to keep pace with increasing needs.[23] By the 1960s the caseloads under Aid to Dependent Children (ADC) had increased from 1,222,000 to 9,660,000.[24]

The unanticipated events that increased the demand for public assistance are not well understood. Robert Peters, for instance, believes that the cause of the rising welfare rolls was laziness and illegitimacy. Few could have predicted that the social-insurance scheme envisioned in the Social Security Act would leave unattended the problems of parental desertion, separation, or divorce; economic insecurity caused by automation; discriminatory practices that prevent ethnic minorities and women from acquiring jobs at a decent wage; and catastrophic illnesses and high medical costs that render families economically vulnerable. These new developments related to the "risks" of modern economic life have actually prolonged the demand for assistance and have helped to institutionalize income maintenance as a first-line responsibility of government.

WAR ON POVERTY

Some of the most ambitious efforts to assist the poor since the enactment of the Social Security Act were visible when the War on Poverty was declared in the 1960s. The dream of eliminating hunger and want, spurred by John F. Kennedy's visit to Appalachia, became embodied in the Equal Opportunity Act, which provided for education, training, and jobs, along with other resources.

The promise of equal opportunity for all in the War on Poverty ignored the fact that equality of opportunity is not commensurate with equality of results. Thus, a system that metes out limited opportunities such as an insufficient number of jobs, produces unequal outcomes. Moreover, the victims of such inequalities are considered to be not only the losers but also the perpetrators of their condition.

Some of the contributions of the War on Poverty cannot be measured solely in dollars. One major impact of the War on Poverty was the empowerment of poor people, who began to define for themselves the kinds of services and programs that were necessary to eliminate discrimination and destitution. The War on Poverty made it possible not only for Mary O'Neill's children to find work in the summers through the Neighborhood Youth Corps, but also for her friends to assume roles as community leaders by serving on community action councils and social service boards. During the War on Poverty, Mary's aspirations to train for a career unfolded. Welfare was supportive of her interests and offered her training as a mortician's aid. She rejected that offer promptly, but did so with great fear that her refusal might lead to the termination of her assistance. She turned to the local legal-assistance office for advice on her right to refuse. Unfortunately, the laws were unclear regarding her right to refuse under the terms of the Work Incentive Program (WIN), which was established in the late 1960s to encouage work among able-bodied AFDC recipients with school-age children. Coercion to take a job was an inherent problem in the WIN program, since aid could be denied if the recipient chose to be selective. Mary knew some welfare mothers whose WIN counselors used tactics of intimidation to compel them to take specific jobs. Despite the benefits of the War on Poverty, the 1960s were not an easy time for Mary, for she, like many others, lived with the constant worry of having her welfare terminated if a man were present in her home. While she never experienced the "midnight raids" that occurred to check for the presence of a man, other forms of harassment were used relentlessly, and this reminded her constantly that aid was not an entitlement but a privilege.

INCOME MAINTENANCE AND WELFARE REFORM

During the aftermath of the 1960s, many plans and strategies were devised to replace the welfare program with a more equitable and more humane income-maintenance system. Several key principles guided these developments. While debates about various income-maintenance proposals continue even today, most people place clear responsibility on the federal government to set uniform standards in eligibility and allotment and thus to eliminate variations in welfare programs among the states. Current inequities, such as the discrepancy in Aid to Families with Dependent Children benefits between Mississippi ($28.29 per child) and Wisconsin ($118.95), should be eliminated.[25] Another principle guiding welfare reform is that mere tinkering with the present structure of welfare cannot resolve discrepancies among welfare benefits from state to state. Another major preoccupation of the advocates of welfare reform centers on designing work incentives that are neither coercive nor punitive, yet remain politically acceptable.

Income maintenance reform has also addressed the issue of what kind of impact welfare reform proposals have on the family. For example, in the states where two-parent families are ineligible for aid, desertion, separation, or divorce must occur in order for a family to acquire assistance.

Another major preoccupation has been to reduce the divisiveness of current welfare programs by reducing the current stigmatizing of the poor as separate and different. Such stigmatizing is a carryover from the Poor Law and is reflected in many policies and programs directed toward the poor, such as the food-stamp program. Grocery store clerks can testify to the personal suffering of food stamp recipients who are subjected to stares of disgust when they pay for their food with stamps. Mary O'Neill recalls her first week of using food stamps.

It was like having a calling card that said to the world, "Look at me, I am poor." People stared at every item that I bought to make sure, I guess, that I wasn't spending money on food too expensive for the likes of me—hot dogs and hamburgers. Dog food? I'd let them wonder whether it was for me or our dog. Once I bought steaks on a special, and I could hear people behind me in the line mutter to themselves when they saw that I was eating well on food stamps.

THE FUTURE

Mary O'Neill would like to eliminate the injury of social assistance programs. She is convinced that much of the animosity and resentment taxpayers direct at programs for the poor becomes focused on the poor and abets their pain. If aid were an entitlement and were provided automatically through an efficient tax credit, the noxious pauperization of the destitute would be minimized. Moreover, millions would at last be assisted who are now ineligible for social assistance because they are not blind, disabled, aged, or members of families with dependent children.

Robert Peters disagrees vehemently with such an approach to aid the poor because he fears that the costs will be exorbitant and will erode his own income. What he does not realize is that less than one percent of the gross national product is spent on welfare payments. When compared to the billions of dollars spent on defense, such increases seem less awesome. On the other hand, as long as American ideologies hold the poor culpable for their condition and divest the nonpoor of responsibility for the persistence of poverty, the struggles to justify aid to poverty's victims will continue. Shaped by such ideologies, the values of individualism, the Protestant work ethic, and self-reliance have caused Americans not only to remain unaware of the facts of poverty, but also comfortably to justify the economic insecurity and victimization that have evolved over the centuries.

NOTES

1. Portions of the vignettes of Robert Peters, Zella Grange, and Mary O'Neill are derived from the lives, experiences, and views of several former students, whose names will remain anonymous.
2. Orshansky, Mollie. "Who's Who Among the Poor," *Social Security Bulletin*, July, 1965.
3. Titmuss, Richard. "Poverty Versus Inequality: Diagnosis," *The Nation*, Vol. 200, No. 1, February 8, 1965.

4. Roby, Pamela. *The Poverty Establishment.* Englewood Cliffs, N.J.: Prentice Hall, 1974.
5. Orshansky.
6. Piven, Frances Fox and Richard Cloward. *Regulating the Poor: Functions of Welfare.* New York: Random House, 1971.
7. Research has shown that many Americans, regardless of whether they have been touched by poverty, agree with Robert Peters. See the research of Joan Huber, William H. Forum, and John Pease. "Income and Stratification Ideology," *American Journal of Sociology,* Vol. 75, No. 4, Part 2, January, 1970.
8. Rainwater, Lee. *The Moynihan Report.* Cambridge, Mass.: MIT Press, 1967.
9. Feagin, Joe R. *Subordinating the Poor.* Englewood Cliffs, N.J.: Prentice Hall, 1975.
10. Lewis, Oscar. *Five Families.* New York: Basic Books, 1959.
11. Banfield, Edward. *The Unheavenly City.* Boston: Little, Brown, 1970.
12. Galbraith, John Kenneth. The *Affluent Society.* New York: Mentor Books, 1958.
13. Kahn, Kathy. *Hillbilly Women.* Garden City, N.Y.: Doubleday, 1973.
14. *Background Papers.* The President's Commission, Income Maintenance Programs, Superintendent of Documents, Washington, D.C.: U.S. Government Printing Office, 1970.
15. Simmel, George. "The Poor," *Social Problems.* Fall, 1965.
16. Gans, Herbert J. *More Equality.* New York: Vintage Books, 1974.
17. Titmuss, Richard. *The Gift Relationship.* New York: Vintage Books, 1972.
18. deSchweinitz, Karl. *England's Road to Social Security.* Philadelphia: University of Pennsylvania Press, 1974.
19. *Ibid.*
20. Mencher, Samuel. *Poor Law to Poverty Program.* Pittsburgh: University of Pittsburgh Press, 1967.
21. Sampson, Timothy J. *Welfare: A Handbook for Friend and Foe.* Philadelphia: United Church Press, 1972, p. 60.
22. Mencher.
23. Steiner, Gilbert Y. *The State of Welfare.* Washington, D.C.: Brookings Institution, 1971.
24. Aid to Dependent Children was changed to Aid to Families with Dependent Children.
25. These data are based on public assistance statistics from 1979. See the report by the Office of Research and Statistics, Office of Policy, Social Security Administration, U.S. Department of Health, Education and Welfare, *Public Assistance Statistics,* July, 1979, Washington, D.C., February, 1979.

SUGGESTED READINGS

Feagin, Joe R. *Subordinating the Poor.* Englewood Cliffs, New Jersey: Prentice Hall, 1975. This book presents prevalent myths about the poor and welfare recipients and analyzes these beliefs in view of data and evidence. Many prevailing assumptions are shown to be erroneous and stereotypical.

Piven, Frances Fox and Richard Cloward. *Regulating the Poor: The Function of Welfare.* New York: Random House, 1971. The authors provide a useful perspective on the interplay of the welfare system and fluctuations in work opportunities created by the economy. Historical and recent evidence cited by the authors of ways in which the welfare system has been a necessary, integral component to the functioning of the political and economic systems help promote a contextual appreciation for the persistence of American poverty.

Ryan, William. *Blaming the Victim.* New York: Random House, Vintage Books, 1971. William Ryan depicts ways in which strategies to help the poor and afflicted actually may encourage change in the individual victim rather than in the system. It is argued that such approaches reinforce the system and its negative impact on the poor.

Sampson, Timothy J. *Welfare: A Handbook for Friend and Foe.* This book presents useful information about the welfare system, experiences of recipients and action steps readers might pursue to become further informed.

STUDY QUESTIONS

1. Visit your local welfare department. Ask for an interview with a welfare worker so you can learn more about the needs and problems of recipients.

2. If you were asked to present your plan for alleviating, if not eliminating, poverty, what might it be?

3. Where do people in your community turn for emergency food, housing, clothing, and transportation? Plan a visit to those agencies that provide such emergency services. It will sharpen your understanding of what it feels like to be poor and to have to ask for help.

4. Survey your colleagues as to their vision about the cause of poverty. How many of these ideas they have are based on inadequate information or may be shaped by the media coverage of sensational cases of welfare recipients?

5. Who are the major poor groups in your community? How do leaders in your community account for poverty in your community? Do they see it as a personal defect of the poor person or as a problem which community leaders need to solve?

3

Economic Insecurity: A Family Problem

Katharine H. Briar

The debates and political sparring set off by the International Year of the Child in 1979 and the White House Conference on Families in 1980 have placed the needs of families sharply before the American people as an agenda for policy and service innovation. Regardless of whether such concerns are prompted by the demise of the nuclear family, the high divorce rate, the growing numbers of reconstituted families, or the decline in birth rates, most would agree that the survival of the family as an institution depends on the degree to which supports provided by society ensure that its responsibilities can be carried out successfully. Since economic resources play a foremost role in the functioning of families, it seems timely to examine consequences of the impact of financial stresses on American families.

Despite the variety of family forms, religious life-styles, and cultural, ethnic, and membership characteristics, all families are expected to perform similar functions. According to the National Commission on Families and Public Policies, these functions transcend diverse structures and characteristics and include unconditional love and affectional ties, economic and other life supports, basic education and socialization, health care, and social services.[1]

The Commission also argued that families are like agencies, such as schools, health, or social service organizations, which are given responsibility and authority to care for their members. Thus, like any agency, each family must have sufficient resources to carry out these functions. Obviously, the more deficient a family is in its resources, the higher the risk that it will not be able to perform its societally allocated responsibilities effectively or even adequately. The persistent incongruity between family needs and availability of resources constitutes perhaps one of the most pressing problems of the decades ahead. The exacting toll and irreversible damage brought about when families cannot provide for their members should command not just the attention of policymakers but the concern of all.

The life chances of each generation of children depend greatly on the abilities of their families to provide for them. Families who falter, it is argued, need resource and support safety-nets to counteract their difficulties and deficits. Yet, even though a simple and self-evident argument, the concept has been difficult to implement because the family has been regarded as a private sphere within the community.

THE FAMILY AND THE PRIVATE SECTOR

The private nature of the family unit, unfettered by government intervention and attention, has been accepted as a fundamental tenet of modern society. Families are not mentioned in the Constitution nor are they explicitly addressed in policies affecting either the public or the private sector. Thus, their problems in functioning have gone unnoticed, except when singled out as deviant, and are often attributed to some pathological aberration within the family unit. For example, a six-year-old child left unattended after school each day and brought to the attention of child protective services is more often seen as a victim of "bad" parenting than of the family's insufficient financial resources to purchase child care. Problems emerging in the family unit are rarely attributed to outside circumstances over which the family may have little control, but instead are seen as a product of individual or family performance. In light of the awesome tasks expected of families, many of whom have insufficient resources, it is a mark of tremendous strength that so many families function successfully.

Increasing stresses, derived especially from external pressures related to employment and economic problems, complicate, if not negate, the ability of families to care for their members. Since poverty and unemployment lead to economic insecurity and thus exert a significant influence on a family's ability to function, an examination of the effects of these two major stresses of modern life will illuminate specific needs of American families as well as the gaps in services to meet them.

FAMILIES AND UNEMPLOYMENT

While most family income is generated from wages for work, other sources include social insurance, public assistance, and allowances for dependents.[2] Since work is the major cornerstone of the well-being and success of families, it might be expected that employment opportunities would be made available for all who wish to work. However, jobs are not provided as automatic entitlements; in fact, in the United States, concerns over inflation tend to mute any implementation of job-entitlement principles. Even the Humphrey-Hawkins Legislation (HR 50), which initially was drafted as a bill to provide jobs as a right, was finally adopted with clauses that reiterate the dilemma of a trade-off between "full employment" and inflation. The proposed economic and budget policies of the Reagan administration leave the impression that unemployment will increase and governmental family support will decrease.

To outsiders, it seems ironic that a nation so committed to the work ethic would persistently cast off millions of people each year into the ranks of the unemployed. It is also startling that the unemployed are viewed as victims of their own inertia. In fact, the inaccurate assumption that "there are plenty of good jobs around" limits the ability of the American public to understand clearly the effects of unemployment and economic insecurity on workers and their families.[3]

If one looks beyond the unemployment statistics to the people which such abstractions represent, one finds that for every person counted in the unemployment statistics, there are several more uncounted victims. Many workers have several children, a spouse, and sometimes elderly relatives who depend on their income from a job. When stripped of a paycheck, not just the worker but the entire family may be devastated. The family side of unemployment has seldom been told, and very little is actually known. However, recent research efforts, which echo findings of studies from the

Depression era, offer a glimpse of the impact of unemployment on families.[4]

A worker's initial response to a layoff may be an indication of what impact impending joblessness will have on his or her family. News of a job termination may be personally devastating. However, the necessity of sharing the news with one's family may produce even more stress. Some workers postpone telling their spouse or children for fear that it would "upset them too much." Family members at first tend to respond optimistically and supportively, even though joblessness signals a crisis of uncertain proportions.

Dependency is more than economic: in fact, family members may never be so acutely aware of the extent of their social and psychological dependence upon the worker and his or her job until employment terminates. With the job loss, the status of the family diminishes in the eyes of neighbors, relatives, community associates, and fellow church members.

Social interaction among children is often shaped by parental judgments about one another's family worth and social status. Thus, children of families where joblessness persists are treated not with empathy as victims of fluctuations in the economic system, but more often as outcasts. Moreover, if such attitudes are not inflicted by other children upon those of the jobless parents, these young victims may actually precipitate their own social isolation. Social interaction in a child's world presupposes the ability to participate freely in sports, birthday parties, and other social events. Since children of the unemployed cannot afford such participation, they may withdraw from events into self-initiated exile during the economic crisis. Name calling, denigration, and teasing of a young social exile may exacerbate the emotional trauma of a family's financial problems.

Similar patterns occur more subtly with adult friends of jobless workers and their spouses. When forced to cut back or curtail their recreational and entertainment activities during an economic siege and thus to withdraw socially, unemployed adults also find that many of their friends recoil from them. Unemployed workers and their spouses complain that their old friends treat them like "poor country cousins" or act as if the unemployed always want something from them, most likely money, or are embarrassed to be around them, treating them as if they have a disease.

The social toll of unemployment continues as a family plunges downward economically, wiping out its life savings and possessions.

Moreover, because of job loss, health coverage for the entire family may be terminated. Cutbacks necessitated by unemployment often include the elimination of expenditures for automobile and home insurance, and soon after, the house or car itself may be sold or repossessed. As the unemployed eliminate expenditures for what they may perceive as "luxuries," such as the telephone and newspapers, they face additional complications, since such cutbacks may further jeopardize their family. For example, the risks of financial loss increase if a calamity such as illness, fire, or accident befalls the uninsured. The absence of a phone reduces the accessibility of a worker to potential employers. The lack of newspapers, which are used so often for job leads, increases the isolation of the unemployed from the network of their friends and from the community of employers.

Moreover, such cutbacks are visible evidence of financial hardships endured by a family that may distance it from, rather than endear it to, the network of potential sources of social support. Friendship support-networks are essential during a period of unemployment. Apart from the emotional sustenance and the modicum of social acceptance such friends provide, the unemployed depend on this network for leads on jobs. In fact, many studies of job seeking confirm that the most prevalent means of acquiring information about job openings is through "word of mouth."

FROM UNEMPLOYMENT TO POVERTY

Financially stricken, a family may go through periods of adjustment and accommodation in its attempts to survive its economic condition. Research has shown that families struggling with long-term unemployment often end up skidding onto welfare or being rescued financially by other family members.[5] Rescue attempts usually consist of job acquisition by the spouse or by the teenagers, who drop out of high school or college to work full-time to help the family. Unemployed fathers have a most difficult time accepting the fact that others must go to work because they "have failed" in their search for a job. In fact, since unemployment is often treated by society as a sign of indolence and laziness, jobless workers have little to counteract the view of themselves as failures. The fact that other family members are driven into the labor market to support the family may be personalized as a crippling reflection of how they have failed or may be harming their family.

Not all families can be rescued by other family members. The wife who has limited marketable skills or who may be caring for a young child or an elderly relative may be restrained by such family work roles from seeking employment. Moreover, job acquisition by another family member may only slow the pace of, rather than prevent, the downward economic skid.

Regardless of the level of income from wages, most workers and their families build their standard of living and life-style, which, in the absence of a paycheck, cannot be sustained without equivalent wage substitutes. Moreover, the credit-card culture of buying now and paying later induces low-income families, who can least afford excessive debts, into additional financial chaos during a period of joblessness. It has been suggested that these workers receiving only minimum level wages may find that the economic skid into joblessness involves less in terms of the actual dollar value of the casualty than middle- or high-income workers, even though their unemployment still constitutes a catastrophe for them and their family.

Unemployment benefits are usually insufficient to stave off the economic plummet for many families, since they are pegged to generate substitute income at only 50% of earned wages, are limited by a ceiling on assistance which varies from state to state but rarely exceeds $600 per month, and do not provide coverage for all workers. Many families, overextended with credit, bills, a mortgage, and car payments, are ill-prepared to tolerate even a slight reduction in their income. Thus, one period of joblessness may constitute more than a temporary fluctuation in their social and economic functioning. The effects may be irreparable, for the years of building a second base for the family, both in material possessions as well as the accompanying social standing, may never be regained.

UNEMPLOYMENT AND SEVERED FAMILIES

Unemployment may contribute to, if not precipitate, deteriorating marital relationships. This seems to be a problem particularly when the male provider in a traditional nuclear family experiences unemployment. For example, having been socialized into becoming the economic provider for the family, the jobless husband has a most difficult time because all family problems may be attributed to him. Initial family support and understanding may wear thin after weeks of unsuccessful job-seeking have elapsed. Encountering one rejection after another, he slides into a depression and becomes self-absorbed and withdrawn. This pattern evolves into a syndrome which is accompanied by self-blame and recrimination. As the worker begins to "give up" to the extent even of becoming physically immobile during the day, perhaps sitting in a corner and staring at the ceiling, family members may become more perturbed. Their frustration may escalate at the sight of the paralyzed "breadwinner," whose behavior they may mistake for indifference to their feelings and the crisis before them.

Meanwhile, once the jobless husband blames himself, he may seek therapy or social service help, believing that if he can change some personal attribute, a job will be forthcoming. When such changes do not occur immediately, family members become despondent in their attempts to survive joblessness. Sensing their desperation and stress, the father may leave, believing that divorce or separation may be the only recourse. Unable to tolerate unresolved marital or family conflict, he may believe that the family will be better off if he leaves. The father may also desert the family in order to ensure their eligibility for welfare. Since less than half the states in the United States provide welfare to impoverished dual-parent families, many such family breakups through desertion are encouraged. While there are debates over the extent of welfare-generated marital and family breakups, eligibility requirements that prevent the provision of aid to two-parent families clearly inflict harm to the highly stressed family unit.

Societal pressures and American values which encourage high living standards add to the stresses on jobless workers and their families. Such persistent family stress may take its toll in a variety of ways. Research suggests that child and spouse abuse,[6] alcoholism,[7] drug addiction,[8] marital conflict,[9] divorce,[10] stress-related health disorders, suicide, crimes of violence (e.g., homicide), mental illness,[11] longevity,[12] and death rates are all precipitated by or related to joblessness.

Recent research on dual-career families describes the emotional toll of joblessness among women.[13] Family income and living standards may be very much affected by alterations in income. Thus, when unemployment impinges on just one of two providers in a family, the same devastating psychological and financial consequences may occur, although in less dramatic ways.

ECONOMIC INSECURITY AND
SINGLE-PARENT FAMILIES

Even less is known about the effects of joblessness on single-parent families, especially those headed by women. Since divorce so frequently propels women into the role of sole provider for their family, their problems with joblessness may be very similar to those of male providers. However, women are often untrained for employment, receive lower wages than men—even for comparable work, and are more frequently the victims of layoffs because of "last hired, first fired" practices in the workplace. Consequently, their hardships resulting from joblessness may be more frequent as rising numbers of women assume the role of single-parent provider for their families. Whatever the source of economic worry—unemployment, inflation, debt, or credit problems—financial problems continue to be cited as one central cause of divorce.

Ironically, the same factors that account so frequently for divorce may continue to rankle the newly divided family. Obviously, divorce may involve factors more complex than coping with finances. However, whatever relief marital dissolution may bring to an interpersonal conflict, divorce may only intensify economic strains. Setting up two households may stretch previous family income to unendurable limits. Thus, lacking sufficient resources or employment income, many single-parent women slide onto welfare after their divorce. Paradoxically, for those for whom divorce is neither an option nor a desire, financial incentives may actually encourage the breakup of a family at rock bottom, who would be eligible for welfare in the father's absence.[14]

Bureau of Labor Statistics data show that one out of every three single-women parents is living beneath the poverty level.[15] Such data emphasize the fact that poverty is an acute problem of single-parent women and their families.

Such women are often young and unskilled and have several children. Together with their families they may be caught trying to choose among three options: (1) taking a low-paying full-time job in addition to their full-time family work roles, (2) stabilizing at rock-bottom poverty through welfare, or, (3) finding a mate whose income may lift them out of poverty.

Many women who slide into welfare are pressed to get off as quickly as possible. Welfare policies encourage work as well as reunion with the ex-husband or the finding of a new mate. A longitudinal study of women on welfare showed that the welfare system is often a revolving door for them, since economic independence is secured neither from one's job nor from remarriage. Thus, a study of mothers receiving Aid for Dependent Children showed that 18 percent of the initial cohort of recipients left welfare through marriage. Of the group who married, 66 percent reunited with their ex-husbands and 34 percent entered a new marriage.[16] However, within six months, 17 percent of this married group had returned to welfare. Such data confirm that finding a mate may not resolve economic problems, since his income may not be sufficient to meet the family's needs.

Of the original cohort of women studied, 48 percent were able to leave the welfare roles because they found jobs. Even so, a number of them (17%) were back on welfare by the end of six months because of employment problems, for example, layoffs and insufficient wages.

Such findings show that marriage is a key determinant in getting on or off welfare.[17] However, marriage becomes an economic necessity rather than a mere choice for such economically insecure women. For some, marriage is not a feasible or desirable option. This is particularly true of unmarried single mothers, for eight percent of all children born "out of wedlock" are raised by very young mothers under the age of 25.[18] Many of these mothers are teenagers who, still in the midst of their own adolescent development, have acquired few skills and lack the ability to compete in the adult work world. In addition, many are reluctant to marry simply because of economic need.

WELFARE LOOSENS FAMILY BONDS

It has been argued that the welfare system forces family breakups and encourages divisive feelings toward fathers. For example, in order to receive aid, women must sign a statement stating their willingness to prosecute their husbands for not paying child support. While complaints abound that such prosecution occurs too infrequently, the requirement itself may connote to children that their mother is "sending their father to jail." Some women, abhorring the destructive nature of such policies, are unable to comply and thus deny themselves and their children the income allotments that may be necessary for their functioning.

Welfare policies tend to create economic incentives for the poor to maintain loose family ties.[19] The bonds so essential for healthy family units may be further eroded by welfare policies which mandate that women with school-age children seek employment through the welfare work incentive program (WIN). Women who may be attending school or who want to remain at home performing family work roles are forced to accept employment as a condition of aid. Refusal may mean that someone else is assigned guardianship of the children as a conduit to permit the receipt of monies by the children while their mother goes without aid.

By comparison with other nations, the United States does little to invest in the life chances of children and their families' ability to care for them. Many Western European policy innovations, designed to support families and children, are not provided in the U.S. For example, Children and Family Allowances, so prevalent in all western industrialized countries, have not been enacted in the United States. Recognizing the added costs of caring for children, other countries have developed such programs as mechanisms of family policy and in recognition of the need for government to invest in children.

Instituted after World War II in such countries as France, Germany, and England, Children and Family Allowances were initially used (altogether not always successfully) to stimulate the birth rate. While such entitlements are provided to all families with children, poor families rely heavily on them as income supplements. Since wages are not allocated according to family need, such supplements are responsive to family size and the costs of childrearing.

As tools of public policy to enhance the economic well-being of children and to invest in families' ability to care for them, Children and Family Allowances have constituted major avenues for policy development in Western European countries as well as Canada. Yet U.S. critics of Children and Family Allowances claim that this modern "aid in wages" would provide families with incentives to have more children and would encourage illegitimate births. Moreover, it is argued that much money would be wasted on families who, because of tax loopholes, neither need the income nor will return it through taxes.

Other Western European policy innovations that promote family functioning include extended maternity leaves, comprehensive child care, and subsidized family and maternal vacations, as well as national health insurance. Like the children and family allowance program, such supports are provided as universal entitlements for all, rather than segregated in programs just for the poor.

POVERTY: A CHILD'S EXPERIENCE

Children of the poor have a difficult time explaining to themselves and to others why their lives are different from those of the nonpoor. As some lie awake at night unable to sleep because of hunger pains, they may remain oblivious to the fact that millions of other children like them suffer similarly each day. They, like their parents, may instead personalize their situation and blame themselves for their condition rather than see themselves as victims of economic injustices and income inequality.

Very little is known about the effects of poverty on the psychological well-being of children. Research has shown how poverty may cripple the young child, who even before birth may suffer brain damage from its mother's malnourishment.[20] Moreover, poverty-stricken mothers are unable to pass onto their nursing babies life-enriching nutrients. Consequently, their babies may show low birth weight, lethargy, inhibited intellectual development, and other consequences of malnourishment.

Compensatory programs reverse only some of the effects of malnutrition. Early findings on the benefits of Headstart programs, which promote comprehensive preschool and parent involvement programs for low-income families, demonstrated the importance of nutrition for children who become more energetic and less educationally crippled because of the nutritional breakfasts and lunches provided.

Receiving Aid to Families with Dependent Children (AFDC) does not necessarily relieve the problems of the poor family. Interviews conducted by Charles Lebeaux with welfare recipients showed that more than half believed their families to be inadequately fed.[21] Despite the relief provided by food stamps, many continue to go hungry. Unless one has sufficient cash on hand, food stamps are the same as no food at all.

Lebeaux found that half of the clothes that poor children wear to school come not from the AFDC check, but as gifts from neighbors, friends, and teachers. Truancy from school may be due to a lack of shoes. Lebeaux's research showed that half the young girls and eight out of ten boys on AFDC had only one pair of shoes.

The isolating consequences of poverty are similar to those caused by unemployment and take on new dimensions when family relationships are severed by divorce, desertion, or death. A study by James J. Lynch offers documentary evidence of the medical consequences of loneliness.[22] He shows how cardiovascular, as well as other, diseases may lead to premature death, not just for the lonely, socially isolated, or grieving adult, but for children as well.

Whether rich or poor, families attempt to prepare their children to endure challenges and disappointments. However, impoverished parents are hard-pressed to counter the psychological and social harm that may accrue from the segregating, name-calling victimization that nonpoor children perpetrate on their poor counterparts and that serve as constant reminders of their inequality. Much has been written about how, at an early age, poor children may be set in the same track as their parents. Inadequate education, housing, and health care conspire to make an escape from poverty highly improbable. Expectations that they will be losers are conveyed by teachers, police, neighbors, and even family members and thus add to their injury. After staying in school as long as possible, these children are confronted with the "ultimate betrayal." Having been raised in a society that requires years of public education as a precondition for eventual employment, these children face rates of unemployment of at least 20 percent among white and up to 40 percent among minority youth. As a result, many of them become frustrated and bored, marry in their teens, and have babies. They either skid onto welfare or fill the nation's jails and prisons. During their adult years, they may live out the "failure syndrome" while being punished for their deviance.

UNEQUAL LIFE CHANCES

Richard H. DeLone, an economist and former associate director of the Carnegie Council on Children, writes: "The most destructive aspect of poverty for a child is not, in our view, the daily hardship, the compounding risks of death, disease, family break-up, miseducation, and the like; it is the fact that for most of them, adult life will not be significantly better." [23] Social mobility that might move poor children beyond the socioeconomic or occupational status of their parents is more an ideal than a reality.

For women and minorities the problems of mobility are even

worse because of discrimination and unequal treatment at critical junctures in the upward-mobility stepladder. DeLone notes that women with similar training receive only 60 percent of the wages of their male counterparts; and black male workers with similar training and educational experiences receive only 80 percent of the salary of white male workers.[24]

While currently only one out of five children is raised on AFDC, there may be an ever-expanding intergenerational group of parents and children permanently consigned to life on and off the dole as the result of poverty related to divorce. Current estimates peg the number of permanent welfare dependents at no more than ten percent of the welfare population. This figure is misleading if one infers that there is only a small group of permanently poor welfare dependents. In reality, many poor persons go on and off welfare. Thus, while preventing the development of a welfare class, economic policies in the United States tend to encourage the persistence of economic insecurity among millions of families and prevent opportunities for them to become self-sufficient above the rock-bottom poverty levels of subsistence.

POVERTY AND FULL-TIME WORK

Full-time work is no guarantee of liberation from poverty. For example, a full-time worker with three dependents who earns minimum wages still will not be able to bring his or her family above poverty level. Such demonstration projects as the New Jersey Income Maintenance experiments and interviews with the poor have shown convincingly that their incentive to work persists despite poverty-level wages and menial, insecure employment. That the poor continue to demonstrate strong work motivation in the face of poverty-level wages and insecure, often temporary, employment suggests that they possess fortitude and determination.

Those poor who are eligible for welfare experience disincentives to work. For example, at one time every dollar earned from work was subtracted from one's welfare check; currently recipients may retain $30 and one-third of the remainder of their monthly earnings. AFDC mothers find themselves constantly watchful of the potential jeopardy that their jobs may encourage, since earning one dollar beyond their welfare allowance means immediate termination of welfare allotments and a precipitous increase in economic worries.

HOUSING AND HEALTH

Despite the Housing Act of 1949, which called for a decent home for every American family, suitable housing is not an entitlement. Census data in 1970 showed that 13 million families or 11 percent of the population suffered from housing deprivation; half of those families were black.[25] Increasingly families must fend for whatever shelter they can afford. Racial discrimination compounds the problem of competing for limited housing in the United States. Among the poor, this may mean living in a rat-infested single-room apartment or a shack without heat or running water. For some, housing problems may cause families to be divided; various members are shipped off to relatives or others to live. Dividing the family is an undesirable solution to the problem.[26]

The larger the family, the greater the incidence of poverty and housing problems. Fixed costs in one's budget, including housing, are those stationary payments which must be made. Too often food and clothing are budgeted as items which must be stretched, postponed, or cut back.[27] Moreover, overcrowding of family members may compound the stress of the parents and psychologically inhibit a child's sense of a physical and emotional space for growth. Overcrowding has been defined by census takers as dwellings in which at least three persons reside with 1.5 or more persons per room. Of the 13.1 million people living in such depressed housing, 700,000 lived in overcrowded conditions.[28]

HEALTH CARE

Like housing, access to health care is not an entitlemenet but comes usually through one's benefits at the workplace. Health-care coverage for the poor has been addressed through Medicaid, which on the surface appears to promote equal access by the poor to health care, but in reality constitutes a program that segregates the poor from the rest of society. For example, welfare recipients encounter doctors who refuse to care for them or who demean and treat them differently from their nonpoor patients. Even with Medicaid, the fact that millions of children and families have no adequate health care has been a major force in the development of health-insurance proposals. In addition, health problems and medical costs may precipitate poverty for families who lack adequate health-care protection or who are crippled by excessive health-care costs.[29]

CONCLUSION

This chapter has examined some of the major consequences of economic and employment policies for low-income families in the United States. Since economic and employment resources are essential for effective family functioning, it seems imperative that a major overhauling of income-support policies in the United States occur to ensure that families survive and their children thrive. To ask for anything less is to subject the future of families and the life chances of children to the potentially harmful vicissitudes of the economic system. By promoting ways to meet families' needs in a systematic yet nonintrusive manner, the U.S. could at least join numerous other nations that have deemed it a national public responsibility to invest in the economic well-being of one of their most precious resources.

It is too early to know the precise effect that President Reagan's budget proposal will have on poverty and poor families. But it seems evident that a good number of families will slip into poverty because of the removal of present support systems. Persons presently living in poverty will have less than before. The problems created by poverty will be experienced by an increasing number of families, and those families in poverty already will have their problems intensified.

NOTES

1. National Commission on Families and Public Policies, *Families and Public Policies in the United States.* Washington, D.C.: National Conference on Social Welfare, 1978.
2. *Ibid.*
3. Walsh, John, Miriam Johnson, and Marge D. Sugarman. *Help Wanted: Case Studies of Classified Ads.* Salt Lake: Olympus Publishing Co., 1975.
4. Briar, Katharine H. *The Effect of Long-Term Unemployment on Workers and Their Families.* San Francisco: R & E Research Press, 1978.
5. Sheppard, Harold L., and Harvey A. Belitsky. *The Job Hunt.* Baltimore: John Hopkins Press, 1960.
6. Light, Richard J. "Abused and Neglected Children in America: A Study of Alternative Policies," *Harvard Educational Review,* Vol. 43, No. 4, November 1973. Suzanne K. Steinmetz and Murray A. Strauss, eds. *Violence in the Family.* New York: Harper and Row, p. 9.
7. Such findings by Kurt Donig from West Berlin are reported in *Parade Magazine, The Seattle Post-Intelligencer,* Oct. 5, 1976, p. 6.
8. *Ibid.*
9. Briar.

10. Brenner, Harvey M. *Estimating the Social Costs of National Economic Policy: Implications for Mental and Criminal Aggression.* Joint Economic Committee, Paper No. 5. Washington, D.C.: Government Printing Office, 1976. Also see S. C. Cobb and S. Kasl, "Blood Pressure Changes in Men Undergoing Job Loss: A Preliminary Report," *Psychosomatic Medicine,* Jan. and Feb., 1970.

11. Brenner.

12. Donig.

13. Rosenman, Linda. "Unemployment of Women: A Social Policy Issue," *Social Work.* Jan., 1979, pp. 20-25.

14. Turem, Jerry S., and Michael Arnow. "Welfare Policy and Family Splitting," *Journal of Social Service Research,* Vol. 1, Fall 1977.

15. McEaddy, Beverly Johnson. "Women Who Head Families: A Socio-Economic Analysis," *Monthly Labor Review,* 1976, 99 (6).

16. Shkuda, Anne N. *Former Welfare Families Independence and Recurring Dependency.* New York: Center for New York City Affairs, New School for Social Research, Sept., 1976.

17. Chambre, Susan Maizel. "Welfare, Work, and Family Structure," *Social Work.* March, 1979.

18. National Research Council, *Toward a National Policy for Children and Families.* Washington, D.C.: National Academy of Sciences, 1976.

19. Durbin, Elizabeth. *Income and Employment.* New York: Praeger, 1969.

20. Background Papers, *President's Income Maintenance Commission Report.* Washington, D.C., 1980.

21. Lebeaux, Charles. "Life on A.D.C. Budgets of Despair," *Poverty in America.* Louis A. Ferman, Joyce L. Kornbluth, Alan Haber, eds. Ann Arbor: University of Michigan Press, 1965.

22. Lynch, James J. *The Broken Heart.* New York: Basic Books, 1977.

23. DeLone, Richard H. *Small Futures.* New York: Harcourt Brace and Jovanovich, 1979.

24. *Ibid.* Also see *Jubilee for Our Times.* Alvin Schorr, ed. New York: Columbia University Press, 1977.

25. Goodwin, Leonard. *Do the Poor Want to Work?* Washington, D.C.: The Brookings Institute, 1972.

26. Frieden, Bernard J. "Housing," *Encyclopedia of Social Work.* Washington, D.C.: National Association of Social Workers, Vol. 1.

27. Schorr, Alvin L. "How the Poor Are Housed," *Poverty in America.* Louis A. Ferman, Joyce L. Kornbluth, Alan Haber, eds. Ann Arbor: University of Michigan Press, 1965.

28. Frieden.

29. The fact that the United States continues to experience high infant and maternal mortality rates, along with insufficient medical care for about 20 million children, constitutes one of several reasons for a National Health Insurance Policy. See the National Research Councils, *Toward a National Policy for Children and Families.*

SUGGESTED READINGS

DeLone, Richard H. *Small Futures*. New York: Harcourt Brace and Jovanovich, 1979. DeLone analyzes the effects of structure, policies and ideology in America on families and the life chances of their children. His analysis offers useful material for discussion, debate as well as implications for structural reform.

Keniston, Kenneth and the Carnegie Council on Children. *All Our Children: The American Family Under Pressure*. New York: Harcourt Brace and Jovanovich, 1977. Problems of children and families are analyzed and suggestions for improved services are presented.

National Commission on Families and Public Policies. *Families and Public Policy in the United States*. Columbus, Ohio: National Conference on Social Welfare, 1978. This report offers timely data and analyses about the stresses and economic problems eroding effective family functioning. Implications for policy and service innovations are presented.

The National Research Council. *Toward a National Policy for Children and Families*. Washington, D.C.: National Academy of Sciences, 1976. Changing needs of American children and families are analyzed and arguments for policy development and future research are presented.

STUDY QUESTIONS

1. Discuss with local welfare department representatives what it is like for a family to live on a welfare budget. Then construct for yourself the kind of life-style, eating, housing, clothing, transportation, and recreation adjustments you or your family would have to make to live on a comparable budget.

2. Compare the rates of unemployment among adults and youth in your local community or your state with the estimated number of jobs available. What is the difference? What solutions is your community developing to assist these unemployed persons and their families?

3. What community day-care resources are made available for low-income, single-parent, female-headed families? Are these resources sufficient to meet the need? If not, what are the consequences of deficient community day-care resources to the work and family needs of these low-income, single-parent families?

4. Develop a list of all the factors that account for successful family functioning. How many of these factors depend on adequate financial resources for families? Interview community leaders to learn what percent of the families in your community suffer from such financial resources problems.

5. List recent public policy decisions which have a negative impact on low-income families that have been developed or implemented in your state. To what extent were the needs of economically insecure families addressed prior to the adoption of such policies? Who speaks on behalf of low-income families in your community?

4

Poverty and Income Inequality: An Economic Perspective

Stanley L. Brue

This quotation previews the central focus of this chapter:

Measures taken to increase the amount of economic equality will often reduce economic efficiency—that is, lower the gross national product. In trying to divide the pie more equally, we may inadvertently reduce its size.

Lesson 1. There are better and worse ways to promote equality.

Lesson 2. Equality is bought at a price. Thus, like any commodity, we must decide rationally how much to purchase.[1]

The "Big Tradeoff" between increased income equality and growth in the size of the national income has pushed itself to the forefront of economists' discussions of poverty and inequality.[2] This chapter describes and analyzes the concepts of equity and efficiency and then provides specific examples of the equity-efficiency tradeoff. Next, it dissects and evaluates the lessons referred to in the opening quotation. Finally, the chapter describes and rejects several policy approaches to poverty and inequality and then briefly sketches policies that either simultaneously achieve both equity and efficiency or minimize the costs of reducing poverty and inequality.

Before proceeding to a discussion of the central issue, a major historical detour is necessary. By examining the poverty and inequality records of the 1960s and 1970s, one can ascertain why the equity-efficiency tradeoff poses a major economic dilemma today.

THE CONTRASTING DECADES

The past two decades in the United States provide an interesting economic contrast. The following facts, which will be referred to in subsequent sections of the chapter, illustrate some of the key differences between the 1960s and 1970s. The facts also demonstrate some important economic trends.[3]

1. Real national income (total earned income adjusted for inflation) increased by 50.6% from 1960 to 1969; it increased by 28.1% from 1970 to 1979.
2. The average annual rate of productivity (output/person-hour) growth was 2.9% in the 1960s; it fell to 1.3% during the 1970s.
3. The average annual unemployment rate was 4.7% in the 1960s; it rose to 6.2% in the 1970s.
4. The Consumer Price Index (a measure of inflation) increased by 23.7% in the 1960s; it rose by 97.7% during the 1970s.
5. Government expenditure (federal, state, and local) as a percentage of gross national product (GNP) was 27.0% in 1960; 31.7% in 1970; and 36.0% in 1979.

These facts about the 1960s and 1970s contribute to understanding the poverty and income inequality records of the same two decades.

The Poverty/Inequality Record: The 1960s

In 1962, Michael Harrington published a profoundly disturbing book, *The Other America*, in which he detailed the plight of the poor in the land of abundance.[4] The poor, observed Harrington, numbered in the millions, yet were largely invisible to the society at large. Poverty was isolated and hidden in the slums and ghettos in the hearts of major cities. It also existed among the aged and infirmed, who rarely left their dilapidated rental rooms, and among the rural population, who were located far from the visibility of those living in suburbia.

FIGURE 1
Progress Against Poverty, 1960-1980

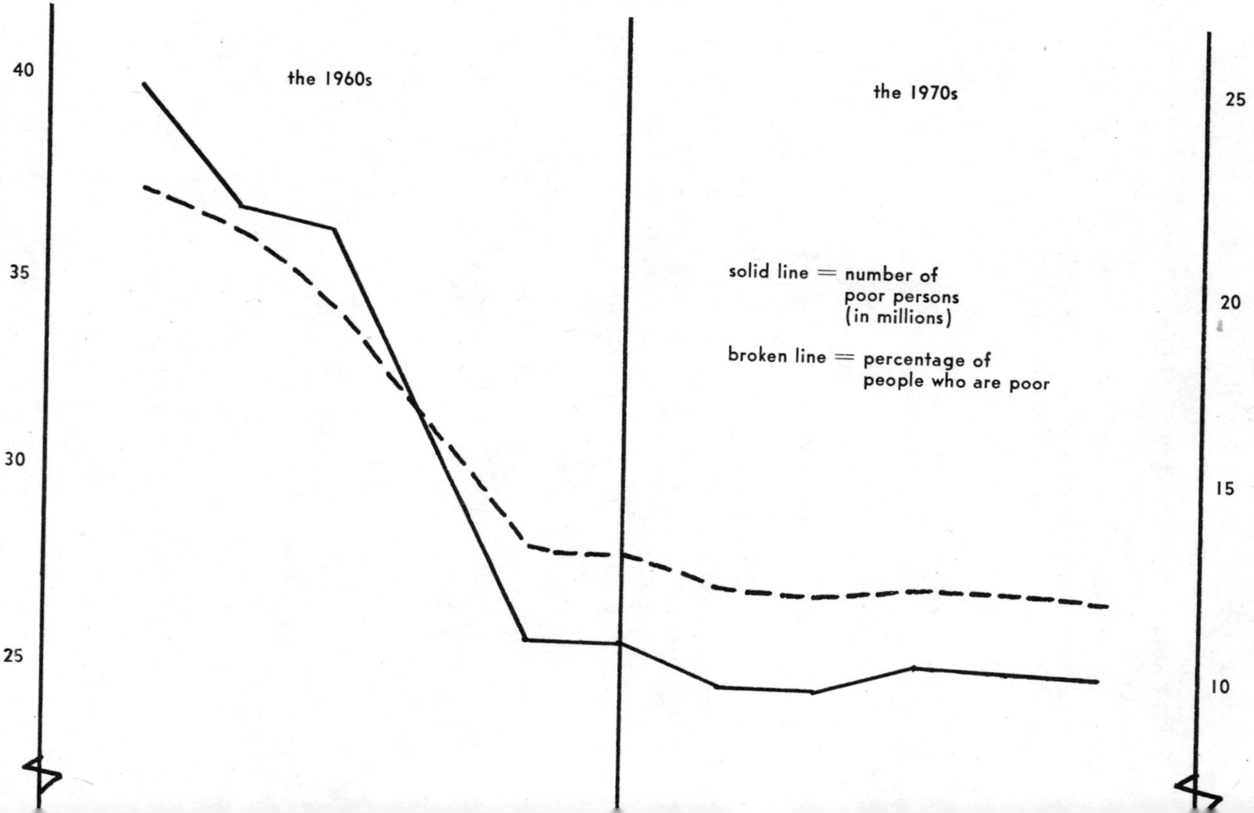

the 1960s

the 1970s

solid line = number of
poor persons
(in millions)

broken line = percentage of
people who are poor

40

35

30

25

25

20

15

10

The Other America, along with efforts by sociologists, ministers, economists, and the media, shook the nation's complacency and opened its eyes to a reality that demanded attention. The ensuing discussion and debate culminated in a War on Poverty declared by President Johnson in 1964. Government officials established a minimum family-income level that represented a poverty threshold and declared those families with less than that income level to be poor. The federal government set the poverty line at $3000 for a typically-sized family in 1964 and adjusted it upward each year thereafter because of inflation. Also, in 1964 Congress passed legislation establishing specific programs designed to reduce the number of Americans living in poverty.

Did poverty decline during the 1960s? Figure 1 helps answer this question.

According to the Census Bureau data used in Figure 1, 39.9 million Americans lived in poverty in 1960. That figure represented 22.2% of the total population. The solid line in Figure 1 shows the total number of poor persons (measured on the left-hand axis) who lived in poverty during each year of the 1960s. The broken line depicts the percentage of total population who were poor (measured on the right-hand axis) during each year of the decade.

The poverty trend was clearly downward during the 1960s. By 1970, based on a higher monetary definition of the poverty line because of inflation, the number of those in poverty had fallen to 25.4 million, and the percentage of the population in poverty had declined to 12.6%. The answer to the question, "Did poverty decline during the 1960s?" is an indisputable yes. But it is also evident from Figure 1 that though much success has been achieved in reducing poverty, the war on poverty remained unwon. In 1970 over 25 million people, one out of eight Americans, still remained poor. Additionally, many of those formerly in poverty were precariously situated only slightly above the poverty line.

Paradoxically, although the number of people in poverty declined appreciably during the 1960s, the distribution of income remained virtually unchanged. This paradox can be resolved by examining some of the "statements of fact" previously listed. The 1960s were a period of relatively high employment and strong sustained growth of national income. Real national income increased by 50 percent, labor productivity rose by 32 percent, the unemployment rate fell throughout the decade, and inflation was relatively mild.

The increase in employment and the expansion of overall income during the 1960s significantly reduced the incidence of poverty. Many of those who were in poverty in 1960 shared proportionately in the general income growth and thereby moved above the poverty line. The economic growth of the 1960s also generated rising tax revenues, a growing proportion of which were used for income transfers and poverty programs. Recall that government expenditures as a percentage of GNP rose from 27.0% in 1960 to 31.7% in 1970.

Thus, the 1960s represented "a positive sum game." Gains for one group did not dictate offsetting losses for other groups, because all groups shared in the income growth. The slices of the economic pie (income distribution) remained proportional to the other slices, but each group found its slice, in an absolute sense, to be larger than before. That increase created an escape from poverty (as officially defined) for many people in the lowest 20% of the distribution of income.

The Poverty/Income Inequality Record: The 1970s

Unlike the 1960s, the 1970s were a period of simultaneous inflation and stagnant growth of real income (stagflation). The decade created difficulties for both the "other America" and for the larger American economy. The nation experienced two major recessions, the 1974-75 one being the worst economic downturn since the Great Depression of the 1930s. The average annual unemployment rate for the ten-year period was 6.2%, the Consumer Price Index rose by 97.7%, productivity slowed to 1.3% annually, and real income growth fell to an average annual rate of less than 3%. By the end of the 1970s, the "positive sum game" seemed to have been replaced by a "zero-sum game," one in which the gains and losses are equal. Under the rules of the "zero-sum game," increases for some income recipients must be financed out of declines in real income for other groups.[5]

How did the poor fare under the economic circumstances of the 1970s? Figure 1, referred to earlier, provides a *partial* answer. According to the solid line, the number of poor in 1970 and 1979 was approximately the same. For example, 25.4 million Americans fell below the poverty line in 1970, and 24.7 million were there in 1977. The percentage of total population in poverty, shown by the broken line, declined only slightly, and ranged between 13-12% throughout the decade.

And what about the distribution of income? According to the Bureau of Census data, the distribution in the late 1970s was nearly a carbon copy of the distribution in 1970—and, for that matter, the distribution for each year since World War II. Had progress in reducing poverty come to a halt?

Superficially, the answer would appear to be yes. But the Census Bureau data are deceptive. Economists now generally agree that more progress was made against poverty in the 1970s than indicated in Figure 1. The major reason that the data overstate the number of people in poverty is that they fail to include in-kind transfer payments. These in-kind transfers differ from cash transfer payments in that the former involve transfers of goods and services. These in-kind transfers include housing assistance, food stamps, Medicaid, Medicare, and child nutrition assistance, all of which serve a similar function as income: they provide means to obtain needed commodities. Federal outlays for in-kind transfers, in dollars adjusted for inflation, increased by over 100% between 1970 and 1977. Federal expenditures on the food stamp program, for instance, increased from $850 million (in 1977 dollars) to $5.0 billion in the seven-year period. None of these in-kind transfers is included in the Census Bureau data used to construct Figure 1.[6]

The Congressional Budget Office has revised the Census Bureau data to include in-kind transfers. If one uses the revised data, the poverty record of the 1970s—the period that has witnessed the largest rise of in-kind transfers—is less disturbing. For example, after the adjustment, the percentage of the total population in poverty in 1976 was 6%, rather than the 11.8% reported in Figure 1.

According to economist Morton Paglin:

> The transfers have been on a sufficiently massive scale to effect a major reduction in the poverty population. It would have been surprising if they had not done so. What is disquieting is the failure to recognize this accomplishment.[7]

In summary, during the full period between 1960 and 1980, there was a substantial decline in poverty. The greatest decline occurred in the 1960s and was caused mainly by economic growth, low rates of unemployment, and the War on Poverty, the latter financed out of expanded tax revenues from the growth of real national income. During the 1970s, the decline in poverty was much less pronounced, and owed less to rising overall real income, and more to increased transfer payments, primarily those of the in-kind variety. The federal government financed these growing transfer payments by re-prioritizing the budget, via increased tax revenues generated because of inflation, and by expansion of the national debt. And although the "other America" had shrunk, it certainly had not disappeared.

Would further efforts to reduce poverty and improve the distribution of income erode economic growth? Had that been the case in the 1970s? These questions, together with the realities of stagflation, focused economists' attention on the equity-efficiency tradeoff.

THE BIG TRADEOFF: THE EMERGING ISSUE

Collectively, Americans profess to value both equity and efficiency —that is, they prefer greater equality in the distribution of income to less equality, and they prefer greater, as opposed to less, growth of real income. Both goals require some elaboration. The following two sections define the terms *equity* and *efficiency* and address the question as to whether the goals are desirable and attainable.

The Efficiency Goal

In discussing poverty, income inequality, and equity-efficiency tradeoffs, economists use the term *efficiency* to describe the optimal production of products and services and the corresponding optimal generation of national income. Such optimums occur when all of society's limited land, labor, and capital resources are fully employed and are allocated to their highest valued economic uses. *Efficiency* also implies an optimal (not necessarily maximal) expansion of national income from one period to the next, or economic growth. Thus, the *efficiency* goal might better be described as the *employment, production, and growth* goal.

A crucial, yet often misunderstood reality, is that greater production of goods or services that people value is the sole source of increasing real national income, viewed in the aggregate. Greater national income is only "real" when it results from greater production of goods and services. Increases in real wages and real national income (both termed "real" because they reflect actual purchasing power) are caused by the increased availability or productivity of land, labor, and capital resources.

High employment, increasing productivity, and economic growth are inherently neither desirable nor undesirable. Participants in the market—consumers, workers, and producers—and voters in elections express their collective judgments on the desirability of these goals. Through observation of the participants in the market and in elections, economists conclude that the great majority of Americans place a high value on employment, production, and expansion of real income (particularly their own!).[8]

To declare that people value something, however, is not to say that they value it at any price, or cost. For example, economic growth might be increased by lengthening the work week from 40 to 60 hours. Economic growth might be increased by allowing factories to pollute the air and water, instead of restricting that activity. Long-term economic growth might be increased by voting to place extremely high taxes on consumption goods in order to increase the prices of these commodities and reduce their production and sales, thereby freeing economic resources to produce capital goods. Or, economic growth might be increased by foregoing all transfer payments and channeling those funds to subsidies for research and development or for the production of new plants and equipment. Few individuals would support these methods for increasing the nation's national income. Most Americans would judge the price to be too high. The benefits simply would not match the costs.

There are better and worse ways to promote economic growth, just as there are better and worse ways to promote equality. Because expansion of real income is bought at a price (the highest of which are reduced present consumption and socially undesirable side-effects), society must decide rationally how much of it to purchase. The election of Ronald Reagan in 1980 and the support for his pro-growth tax and expenditure policies suggest that a substantial number of Americans desire to purchase a faster growth rate than that of the 1970s.

The Equity Goal

In this discussion, the term *equity* is loosely used. It refers to a more equal distribution of personal income, presumably a distribution that conforms more closely to society's collective sense of fairness and justice.

Ascertaining what Americans mean by equity in the distribution of income is not a simple task; in fact, detective work is necessary. The following approach comes to mind:

> I learn a good deal by merely observing you,
> And letting you talk as long as you please,
> And taking note of what you do not say.
>
> —T. S. Eliot

What is it then that Americans do not say? Americans, taken collectively clearly do not say, "Everybody has won, and all must have [equal] prizes," as did the dodo bird in *Alice in Wonderland*. Equity, for most Americans, does not mean complete income equality. Nor do most people say, as did Alexander Pope, "Whatever is, is right." For most Americans, equity is apparently not the status quo.

The present concept of economic equity in the United States, as judged by market behavior, charitable giving, recent laws, and public policies, appears to be: (1) a fair economic race, with an equal start, equal access to advantage, and equal protection from disadvantage along the course, and (2) a modified system of rewards via private charity and public policy so that absolute poverty does not exist and so that the distribution of income is more, but not totally equal. The commitment to achieve the *equity* goal, however, appears to be weaker than that of achieving the *efficiency* goal.

The traditional economic rationale for greater equality in the distribution of income rests on the concept of diminishing marginal utility of money. Utility is a personal, subjective, difficult-to-measure value that influences the economic decisions of consumers, producers, workers, and other participants in the economic system. Economists define utility as "want satisfying power," or "satisfaction." The term "marginal" refers to "extra" or "added." Thus, the marginal utility of money is the extra satisfaction from the last dollar earned and spent.

As a person consumes successive units of an item, the marginal utility tends to decline. For example, one's extra satisfaction from the consumption of a fifth successive fast-food hamburger is unlikely to yield as much marginal utility as did the fourth, the fourth less than the third, and so forth. Several early economists applied this concept to the equity question. For instance, A. C. Piguo commented in 1848:

> It is evident that any transference of income from a relatively rich man to a relatively poor man of similar temperament, since it enables more intense wants [higher marginal utility] to be satisfied at the expense of less intense wants [lower marginal utility], must increase the aggregate sum of satisfactions.[9]

Does a reduction of a dollar of income for a person earning $100,000 a year yield as great a loss of marginal utility as the gain in marginal utility for the recipient of the dollar who earns $3000 a year? Piguo, and others, answered no, and thereby established a rationale for income redistribution.

Contemporary economists, including those who strongly favor redistribution, reject this traditional rationale. The technical problems in applying the concept of diminishing marginal utility to money and to redistribution are many, but two are paramount. First, money buys an amazing array of products and services. Diminishing marginal utility applies to all individual goods, but it may not apply to money, an item that can be used to purchase the full range of products and services that are available. Second, the personal, subjective nature of utility makes it impossible to make utility comparisons between and among separate people.

What rationale then can be provided for the equity goal? The best economic rationale is amazingly simple. If society values something, and the private sector cannot or will not provide it, public provision is warranted so long as benefits exceed costs. For a variety of reasons, many people value a reduction in poverty and a more equitable distribution of income, just as they value weather-warning systems, police protection, public disease-control, national defense, and other "public goods." These goods are poor candidates for private production and sale because they cannot be marketed in a profitable way. The benefits from these public goods are indivisible; no one can be excluded from receiving them, regardless of whether or not one pays for them. The solution: public sector provision. If society values and is willing to pay for poverty reduction and improved income equality, then the public sector should finance the production of these public goods via general taxation and provide them efficiently and effectively.

The public sector has the tools for providing greater income equality. But, the same caution provided in reference to society's desire for economic growth applies: to state that we desire more equality is not to say that we desire it at any cost. "There are better and worse ways to promote equality. Equality is bought at a price. Thus, like any commodity, we must decide rationally how much to purchase."[10]

The Tradeoff: Graphic Representation

Having discussed efficiency and equity, we can next examine the tradeoff itself. Figure 2 helps us understand the situation. Please note that the graph is intended only as a conceptual aid. The actual shape of the concave curve in Figure 4-2 has not been determined empirically.

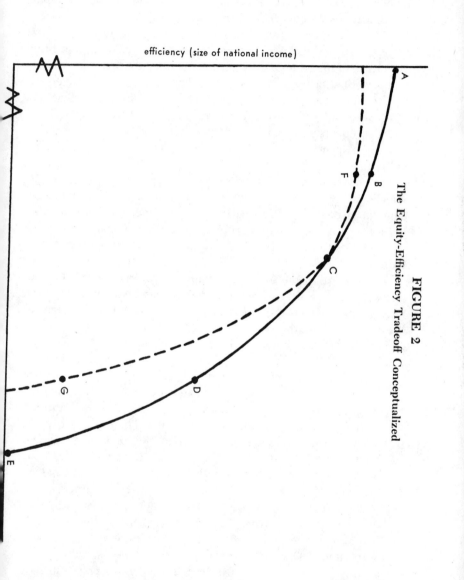

efficiency (size of national income)

FIGURE 2

The Equity-Efficiency Tradeoff Conceptualized

The vertical axis in the figure measures *efficiency* (size of national income) and the horizontal axis measures *equity* (the degree of equality in the distribution of income). The solid curve represents the best tradeoff between efficiency and equity, and the broken-line curve depicts a poorer tradeoff. First, focus on the solid curve and Point C. Assume that the economy is initially at Point C, and there is a desire to increase national income. Policies that promote the expansion of national income may reduce the degree of income equality. At Position B on the solid curve, national income is higher than at C, but equality is lower. To accomplish the extra growth of national income, society must give up some equality (a notion which in some respects resembled the present policy of the People's Republic of China).

Next, observe the opposite situation—a desire to increase equality. Policies that increase equality (a move from C to D) may reduce national income. Point D clearly represents more equality than C, but it just as clearly comes at the expense of less national income (a situation possibly reflected in U.S. transfer payment policies during the 1970s).

Which point on the solid line should society choose? That is not for economists to decide. Society at large must make that decision through the market and the ballot box. Several other chapters of this book examine the political, social, ethical, and religious values and frameworks that shape and implement our collective decision making.

The two lessons first cited in the opening quotation and then again discussed in the foregoing examination of equity and efficiency goals are also clearly shown by the figure. First, "there are better and worse ways to promote equality." There are two paths from Point C to greater equality: (1) along the solid line to D, and (2) along the broken line to G. Both D and G represent the same amount of equality, yet D produces a greater level of national income than does G. Second, "equality is bought at a price. Thus, like any commodity, we must decide rationally how much to purchase." Most citizens have no desire to maximize national income at all costs, including zero equality, such as at Position A; nor do they desire to attain 100% equality at all costs, including no national income, such as at Position E. Instead, they search for points such as B, C, and D, or other compromise positions on the solid curve, and strive to achieve policies that shift the entire curve outward—policies that expand the size of the income pie *and* slice it more equitably.

The Leaky Bucket Analogy

In 1976, economist Arthur Okun, using an analogy of a leaky bucket, proposed an interesting hypothetical experiment by which to test attitudes toward the tradeoff between efficiency and equity. The experiment involves the transfer of income from the wealthiest 5% of families to the poorest 20%. A proposal is made to tax the top 5% an added $4000 each and to redistribute the proceeds to the lowest 20%. The latter group contains four times as many families, therefore, each family would receive $1000 of extra income. "However, the program has an unsolved technological problem: the money must be carried from the rich to poor in a leaky bucket. Some of it will simply disappear in transit, so the poor will not receive all the money that is taken from the rich." [11] Much of the income is an efficiency loss that disappears and is lost to society forever. The rest of it is money that stays within the overall economy but fails to get to the poor.

Suppose 10% of the money leaks out, leaving $900 for each poor family and a national income loss of $100 for society at large. "Should society still make the switch?" asks Okun. "What if 50% leaks out? What if 75% leaks out, or even 99%?" Would one still favor the redistribution?

Okun contended that one's answer cannot be right or wrong because it depends on personal valuations of equality vs. efficiency. Of course, the formation of these values is complex, influenced by the economic system itself as well as by religious and humanitarian beliefs.

What are the sources of leakage from Okun's tax-transfer bucket? Several economists have addressed specific aspects of this topic. Essentially, there are six sources of leakage: administrative costs; reduced work incentives for taxpayers; avoidance and evasion of taxes; disincentives to save, invest, and take risks; disincentives for transfer recipients to work and acquire skills; and welfare fraud. Some of these leakages are substantial, while others are of lesser consequence. An examination of each of them follows.

1. Administrative costs

Federal, state, and local governments employ thousands of workers to design, administer, and audit the many social programs that are designed to reduce poverty and inequality. The salaries paid to these workers, along with other costs such as office construction, computers, typewriters, desks, heating bills, janitorial services, and so forth, represent money that leaks from the tax-transfer bucket. These expenses are paid via tax revenues, but do not get transferred to the poor. This is not to suggest that such a use of resources is unproductive, for these resources are producing services that are valued. But the land, labor, and capital resources employed for this purpose are unavailable to use for other purposes, some of which might generate greater growth of national income, for example, research and development or the production of capital goods. To that extent, there is an actual loss of potential income for society itself.

2. Reduced work incentives for taxpayers

The impact of high-marginal tax rates (rates on the last dollars earned) has received much recent attention. Economists, including Arthur Laffer and other advisors to the Reagan administration, contend that Americans have responded to higher real taxes over the past decade by reducing their work time and increasing their leisure.

The rapid inflation of the 1970s increased real tax burdens for many individuals and families. People's monetary income tended to rise with inflation, but their real income (purchasing power) remained relatively stagnant. Yet the increase in monetary income placed people into higher and higher personal income-tax brackets. For example, people earning a taxable income of $20,000 a year may have received a ten-percent pay raise, boosting their taxable monetary income to $22,000. But if inflation was also ten percent during that year, their real income remained the same; $22,000 could buy no more than $20,000 bought the year before. Yet these people were propelled into a higher income-tax bracket and were forced to pay a greater real tax for each hour worked.

Laffer and others argue that these rising real tax rates, the revenue from which is used to finance larger transfers (among other things), substantially reduce incentives to work, thereby reducing national income. According to this view, the increased tax rates make work more expensive and leisure relatively cheap. Some workers exchange their full-time jobs for part-time ones; refuse overtime work; demand longer vacations, holidays and special leaves; increase their absenteeism; reduce personal investment in the acquisition of education and skills; demand shorter work weeks; and abandon the motivational influence of trying to get ahead.

This view suffers from a major weakness—to date, most economic studies do not support it. It is true that an increased tax rate does reduce one's after-tax return from an hour of work and therefore does make leisure less expensive, but this is only one of two possible effects. The other is that a higher tax rate reduces one's total after-tax income. If a person desires to maintain that previous level of income, he or she would have an incentive to work more. Statistical studies show that the structure of the American tax system, replete with its numerous deductions, credits, and regressive local taxes, has no appreciable overall impact on work effort. That is not to deny the reality that there exists some tax rate above which the work reduction impact would dominate and the total size of the leak from the tax-transfer bucket would become substantial. Some economists suggest that one or two European countries may have tax rates in that range.

3. Avoidance and evasion of taxes

A third potential leak in the income transfer bucket is the effort to avoid or minimize tax payments. As Okun colorfully observed, high tax rates are followed by attempts of ingenious people to beat them as surely as snow is followed by little children on sleds.

Efforts to avoid and evade taxes take many forms. Examples include: insisting on more of one's total compensation in nontaxable forms, such as use of company airplanes, liberal expense accounts, and other perquisites; hiring legal specialists to discover loopholes in the tax code; establishing "tax shelters"; failing to report tips and other types of "informal" income; engaging in bartering; skimming retail sales; renting property covertly; and taking unwarranted deductions and tax credits.

Several economists report a substantial rise of this "underground," "subterranean," or "irregular" economy in the United States. A 1976 IRS study, for example, determined that 36 to 40% of all income earned by self-employed people, 35 to 50% of all rental and royalty income, 17 to 22% of all capital gains on sales of property, and 8 to 16% of interest and dividend income went unreported.

The growth of the "underground" economy has many causes, only one of which is tax-transfer programs. But, as economist Melvyn B. Krauss of New York University has pointed out, high taxes severely tax the honesty of ordinary citizens as well as their incomes. He points out that a leading Dutch newspaper recently reported that the national motto in Holland has become "Paying taxes is for jerks," and that two prominent Swedish Social Democratic economists, Nobel Prize winner Gunnar Myrdal and highly regarded Assar Linbeck, have noted that the corruption of the value of honesty caused by high Swedish taxes is one of the welfare state's most pressing problems.[12]

In summary, the tax-transfer bucket may have a third general form of leakage: evasion and avoidance of taxes. This may (1) reduce the size of the water in the bucket (national income) by channeling efforts toward less productive uses, (2) reduce the flow of tax revenues which are used for the transfers, and (3) undermine traditional values of honesty and fairness.

4. *Disincentives to save, invest, and take risks*

A fourth potential area of leakage from the tax-transfer bucket is a reduction in saving, investing, and risk taking caused by high marginal tax rates. Economist Martin Feldstein of Harvard contends that tax-transfer programs, especially the Social Security program, retard saving. Workers believe that their Social Security taxes represent an amount of current income set aside for retirement. But Social Security is not a pension fund, and the tax payments generate no added savings or loanable funds for society. Feldstein contends that people save considerably less than they would in the absence of the Social Security program. This reduces loanable funds, causing an increase in the interest rate, which produces declines in investment, capital formation, and growth of the national income pie.[13]

Feldstein and other economists also contend that high personal and corporate tax rates reduce incentives for individuals and firms to take risks and to expand their capital stock. Risk taking and capital formation, of course, are both vital elements for economic growth.

Many liberal economists echo some of the same concerns as their more conservative colleagues. They point out that U.S. stagflation is partly the result of investment (purchase of new capital) falling to 10% of the GNP, compared to 15% in West Germany and 20% in Japan. To adjust the investment ratio to 15% in the United States, well over $100 billion would have to be shifted from present consumption to saving and investment. Policies to accomplish that shift pose difficult problems for present efforts to reduce income inequality.

5. *Disincentives for transfer recipients to work and acquire skills*

Perhaps the greatest leak in the tax-transfer bucket is the impact of the transfers on recipients' incentives to work and acquire skills. People receiving cash or in-kind transfers face a marginal tax rate, just as do those in higher income brackets. For the transfer recipients, the marginal tax rate involves no taxes at all, but rather losses of welfare or in-kind benefits when work income rises. For example, in many states a recipient of Aid for Dependent Children benefits loses 67¢ of welfare for each extra $1 of income earned. That represents a 67% marginal tax rate on work income. (The highest marginal tax bracket for work income under the federal income-tax law is 50%.) When transportation, food, child care, and clothing costs are considered, the effective marginal tax rate may even approach or exceed 100%, that is, to earn a dollar of income, one incurs costs and loses transfers that equal or exceed $1. Can there be any doubt that work incentives are impaired under such a system?

This leak in the tax-transfer bucket may be seen in a hypothetical example. Assume that society defines the poverty line for a family of four at $7000 and enacts a program to plug the "poverty gap" by bringing all such families up to that income level. Assume that Family A earns $6000 a year and Family B earns $8000. If work disincentives are ignored, government might conclude that it needs only to transfer $1000 of income to eliminate poverty. Family A, however, can get $7000 of transfer without working. If it takes that option, $7000, not $1000, must be transferred to fill the poverty gap. The extra $6000 is a leak from the tax-transfer bucket. And what about Family B which is earning $8000? Might it not be tempted to accept $7000 of income supplement rather than work forty hours a week and earn $8000? If it succumbs to that temptation, a family theretofore not in poverty, will fall into it, and the tax-transfer leak will rise by another $7000. Is it possible that the more the government transfers, the more it will still have to transfer to accomplish income distribution goals?

The U.S. Department of Health and Welfare has carried out several experiments to test the feasibility of proposed tax-transfer schemes that would reduce the work disincentives of existing programs. Based upon the most recent and longest experiment, the Seattle and Denver test, analysts concluded that the cost of a national income-supplement program would be 16 to 31% higher than if participants maintained exactly their preexperiment work effort.[14]

Several other examples of this leak in the tax-transfer bucket can be cited. Recipients of Social Security Disability (SSD) benefits must under the terms of the law be medically incapable of holding a job. But in a study of men aged 45 to 54, Harvard economist Jonathon Leonard discovered that higher benefits cause men to drop out of the labor force and become SSD recipients. His study controlled for other variables and found that a $180 increase in "real" annual benefits caused a one percentage point increase in the proportion of men on disability. Leonard contends that 43% of the observed decline in the proportion of men 45 to 54 in the labor force during the past few years is caused by liberalization of real SSD benefits.

The same policy dilemma arises with respect to another important social program—unemployment compensation. Feldstein and others observe that unemployment compensation benefits, pegged at 50% of one's lost *gross* income actually replace 65 to 75% of *after-tax* income for many recipients. These economists question whether or not the system provides sufficient incentive for recipients to seek employment at salaries that are lower than those of their previous jobs. According to Feldstein's study, nearly 1.25 percentage points of unemployment can be explained by unemployment compensation.[15] Other economists, such as Stephen Marston of the Brookings Institution, accept Feldstein's major premise, but reject his 1.25 percentage point figure, replacing it with one in the .25 to .50 percentage point range.

Several other examples of distinctive leaks can be presented, including those associated with the in-kind transfer programs, but the examples would here be redundant. To do away with disability and unemployment-compensation programs would be a tragic error. The purpose of this discussion is to reinforce the point that the tax-transfer bucket leaks. Society must recognize that reality in order to make a rational decision on how much leakage to accept in accomplishing redistributional goals.

6. Welfare fraud

The final leak in the tax-transfer bucket is welfare fraud. This involves the illegal receipt of payments either by those providing services to the poor or by those not truly eligible for benefits. These funds are siphoned away from the poor and represent money that leaks from the income transfer bucket. Recent studies indicate that the dollar amounts involved in Medicaid and food stamp fraud are substantial. Fraud, however, is confined to a small percentage of providers and recipients.

Equity vs. Efficiency: A Word of Caution

Tax and transfer programs can and do reduce poverty and income inequality. They also may reduce the size of the national income pie in the process. But the size of this reduction is a matter of considerable dispute, for nobody has successfully estimated the dimension of the tradeoff. As a result, the equity-efficiency tradeoff notion is subject to misuse. Those people who value efficiency highly, and equity hardly at all, have a tendency to *overstate* the degree of the income loss from redistribution. Rather than admit their values, they contend that they favor redistribution in principle, but oppose it in practice because the price is too high. Many economists (this writer included) may inadvertently overestimate the tradeoff because of their training and their focus on efficiency. On the other hand, those people who value equality highly, and efficiency very little, have a tendency to *understate* or even *dismiss* the extent of income loss from redistribution.

Statements such as, "Redistribution schemes threaten the very existence of the United States' economy," and "Greater equality is absolutely essential for the very survival of the mixed-market economy," usually reflect deeply ingrained biases rather than carefully thought-out appraisals. If society truly desires greater equality in the distribution of income, it surely has the means to accomplish that end. To say that something has a price (the loss of national income), even a high one, is not to say that it should not be bought.

BETTER AND WORSE WAYS
TO PROMOTE EQUALITY

It is not the intent of this chapter to outline a comprehensive program for reducing poverty and promoting income equality. That is a task that has befuddled teams of experts for decades. But based on the concepts developed in this chapter, we can reject some broad approaches. Our criteria for rejection and acceptance are as follows:

Criterion 1. A policy is acceptable if it increases both efficiency and equity (shifts the curve in Figure 2 outward).

Criterion 2. A policy is acceptable if it increases equity at the lowest possible loss of efficiency (moves society along the outermost curve in Figure 2). This criterion assumes that society is willing to bear the cost of that efficiency loss.

Worse Ways

Several general approaches to poverty and inequality must be rejected for their failure to meet Criteria 1 and 2. These approaches are given vivid names to reflect their extreme manifestations.

The first of these policies might be termed the *Pol Pot Approach.* Pol Pot was the Cambodian leader whose attempts to restructure society, presumably to create equality, led not only to a decline in income for the wealthy, but also to a complete collapse of income for the poor. Starvation for the masses followed. Policies that aim at making the rich poor, when that also makes the poor poorer, should be rejected on the basis of the two criteria as well as on the basis of religious and humanistic values. Hatred of the rich, and stereotyping of how they got that way, is just as much a vice as lack of compassion for the poor and stereotyping of why they are that way. In its extreme manifestation, the folly of the Pol Pot Approach is easy to see, but in its less extreme forms the approach possesses considerable public policy appeal and presence in the United States. For example, many people support policies that reduce rental income for the wealthy even though those same policies worsen the long-run housing prospects for the poor. Often policies that would reduce absolute poverty are rejected solely because they would enhance corporate profits.

A close variation of the Pol Pot Approach might be termed the *Handicapper General Approach,* so named after Kurt Vonnegut's character, Harrison Bergeron, in *Welcome to the Monkey House.* An excerpt from this source makes the point. Policies that handicap the talented may reduce income inequality, but will do so at an extremely high cost in terms of lost total income.

> The year was 2081, and everyone was finally equal. This was due to . . . the unceasing vigilance of agents of the United States Handicapper General . . . .
>
> George [Bergeron, whose] intelligence was way above normal, had a little mental handicap radio in his ear. He was required by law to wear it at all times. It was tuned to a government transmitter. Every twenty seconds or so, the transmitter would send out some sharp noises to keep people like George from taking unfair advantage of their brains . . . .

On the television screen were ballerinas. They weren't really very good—no better than anyone else would have been anyway. They were burdened with sashweights and bags of birdshot and their faces were masked, so that no one, seeing a free and graceful gesture or a pretty face, would feel like something the cat drug in. George [began thinking] that maybe dancers shouldn't be handicapped. But, . . . a twenty-one gun salute in his head stopped that.[16]

A third general approach that must be rejected because of its failure either to improve both equity and efficiency or to minimize the cost of achieving equity may be called the *Slavery Solution.* This approach reduces income inequality and poverty, but intentionally or unintentionally does so by creating a permanent caste of people almost totally dependent on the state and almost totally subjected to the state's agents, the social work bureaucracy. The Slavery Solution to poverty not only violates Criteria 1 and 2, but is repugnant to religious and humanistic values. It is shortsighted and ineffective to help people by subjugating them. Some observers are concerned that several poverty programs, with their high marginal tax rates, in-kind benefits, and bureaucratic strings, come dangerously close to this approach.

A final nonsolution to the poverty and income inequality problem might be called the *Do-It-with-Mirrors Approach.* Several specific policies fit within this category. For example, some economists have ended poverty in the United States by defining it away. Indeed, one must use proper definitions of income and include in-kind transfers, but the human reality of poverty cannot be reduced by means of mere statistical manipulations.

A second example of a Do-It-with-Mirrors Approach is the notion that general, massive tax cuts will increase work effort, saving, and investment so dramatically that government will end up with more tax revenue to distribute to the poor. Poverty and income inequality are real problems, requiring practical, not Do-It-with-Mirrors, solutions.

Better Ways

Three broad interrelated approaches to poverty and income inequality fit either Criterion 1 (improve both equity and efficiency), or Criterion 2 (minimize the efficiency costs of achieving equity). These approaches are better ways to attack the problem.

At the risk of great oversimplification, this final section provides a brief sketch of these three approaches.

1. *Targeting policies to remove the causes of poverty and inequality*

Lack of sufficient income is a symptom of poverty, not a cause (although, of course, it can be a cause of subsequent poverty for children of the poor). Often only the symptoms of poverty are treated by people who think erroneously that they have treated the cause and then wonder why the problem seems to recur and why continuing treatment is necessary.

As pointed out in previous chapters, the causes of poverty are numerous and complex. Many of the causes cannot be treated directly, and treatment of symptoms becomes the optimal approach. For example, most—but not all—people who are in poverty because of severe handicaps or disabilities require recurring, direct cash assistance. The present Supplemental Security Income (SSI) program is an efficient method for reducing poverty caused by blindness, disability, and old age. In other instances, the causes of poverty and low income are treatable and greater efforts should be made toward that end.

One such cause is lack of education, training, and skills. Several human resource programs aimed at this cause have provided a good return on society's expenditure. Much more could be done in this area. For example, government could subsidize paid, on-the-job skill training directly in the private sector, just as it now does, indirectly, for college students who are acquiring job skills at public institutions of higher learning. To produce an incentive to enter such programs, transfer programs could be restructured for the able-bodied so that benefits would decline at a set schedule.

A second treatable cause of poverty and income inequality is unemployment. Full employment, maintainable in the long run only by the expansion of capital, must remain the central priority of economic policy. That does not mean that temporary employment gains should be bought via fiscal and monetary policies that accelerate inflation, for the recession that would eventually follow would produce more unemployment losses than the temporary gains. Policies that vigorously promote full employment of the nations' economic resources should be legislated and executed. A strong, stable economy, characterized by price stability, high employment, and balanced economic growth, is a powerful antipoverty force. This is not a "trickle down" concept; it is a "rising tide raises all boats" idea. More of the efforts to eradicate poverty should be directed toward employment and skill acquisition, both of which boost production, rather than toward transfer payments that mainly boost consumption.

A third treatable cause of poverty is discrimination against racial minorities, women, and elderly workers. Antidiscrimination measures that guarantee equal access to quality education, job training, employment, promotions, and housing serve to reduce poverty and improve the distribution of income. Additional resources should be devoted to this purpose. Discrimination impedes attaining both the equity and efficiency goals.

A final treatable cause of poverty and inequality is family breakup and the resulting loss of income for many families headed by females. In 1959 only 20% of all poverty families were headed by females; in 1980, the percentage was 50%. More programs and resources should be targeted directly at this group. Possibilities include subsidized child care, skill-training programs, subsidized on-the-job training in the private sector, public-sector jobs programs, and tax concessions to businesses which hire heads of poverty households. To satisfy Criteria 1 and 2, these programs should emphasize employment and skill acquisition and deemphasize transfers.

2. Treating the symptoms of poverty efficiently

The approach to poverty and income inequality discussed in the previous paragraphs is for the long term. Causes of low income are not eliminated easily nor quickly; symptom relief is also necessary. A delicate balance is required here. The treatment of the symptom (low income), regardless of the purity of its motivation, must not contradict the treatment of the cause. That is, transfer payments should not be structured in such a way as to reduce the incentives to participate in training or employment. Likewise, the treatment of symptoms should be accomplished in a way that minimizes the efficiency leaks referred to earlier.

A majority of economists believe that the most efficient way to transfer income is through a negative income tax or an income supplement scheme. Such a plan would establish a guaranteed base-income level reflecting family size. Table I describes a hypothetical plan for a family of four.

Table I

Typical Income Supplement (Negative Income Tax) Plan
(Family of Four)

Earned Income	Income Supplement (negative tax payment)	Total Income
$ 0	$6000	$ 6000
2000	5000	7000
4000	4000	8000
6000	3000	9000
8000	2000	10,000
10 000	1000	11,000
12,000	0	12,000

As income is earned, the base-income supplement of $6000 declines by 50% of the family's earned income. For example, as earned income increases from $4000 to $6000, the income supplement declines from $4000 to $3000. As the "break-even" level of income ($12,000) is approached via earned income, the supplement (negative tax) diminishes and then disappears. A well-designed program would establish a minimum income for all, guarantee uniformity of benefits throughout the nation, maintain anonymity for recipients, reduce administrative expenses, and provide work incentives that are greater than those under the programs that would be replaced. The plan could contain a work requirement for the able-bodied and could be coordinated with the long-run programs such as subsidized employment and on-the-job training.

3. Reforming the tax system

Tax reform, a third general method of reducing poverty and income inequality, can be structured to meet Criterion 1 (promoting both equity and efficiency), and Criterion 2 (minimizing the efficiency costs of achieving equity). The overall tax system in the United States is proportional rather than progressive, as many people erroneously believe. The personal income tax is progressive statutorily, but much less so in reality owing to the many tax exemptions, deductions, and credits that disproportionally benefit high-income taxpayers. The regressive nature of the state and local tax system offers the remaining progressiveness of the federal personal income tax. For example, low-income people tend to pay a higher proportion of their income to sales and property taxes than do higher-income people. Redistribution occurs only on the expenditure side of the overall federal, state, and local budget.

The tax system should be scrutinized to insure equity. Special tax provisions sometimes benefit the wealthy at little benefit to society at large. Several examples can be given, but the following two illustrate the point. First, the personal income tax deduction for mortgage interest aids those who have the highest mortgages and may discriminate against renters. This could be solved by eliminating the deduction or permitting renters to deduct a portion of their annual rental payments. Second, interest income from state and local government bonds is exempt from the personal income tax. The holders of these bonds, generally the wealthy, can earn considerable income that is completely untaxed.

Not all special tax provisions, or "tax expenditures," are loopholes. For example, capital gains provisions, energy credits, investment tax credits, and child-care credits are designed to promote activity that expands the total level of national income. The tax benefits go to the taxpayers, but the broader benefits of the promoted activity are shared by all income groups. And, of course, few people who express indignation about "tax expenditures" and "welfare for the rich" have in mind eliminating the deduction for charitable contributions. The task is to isolate and eliminate those tax provisions that reduce equity and add nothing to efficiency, not simply to assume that all tax expenditures are government "giveaways."

In summary, a comprehensive approach to reducing poverty and improving the distribution of income should have three elements: targeted programs that treat the causes of poverty, efficient systems of transferring income to alleviate the symptoms of poverty, and tax law changes that eliminate special provisions which benefit the wealthy at the expense of other taxpayers.

THE UNCERTAIN FUTURE: REAGAN POLICIES

The Reagan administration's comprehensive economic program contains some (definitely not all) of the elements of the poverty policies suggested in the previous section. For example, the Reagan program emphasizes economic growth and expanded private-sector employment, as opposed to transfers, as a general strategy to improve the economic position of low-income persons. The massive spending and tax cuts, however, launch the economy into unchartered waters. The outcome of the voyage and the implications for poverty are unclear and uncertain. The reductions in expenditures for transfer programs (such as food stamps) and public sector employment programs (such as CETA), if enacted, will increase poverty in the short term. But, if the overall Reagan strategy succeeds in reducing inflation and creating 1960-style economic growth, the poor are likely to benefit over the long term.

The Reagan administration's program is a rather dramatic policy tilt toward the *efficiency* goal (growth of national income) at the expense of the *equity* goal (a more equal distribution of income). Will this shift retain political support? Will it succeed in reducing inflation and expanding real national income? Will poverty increase or decline as a result of the policies? The answers await the future.

NOTES

1. Baumol, William J., and Allan S. Blinder. *Economics: Principles and Policy*. New York: Harcourt Brace and Jovanovich, Inc., 1979, p. 567.
2. See, for example, Okun, Arthur M. *Equality and Efficiency: The Big Tradeoff*. Washington, D.C.: The Brookings Institution, 1976.
3. These data are taken or derived from *The Economic Report of the President* and the *Monthly Labor Review*.
4. Harrington, Michael. *The Other America*. Baltimore: Penguin Books, Inc., 1962.
5. Thurow, Lester C. *The Zero-Sum Society*. New York: Basic Books, 1980.
6. While nearly all economists agree that in-kind benefits should be included as part of one's income, they disagree on how the in-kind transfers should be valued. Studies show that recipients prefer cash transfers to equal dollar amounts of in-kind transfers. This indicates that the full cost of in-kind transfers should not be included in computing the recipient's total income for poverty statistics purposes. See *Economic Report of the President*. January 1978, p. 224.
7. Paglin, Martin. *Poverty and Transfer in Kind: A Reevaluation of Poverty in the United States*. Stanford, CA: Hoover Institution Press, 1979. Chapter 6, as quoted in James D. Gwartney and Richard Stroup. *Microeconomics: Private and Public Choice*, 2nd ed. New York: Academic Press, 1980, p. 334.
8. For a standard discussion of the costs and benefits of economic growth, see Campbell R. McConnell. *Economics: Principles, Problems, and Policies*, 7th ed. New York: McGraw-Hill Book Co., 1978, pp. 422-432.
9. Piguo, A. C. *Economics of Welfare*, Fourth Edition. London: Macmillan, 1948, p. 89.
10. Baumol and Blinder. *Economics*, p. 567. The graphic representation that follows is also from this source.
11. Okun, p. 91.
12. Krauss, Melvin B. "The Social Democracies: Equality Under Strain," *The Wall Street Journal*. February 1, 1980.

13. Feldstein, Martin. "Social Security, Induced Retirement, and Aggregate Capital Accumulation," *Journal of Political Economy,* September-October 1974, pp. 905-926.
14. U.S. Department of Health, Education and Welfare. *Summary Report: Seattle-Denver Income Maintenance Experiment.* Washington, D.C.: Government Printing Office, February 1978.
15. Feldstein, Martin. "Temporary Layoffs in the Theory of Unemployment," *Journal of Political Economy.* October 1976, pp. 937-957.
16. As quoted in Paul Wonnacott and Ron Wonnacott. *Economics.* New York: McGraw-Hill, 1979, p. 677.

SUGGESTED READINGS

Blinder, Allan S. *Toward an Economic Theory of Income Distribution.* Cambridge, Massachusetts: MIT Press, 1974. A rigorous, but excellent source for the statistically minded. The author attempts to quantify the extent to which factors such as age, salary, wealth, etc., explain income inequality in the United States.

Friedman, Milton and Rose Friedman. *Free to Choose: A Personal Statement,* Chapters 4 and 5. New York: Harcourt, Brace, Jovanovich, 1980. A controversial best-seller by a leading conservative economist. Friedman argues that the existing welfare system destroys incentives to work and invest in oneself and creates a class of subjugated dependent Americans cut off from the mainstream of society.

Okun, Arthur M. *Equality and Efficiency: The Big Tradeoff.* Washington, D.C.: The Brookings Institution, 1976. A widely praised and quoted analysis of the equity-efficiency tradeoff. Assumes a basic understanding of economics, but is assessable to the nonexpert. Used in many economic issues courses in U.S. universities.

Shiller, Bradley. *The Economics of Poverty and Discrimination.* Englewood Cliffs, N.J.: Prentice-Hall, Inc., 1980. A widely used text for courses on the economics of poverty. This short paperback discusses the causes of poverty and analyzes present and proposed antipoverty schemes. Quite comprehensive for a short book. Treats many current issues concerning the measurement and treatment of poverty.

Thurow, Lester, *Generating Inequality.* New York: Basic Books, 1975. A 250-page book by a leading liberal economist. The author criticizes the prevailing income distribution theories (marginal productivity, investment in human capital, etc.) and develops alternative theories based on randomness (luck) and the competition for jobs. Concludes that much of the existing rationale for inequality lacks validity.

STUDY QUESTIONS

1. Determine the official poverty line in existence at the time you read this book. Do you think this line is too low? too high? Do you think in-kind

transfers should be included as income for purposes of poverty statistics? Why or why not?

2. How is it possible that poverty has been reduced, yet the distribution of income has remained approximately the same during the past two decades? Which is more politically difficult: to reduce absolute poverty or to reduce income inequality via redistribution?

3. Do you value efficiency, that is, a higher standard of living for yourself and for society? What personal actions can you cite that reflect this valuation? Do you value equity, that is, a reduction of poverty and a more equal distribution of income? What personal actions can you cite that reflect this valuation?

4. Consider the leaky-bucket experiment proposed by Okun in this chapter. How far would you be willing to go before concluding that the trade-off is too large? Do you think that generally speaking that point has been reached in the United States? On what basis do you reach this impression?

5. Study Table 4-1 in this chapter. Would you support this income supplement plan if it were substituted for present welfare programs? What do you see as the plan's greatest strength? Do you foresee any problems should the plan go into effect? What additional information would you need to know before deciding whether or not to support such a plan?

5

Political Power, the Poor, and Poverty Policy

Wallace H. Spencer

Harold Lasswell once defined politics as "Who Gets What, When, and How." [1] As much as its brevity recommends it, Lasswell's observation is more important because of the perspective it provides regarding political life. While neutral in tone as compared to Ambrose Bierce's definition of politics ("The conduct of public affairs for private advantage"),[2] Lasswell also reveals that a central element in politics is in the "getting" of something by someone. While it could be usefully expanded to include such additional questions pertaining to the "getting" as "from whom?," "at what cost?," "why?," and "with what results?," he has provided an excellent framework for inquiry into the relationships between political systems, processes, and actors (on the one hand) and political decision, public policies, and beneficiaries (on the other).

The essence of Lasswell's conception of politics is the notion that the "getting" involves the use and application of political power, that politics involves conflict and competition for societal values from which those with the most power emerge with the greatest gains. If power is central to political life and crucial to determining results, it should be a useful focal point for an examination of poverty policy. At least, that is the assumption of this chapter, which will attempt to explain some important aspects of poverty policy as it relates to the political system and the power position of those participants, poor and nonpoor alike, who seek to use the system to alleviate or solve the poverty problem.

Such a statement of intent has perhaps revealed an implied bias which should be admitted openly. The goal of eradicating poverty is assumed to be a worthy one, which should be among the highest priority items on the public agenda. However, this does not assume that the means to the goal are known or even possible. There is certainly enough disagreement about those matters to invite some degree of caution.

THE POLITICAL POWER PERSPECTIVE

At the outset, some effort should be made to clarify what is meant here by the term *power*. It is a term which has been used extensively in an extraordinary variety of contexts throughout history. Political scientists have drawn certain conclusions about power and its exercise: (1) there is no uniform and universally accepted definition of power; (2) political power is virtually impossible to measure; (3) everybody seems to want power, but fear it in the hands of others; and, (4) it seems to be important.

If it has been exceptionally difficult to develop agreement as to what power is and how it manifests itself, there have been two conceptions of power which have emerged with regularity. Power has been treated in terms of *results*, which is the essence of Lasswell's approach, for example, who gets what. Power has also been treated as *resources*, for example, who has what in order to compete in the political arena to get more or to protect what is already possessed. These conceptions are useful, but also flawed.

The principal difficulty with the results orientation is that it is absolutist and inadequate to cope with the relativism that constitutes most human affairs. Within the framework of such definitions, one is either powerful or powerless. Wants either are achieved or they are not. If they are achieved, the individual has power. If wishes, wants, or demands are not satisfied, power is presumed to be absent. However, the equation of power with results must be modified to take account of both circumstances and sufficiency. Under some circumstances, one may have formidable power which is nonetheless insufficient to secure the ends sought at that time. In other words, power is relative to time, events, and competition, among other things. This is particularly significant in the American political system, where bargaining, accommodation, and compromise are such pronounced features of the political landscape that the attainment of all one's desires is highly exceptional. Power must be perceived in relative terms, even when assessed in terms of results.

The problem with the power-as-results formulation of political power is further illustrated when one looks at the array of public policies which have been enacted over the years as efforts to cope with poverty and its effects. By simply noting the measures which have been enacted by the federal government in the areas of health, housing, education, and income sustenance, maintenance, and support, one recognizes that the poor have not been ignored. Nevertheless, despite the impressive list of policies articulated and enacted on their behalf, one cannot therefore conclude that the poor are indeed powerful in America. However, the political successes of antipoverty policies do suggest that the poor are not altogether powerless either, in spite of the facts that poverty has not been eradicated, that policies have not always been particularly effective, and that some policies have had negative effects.

The poor have, nonetheless, frequently been portrayed as powerless—often as *the* powerless of society. Such a representation of the relationship between power and poverty derives in part from the continuance of poverty and in part from the conception of power based on *resources*. From this perspective, if one has the resources (money, prestige, etc.), one can achieve one's desires. The resource orientation has underpinned most of the efforts to identify the powerful in our society—those with the most resources tend to stand out and are therefore identified as the most powerful. The converse, of course, would have to be that those with the fewest resources would be the least powerful.

There are a number of problems with the resource approach to power. As is also true of the results approach, the resource approach is too simplistic and too narrow. Usually resources are regarded as being based on wealth. However, as important as money is, it is not the only political resource of importance.

In addition, resources are politically relevant only when applied politically. Potential which remains mere potential is not power. No political actors spread their resources across the entire range of political life. They must be selective according to interest and need. Where actors choose not to invest their resources (or where they are not permitted the opportunity), those resources generally cannot be translated into power.

Political power is a relationship between the resources an actor (whether an individual or a group) possesses, the application of those resources, the opposition's resources and application, and the environment. The relationship can be presented in the form of an equation:

$$P = \frac{R\,A}{O\,(RA)} \pm E$$

Power equals Resources as Applied, divided by the Opposition's Resources as Applied, plus or minus the effects of the Environment.

Such an equation is not meant to be quantifiably exact or applicable. The elements of resource bases, their application, or the environment cannot be reduced to numerical units of like value. The equation is simply a shorthand way of representing power relationships. Power consists only in part of the resources available to a political actor. Their application depends in part on the appropriateness of the resources for the situation at hand, but even more crucially on the will and skill of the political actor, or the intent and abilities of the actor in directing those resources in a productive, effective manner. However, political actors often must contend with opposing actors, competitors who either are in direct disagreement or are seeking the same public goods for their own purposes. Thus, the applied resources of the opposition can offset one's own efforts and capabilities. The competitive nature of politics is central to democratic activity and is a major source of the compromising so characteristic of the political system.

Thus, the applied resources of proponents must be set against those of opponents in assessing power relationships. However, the formula is incomplete unless one also considers the political environment, which may either add to or detract from the prospects of political actors. The political system and its processes may work to the advantage of some actors more than others. The times, events, or conditions of the moment may similarly enhance or jeopardize prospects. The environment, then, has both long- and short-term characteristics which may bias, positively or negatively, the activity of participants in the political process.

The equation will provide the framework for assessing the conditions in which antipoverty proponents must operate. Before examining their resources and their various applications, however, a few words are in order about the political environment in which poverty policy is formulated.[3]

THE POLITICAL ENVIRONMENT

Systemic Bias

Every political system, as well as every political subsystem, carries biases which have effects on who gets what out of the political system, how they get it, when they get it, what it will cost in the getting, and who will pay. Biases are characteristics which, all other things being equal, work to help or hinder the attainment of objectives. Biases may be either positive or negative in their effects, though not always consistently or predictably. Nonetheless, students of politics and practitioners alike must take them into account.

Fragmentation and complexity. The American political system is highly fragmented in that legitimate governing authority exists among many institutions at various levels of government. In part, this is due to conscious design, with roots in the foundation of the constitutional system. The framers of the U.S. Constitution, to a significant degree in response to the pressures of political reality and political feasibility, provided that formal political authority would be divided among the different levels of government in the federal system and among the separate branches of government at the national level.

The political reality of ratification by the states and the premise that power is both necessary and dangerous, led the framers to propose that the institutions of government be given powers appropriate to their responsibilities, but that the responsibilities would, in most cases, be parceled out to the separated institutions and levels of government. However, complete separation would not occur; the framers, through schemes of representation and through specific delegations of tasks, duties, and authority, devised a complex system whereby the parts of the system could overlap and check other parts, thereby making the whole safer from tyranny. In essence, they assumed that the powerful could be trusted only when they were restrained by other centers of power.

While such fragmentation and complexity is beneficial insofar as it safeguards liberty, it does impose costs in terms of the system's ability to act. Where the concurrence of two or more parties is necessary for the achievement of a task, each party may frustrate the endeavor by withholding its approval. The American political system thus consists of multiple mutual dependencies and veto points. In such a system, it tends to be more difficult to act positively than to thwart, to effect change than to preserve the status quo, to attack successfully than to protect and defend.

The U.S. political system had fragmentation and complexity built into it. Subsequent history has augmented those qualities multifold. In terms of physical, social, economic, political, and technological growth, the U.S. has become far more complex and fragmented than eighteenth-century ancestors could have imagined. Society has become bureaucratized, dominated by great public and private institutions with a host of smaller institutions providing the supporting cast. As society has grown and become more complex, and as the demands on government have increased in scale and difficulty, one of the principal responses (not always intentional) has been to specialize and to organize institutions and activities along functionally distinctive lines.

The result has been that institutions are masses of fragmented, functionally specialized domains, often existing more separated from than united to their fellow components of the same institutions. Since power tends to accompany function, a system of government has developed in which most of the decisions made by government are shaped by functionally specialized subunits.

Historical development in particular has enlarged the functional fragmentation built into the American system under the Constitution. Relations between the national, state, and local levels of government have become increasingly intertwined in terms of overlapping areas of policy activity. Indeed, in a number of policy areas, the federal government makes policy (or at least establishes goals and guidelines), then relies on states and localities to implement policy (often with the aid of federal dollars). Thus, although many policy goals are nationalized, the means to attain them may permit a generous amount of local or state discretion.

Functions are also shared between government and the private sector. Government may provide incentives and assistance, but it is left to actors in the private sector to accept the incentives and to carry those programs into effect.

The importance of shared policy functions is significant because policy outcomes become dependent on so many different actors. The upshot is that there are many points in the system which give definition to policy and determine what the nature of policy will be in fact and practice.

The effects of systemic fragmentation and complexity on the making of poverty policy are several and varied. The negative biases, in the sense of inhibiting new policies to aid the poor, are generally more prominent and potent than the positive biases. Nonetheless, there are also positive biases. For example, the system's complexity does provide for many points of access into the political system; if one route proves to be unresponsive, others can be attempted. Failure at one level of government or with respect to one institution may be compensated by success with another level or institution. However, the systemic biases are largely negative if one's goal is major changes in poverty policy, particularly if such changes are comprehensive in scope. The many points of access are double-edged, for they may also serve as veto points against major change. Moreover, to the extent that existing agencies and programs are perceived to be part of the problem rather than the solution (a charge made for different reasons by both liberals and conservatives), the systemic bias against change may be a truly formidable obstacle.

Political Stakes and Legitimacy. A second important systemic bias arises from a powerful predisposition in American politics to confer more legitimacy on the political demands, proposals, and presentations made by groups or individuals with direct, especially concrete or material, stakes in the issue and its outcome. Representations by second parties (except for hired lobbyists, who are regarded as extensions of directly involved parties), made on behalf of interests more directly involved in the issue, are regarded as less legitimate in character and therefore less worthy of serious consideration.

In American politics, people are expected to represent their own interests, an expectation which is only mildly softened by the fact that not all Americans have comparable resources to compete, to gain access into the system, and to derive satisfaction from the system. That fact is generally known and recognized, at least in the abstract. Yet the system is more generally and more profoundly believed to be an open one in which obstacles may be overcome by determined and deeply interested participants. As far as policymakers are concerned, such participants deserve a hearing. Further, since most policymakers act most often in response to demands that come to them rather than going out and discovering needs and problems, and since most policymakers have sufficiently heavy demands on their time and attention, political participants who can carry their own demands into the system are far more likely to be heeded.

To greater or lesser degrees, all policymaking takes place under conditions of partial and incomplete information. Decision makers tend to be acutely aware that their decisions have tangible, often profound effects on people's lives. Most are deeply interested in knowing who will be affected and what the impacts will be. They want to know that assumptions and "facts" are correct and complete. They are also acutely aware that decisions must be made on the basis of and in spite of incomplete information. Hence, they must seek as many reassurances as possible from the decision-making process. Of such reassurances, none is more soothing (for purposes of closing the information gap) than hearing it "straight from the horse's mouth," from parties directly involved.

This bias in favor of self-promotion of self-interest in political life imposes considerable hardship on the poor. Since they are have-nots or have-littles to begin with, their resource base is not promising. The obstacles in the system are relatively more difficult to surmount than is the case for more well-off interests.

Moreover, since organization is generally essential to effective political activity, the poor are further disadvantaged from effective self-representation by the difficulties inherent in effective organization. The general lack of resources, of course, means that organizations are difficult to support and maintain, but the problem goes even more deeply into the nature of the poor as an identifiable constituency. Most politically active organizations represent voluntary associations of rather enduring commitment. The constituent membership of the association is identifiable and relatively permanent. While some of the poor endure poverty on a seemingly permanent basis, many do not; they move in and out of the ranks of the poor and are, as a result, difficult to identify, organize, and mobilize. In a sense, the poor are an anomaly in the political system, a constituency in need of policies to remove them from that constituency.

The major paradox is that when people talk about the poor organizing to compete in the system on their own behalf, they generally refer to the poor as passive recipients; the poor must be organized rather than organizing themselves. Because political organizations are seldom spontaneously generated, it is not surprising to discover that many of the nonpoor, with advantages in such resources as money, information, and skills, assume a leading role in attempting to organize the poor. While resultant organizations probably are more effective than no organization at all, their legitimacy and credibility may be subject to question on the grounds of the involvement of "do-gooders" and "outside agitators."

Another significant paradox resides in the need for effective self-representation and its potential effect on the support base of the constituency. If effective self-representation leads to policies which significantly reduce poverty or alleviate its effect, the result should be a reduction in the scope and intensity of the poor's commitment to continued political action. That could have the further result of reducing the effective self-advocacy of those who remain poor.

Political Inertia. A third systemic bias reposes in the political equivalents of Sir Isaac Newton's laws of physical motion, particularly the First Law of Motion or the *principle of inertia.* Translated into a political frame of reference, the principle of inertia suggests that the status quo is always of moment and of consequence in maintaining conditions in place and in line. In the patterns of their social and political lives, people develop habits of behavior, relationships, and expectations which, in their familiarity, predictability, and regularity, become comfortable. Deviation becomes viable only when external pressures match or exceed the inertia that perpetuates the status quo.

Another way to look at this bias is to frame it in terms of the weight of history. Governments, like other social institutions and practices, are products of historical development, as are the policies they promulgate and enforce. Governments, again like other social institutions and practices, do not lightly or easily depart substantially from the behaviors familiar to them. Precedent, tradition, and commitment to the current order of things influence how and why people behave as they do and set the boundaries of their perceptions of the possible, not to mention the acceptable.

In the area of poverty policy, the principle of inertia has substantial significance. Over the course of American history, there has been considerable movement and change. At one time, social responsibility for the poor was regarded as a matter for limited local action, but gradually the public role in helping the poor has increased, even if unsteadily, over time and with considerable inconsistency over geographical areas and among jurisdictions. Actions by local governments, the states, and the federal government have created layers of policy related to poverty and the poor.

Critics of these policies and programs range from those who are against the whole idea of government activity in these areas, to those who accept the government role but argue that it is misdirected or misapplied, and also to those who believe that the policies either have no significant effect or are counterproductive. But the programs also have their adherents, in addition to the weight of inertia. In the case of poverty policy, the inertial factor is immense, and critics who want to "get the poor out of the public trough" or who want to revamp the whole system will be hard-pressed to supply enough force to overcome the inertia. In a multilayered system of poverty policy, each layer has contributed to a sum of mass that is truly ponderous.

Political Symbol and Political Substance. The American political system contains a number of incentives that encourage responses from policymakers which can variously be called symbolic, cosmetic, or "quick-fix" responses. Whichever label is used, the result is policy which is designed to provide some satisfaction to policy advocates that something is being done, with costs which may fall into either or both of two categories: (1) an inadequate response which, however emotionally satisfying to participants, does not effectively address the real problems in a fundamental fashion; or (2) a response which has been so oversold by its adherents that it is bound to fall short of fulfilling its promises, generating frustration, disappointment, scapegoating, or cynicism in its wake.

Part of the pressure for symbolic, superficial action stems from the highly competitive nature of the system. Such competition is inherent in a relatively open democratic process in which there are no absolute limits on the roles government may be asked to play and in which rewards and penalties are issued according to the responsiveness of decision makers to political demands. The products of these pressures can be expressed in a variety of ways.

For example, decision makers tend to be besieged by more demands than they can possibly respond to. Just getting their serious attention is a battle; getting on the public agenda is a necessary first step, but a difficult one. Getting on the agenda requires that policymakers be convinced that the subject is worthy of their attention.

However, just getting the attention of decision makers is insufficient. Having little enthusiasm for futility, they must be assured that something fruiful can be done. Thus, they must be sold on the problem and on the chances for solving it. This results in the dilem-

ma of what can be called "the escalation of rhetoric." [4] Developing
support for political causes in a highly competitive political marketplace tends to lead advocates to exaggerate the nature of problems
and to oversell the feasibility of proposed solutions. The escalation
of rhetoric in turn tends to generate ongoing or recurring credibility
gaps as programs fail to "solve" the problems as advertised and as
the country avoids collapse in spite of the continuation of the
problems.

Lyndon Johnson's War on Poverty is a classic case in point. In the
few years before he assumed the presidency, the stage had been
set by growing revelations and awareness that there were embar-
rassingly large numbers of Americans living in poverty. Believing
that existing programs were inadequate, Johnson expanded existing
programs, embraced the Kennedy proposals, added a host of his
own, and declared war on poverty in America.

The War on Poverty did not eradicate poverty in America and
has therefore been judged a failure in spite of substantial evidence
that, for all its complications, confusion, and other problems, it had
an impressively positive impact on both reducing poverty and alleviating some of its effects.[5] It could not "solve" or "destroy" poverty,
partly because of the enormously complex nature of the problem
itself and partly because of the inevitably limited resources to cope
with it. In short, when measured against the rhetoric that accompanied it, and indeed induced its birth, the War on Poverty was a
failure.

The incentives for overstating problems and solutions and for
provided highly visible results in short order are not conducive to
good policymaking. It is even difficult clearly to articulate goals
and their relationships to the means used to attain them. In practice,
goals tend to follow policy rather than the reverse. And all of this
is complicated by the necessities of political compromise, which
normally means that however serious the problem and however
comprehensive and sound the solution, one will probably have to
accept less than is desired. The system encourages exaggeration of
problems and solutions before even considering them, but denies
the adoption of policy on an appropriate scale, as it stimulates
rhetoric to the contrary. The consequence is disillusionment, judgments of failure, and cynicism.

In the case of poverty, and in spite of a substantial body of literature on the subject, these considerations are neither simple, suffi-

cient, or complete. Difficulties begin at the definition stage. Poverty may be defined in relative terms (the bottom X percentage of the population) or in absolute terms (persons below X dollars of income). In neither case is the X self-evidently "right." While American policy has used income levels as the indicator of poverty, the public debate often incorporates the relative percentage standard. In either case, lines are drawn arbitrarily—not necessarily unreasonably, but arbitrarily. However drawn, the lines also reflect assumptions regarding equity, equality, standards of living, and economic performance which may be equally arbitrary and based on estimates. Perceptions of the problem may shift substantially as differing assumptions and estimates are used.

The difficulties of developing adequate definitions of the problem of poverty extend to understanding its causes. This is not for lack of effort in developing explanations. Throughout history, some have blamed the poor themselves, arguing that they are lazy, shiftless, inept, or otherwise lacking in virtue. Similarly universalistic approaches at the other end of the ideological spectrum regard the individual as blameless and exclusively fault "the System." [6] In between are a plethora of theories that vary in the proportions of cause they attribute to either individuals or the System.

No one explanation has proven to be entirely satisfactory, perhaps because a number of causes have different impacts on various portions of the population. To be sure, the poor have their poverty in common, which is significant. But the differences among the poor may be equally significant, and they are still too little understood.

With these problems of definition and explanation, it is not surprising that policy has fallen short of solution. Nor, for that matter, is it surprising that some have retreated to the security of simplistic theories. By and large, however, policymakers have embraced no single theory, but have pursued a profusion of approaches whose programmatic scope has been limited. Even with modest pretensions about outcomes, it has been extraordinarily difficult for policymakers to anticipate the effects, both positive and negative, of their policies. Many programs, ranging from income maintenance to job training to minimum wages to public housing and urban renewal, have had side effects that were generally unexpected and disturbing, while frequently falling short of delivering the anticipated benefits.

Policy failures, even partial failures, contribute to the pressures to produce symbolic policy at the expense of substantive policy.

Both the uncertainties which attend substantive policy and the short-term rewards for "quick-fix" action-oriented responsiveness induce policymakers to respond symbolically. Since the rewards are greater and the short-run costs less, and since the long-run political costs may be no less, symbolic policy may be highly attractive.

Incremental and Comprehensive Policymaking. The biases of the system and of the processes by which it operates point to a political system that is essentially conservative in nature. It tends not to move quickly and not to undertake change of considerable magnitude. It affords favored defensive protection to the status quo.

Nonetheless, the system will undertake change. The forces for change can be successfully mustered and deployed, but the scope of success is rarely major. Rather, change comes about one step at a time. Change is incremental rather than comprehensive. It builds on previous efforts as they become the status quo and condition the climate for further movement.

There *are* exceptions to the rule, however. On occasion, government will launch a major policy program or series of programs which are substantial departures from what has gone before. However, such efforts normally require a unique political environment: a fortunate conjunction of perceived need, the available political support to push the issue, and an issue that represents a relatively new endeavor for government.

With respect to poverty policy, the incremental nature of change in the system may be regarded positively or negatively. It depends on one's perspective. To some, modest approaches make sense in an uncertain world; negative effects can be diminished. Also on the positive side, particularly for those who perceive that existing policy to aid the poor is constantly under attack, the incremental nature of change in the system provides a defensive buffer to protect past gains. Finally, the accommodations which are made between contending political forces and which thereby limit the scope of policy tend to reduce the number of situations in which political forces seem to be playing for all or nothing, a volatile situation that poses considerable dangers to the stability of any system.

For many, however, the incremental nature of policymaking in the political system is a source of irritation. Problems seem to go on and on with only minor treatment; the system seems insensitive because its cautious concern for keeping things manageable assures that millions of people will continue to suffer. From this perspective, accommodation becomes cruel expediency. For many critics of existing poverty policy, whether they come from the political left or right, incrementalism is simply an obstacle to sweeping reforms which would, from their perspectives, solve the problems that concern them.

Circumstances and Timing

The systemic biases may be either reinforced or mitigated by the forces of circumstance at any particular time. Systemic processes do not occur in a vacuum divorced from conditions elsewhere in society. Consequently, circumstances and the timing of political efforts are an important aspect of the political environment. They help to set the bounds of the possible and the probable.

While circumstances need not be major cataclysms in order to be felt, major events are more familiar and lend themselves better as examples. As a case in point, the widespread economic problems of the Depression helped condition greater acceptance for the initiatives of the New Deal. Changes in society which are relatively sudden or severe can be a potent stimulus for new or expanded policy efforts. For example, the recession of the early 1970s prompted Congress to provide for emergency extensions of eligibility to receive unemployment compensation benefits. The unemployed were suffering no more greatly than they had before the recession, but there were more of them. Thus, Congress became more disposed to act in their favor.

The circumstances conducive to antipoverty policy need not, however, always be dire in nature, although crisis does tend to generate enhanced responsiveness, often reflexive and unproductive. The development and adoption of the Great Society was greatly enhanced by a combination of circumstances that were not particularly related to the condition of the poor at that time: (1) an economy that was relatively prosperous, encouraging a vibrant optimism that no great purpose was beyond the capacities of the American system; (2) widely publicized revelations regarding the large-scale existence of poverty in America, which helped to set a climate of expectations that such conditions ought not be tolerated; (3) a national tragedy in the assassination of President Kennedy, who had helped lay the groundwork and give a policy direction, and whose death generated considerable sympathy to continue and complete his unfinished work; (4) the accession to the presidency of Lyndon Johnson, a consummately skillful legislative leader who made Kennedy's agenda his own, then added to it; and, (5) the national election of 1964, in which Barry Goldwater's candidacy split the Republican Party and helped carry Democrats, particularly liberal ones, to congressional triumphs in numbers sufficient to overcome the so-called "conservative coalition" of Republicans and Southern Democrats which for years had frustrated liberal social legislation, even in Congresses nominally controlled by the Democrats.

By 1967 circumstances had become less favorable to Johnson. In the off-year elections of 1966, a smaller and more normal Democratic majority was restored in Congress, which, in combination with the progressively troublesome Vietnam War, an emerging preoccupation with law and order in the wake of domestic upheavals, and a characteristically American conservative reaction to the tremendous activity of the previous three years, served to dampen the ardor for further development of the Great Society.

The previous example also suggests the importance of individual personality as a circumstantial factor. It makes a difference who holds which offices on what occasions. The individuals who participate in political events, their perceptions, their skills, and related characteristics, all help shape a political situation and thereby affect power relationships for others. On occasion, a single individual in the political environment can determine the outcome.

Clearly, circumstances and events are crucial elements which condition the environment and thus induce varying states of receptivity to poverty policy initiatives. To the extent that they cannot be controlled by policymakers and advocates, they represent adjustments to which policymaking must adapt.

One such condition which may figure prominently in the calculations of policymakers and policy advocates is the growing dilemma of resource scarcity, which may force reassessment of many assumptions relating to production, growth, wealth, and distribution. More specifically, resource scarcity may impose tighter limitations on the economy's ability to spread the wealth by enlarging the pie than Americans are accustomed to face. It is reasonable to expect that conflict over the issue will be sharper under conditions in which redress occurs by rearranging slices of the same pie, as opposed to spreading the wealth by enlarging the pie. The former is considerably more threatening to the nonpoor than is the latter.

POLITICAL RESOURCES, APPLICATION, AND COMPETITION

Resources are the raw material of political influence and power. The absence of resources prohibits participation. The shortage of resources inhibits effective participation. A relative preponderance of resources permits participation with reasonably good prospects most of the time. Consequently, competitive situations must be framed in terms of relative balances and inbalances and of degrees of shortage or dominance.

However, political resources represent potential only. To be effective, they must be employed; and vigorous, skillful, even lucky application can offset superior potential. In fact, application need not have a particularly high quality to offset superior resources which remain dormant or unused. Moreover, since there are different kinds of political resources, a weakness in one kind of resource may be offset by the application of others.

Financial Resources

In all probability, most Americans view money as the most fundamental, pivotal, and effective source of political power. While perceptions of its importance are probably exaggerated, money is important in political endeavors. Because money is a principal indicator of success and conveys social status in this country, those with wealth are accorded some political advantage in terms of prestige and credibility. Wealth increases their prospects for seeking public office successfully and for engaging in other forms of political participation.

But the real value of money is not in the direct ways that it can be used to exert political influence. Money is the primary fuel for political engines because it can be converted into so many other useful resources. Money is necessary to support organizations and to develop and transmit information. It is crucial to most political campaigning, to most lobbying activities, and to other efforts to mobilize people and material toward political ends.

By definition, the poor are short of this resource. The problem for which they seek redress is also their principal political liability. They are handicapped at the outset of any political contest. They need not be confronted by opposition, for the lack of money makes difficult the overcoming of systemic inertia.

However, as important as it is, the correlation between financial resources and political success is by no means direct. Other resources must be employed to compensate for financial deficiencies if the poor are to stand a chance of being reasonably well served by public policy.

Ideological Resources

"For all their bragging and their hypersensitivity," wrote Richard Hofstadter, "Americans are, if not the most self-critical, at least the most anxiously self-conscious people in the world, forever concerned about the inadequacy of something or another—their national morality, their national culture, their national purpose." [7] The anxiety to which Hofstadter refers is the foundation for the ideological component of American politics.

This is not to suggest that Americans are short of normative values and principles in their lives, including their political lives. On the contrary, an abundance of values underlies the insecurity and anxiety which stimulate the American passion for self-examination and self-criticism. However, American values are not always compatible with each other; indeed, some are mutually contradictory. Moreover, Americans can be highly selective in the application of their values. As if implicitly admitting an awareness of these contradictions and their selectivity, Americans devote substantial energy to examining their virtues and shortcomings in terms of their values, and frequently excel in the art of finger-pointing. Much political rhetoric, whether positive or negative, is an exercise in reaffirming important values. It is also tactical when values are used to substantiate and legitimize one's own posture in the dialog of political competition.

In the development of poverty policy, the values and principles which comprise American ideology are important resources. But they are not unmixed blessings for advocates of policy to benefit the poor. Those advocates have impressive ideological resources at their disposal, which must be employed vigorously if only to compensate for resource deficiencies elsewhere. But advocates should not be surprised to find ideological resources used by the opposition as well. Americans express mixed feelings about their values, and that supplies ideological ammunition in generous quantities for most political participants. A few examples should illustrate the point.

Americans have complex, contradictory feelings about wealth. A long cultural, religious, and historical tradition of suspicion, disdain, and fear of wealth and the wealthy persists. There is a long tradition of sensitivity to, and sympathy for, the suffering of the poor, as well as an inclination to give aid and comfort to those who have come to grief through no fault of their own.

At the same time, however, Americans display an almost morbid fascination with wealth and the wealthy. Few Americans would refuse to swap incomes with someone more wealthy. Wealth and security are intermixed, and therefore the wealth is sought to provide for security. Wealth is a sign of success, and Americans honor winners, even though they may turn in the next moment to root or fight for an underdog.

Americans' perceptions of wealth and poverty are structured around considerations of the relationship between economic status and individual responsibility and worth. They tend to believe that individuals can control their own fate, that they can choose the paths they will pursue, that ambition, perseverance, talent, and skill will be rewarded. Yet they also suspect that luck, circumstance, the System, and similar external factors really determine who wins and who loses. Such ambivalence makes Americans receptive to the view that the poor are that way because of their own inadequacies, but it also provides fertile ground for the argument that the poor are victimized by forces beyond their control and are therefore deserving of external assistance.

This ambivalence extends into considerations of the goals of poverty policy. If the acquisition of wealth or poverty is entirely a matter determined by outside forces, whether arbitrary or capricious, there is no individual vindication or merit in wealth and no logic or reason to sustain wealth disparities. Thus wealth ought to be equalized in some manner. If wealth or poverty is strictly a matter of individual merit, then the Social Darwinism of the 19th century would not appear to be an unreasonable response. If the System imposes handicaps or favors on some, but also retains considerable leeway for individual choice and achievement, an appropriate policy might call for equalizing only the structure of opportunities, reserving a humanitarian caretaker function for those who are simply unable to cope despite their best efforts. This last approach, the more ambivalent and compromised, has characterized the American approach to poverty policy, although American policy has also made limited movement toward redistribution and has provided a broad range of services to ameliorate the effects of poverty.

A discussion of ideological resources based on normative values germane to the poverty problem must address the work ethic. The work ethic is regarded as problematic by many antipoverty advocates because it generates opposition to welfare. The work ethic, they claim, desensitizes Americans to the real extent of poverty and misdirects their attention from real issues to artificial ones, such as welfare cheating. The work ethic therefore undermines attempts to cope with poverty and ease the suffering of the poor.

Reducing the obstacles posed by the work ethic is no easy task, in part because there are grounds for considerable disagreement as to the nature of the obstacles. The work ethic is a deeply embedded cultural phenomenon, not restricted to Americans, capitalists, or Protestants, as is evident by its presence in the Soviet Union and China.

Moreover, it can be argued that the work ethic is not an entirely irrational societal standard (or set of standards) for guiding individual production and reward in a society. An individual produces something of value to others in society, by which that person in turn acquires the wherewithal to purchase and consume the produce of others. Work, therefore, rationalizes survival in a social context; the individual contributes, and that justifies the contribution of others in return. By consuming without producing, an individual may be perceived as stealing from others, which is the essence of concerns about "welfare slackers," work incentives, means tests, and eligibility standards and their enforcement.

The work-reward relationship becomes more complex when levels of assistance are considered. Even those who are victims or otherwise "honestly needy" can get caught here. The issue raised particularly in conjunction with income maintenance and guaranteed-income programs is how much can be made available as entitlements before the incentive to work for one's income is seriously eroded. The results of several demonstration projects to test the effects of a guaranteed income on work incentives have been mixed and inconclusive. More information is needed on the relationships between incentives and work, income, production, investment, consumption, and so forth.[8] For the time being, at least, the work ethic remains a potent economic and social value and therefore an equally powerful element in political life.

For the public and public officials alike, the struggle over poverty policy is an ongoing contest to shape two related sets of perceptions: (1) perceptions about which values are or ought to be an issue; and, (2) perceptions about the nature of reality—past, present, and future—in terms of which societal values have been shaped.

Informational Resources

"Knowledge is power." Information is a crucial ingredient in policymaking. Decision-makers desire it in order to reassure themselves that their decisions in this complex and uncertain world are reasonably sound. Other political actors use information as a tool to guide decision-makers in developing policies favorable to their own interests and points of view.

Information is crucial from another perspective. Information about the political system and its processes is as crucial to success as is information that is issue-oriented. Those interests which are successful over the long run are normally those which know how the system works and what is happening within it at any given time. They are therefore better able to promote and defend their interests as occasion and need require.

The poor are not particularly well situated with respect to having information. They are generally less knowledgeable about the political system than are more affluent members of society. That condition is aggravated by the fact that the poor tend to have less interest and less confidence in the political system. Their knowledge of it is in turn diminished, as is their ability to participate effectively. As a consequence, they get less out of the system, and that tends to reduce their interest in it. And so it goes.

Even if the poor were more interested and knowledgeable than they are, they would still face difficult obstacles to effective participation because of the shortage of other resources, particularly money. Information is costly to develop, package, and transmit.

Much information generated about the poor has found its way into the political system. Relatively little of that has been produced by the poor, however, and the absence of information coming from them bears directly on the stakes-in-the-issue basis of credibility mentioned earlier.

Numerical Resources

Numbers can count in any political system, but in a democratic, representative system, they may acquire particular importance, especially where elected policymakers are concerned. Numbers are central to elections because they determine electoral outcomes. Numbers are also a campaign resource, which may be employed in a variety of endeavors and which may serve to offset disadvantages in other resources.

Finally, numbers are important as a scale to measure sources of information. While elected policymakers are properly skeptical of orchestrated campaigns in which similar or identical postcards came flooding in, evidence that a sizeable constituency is concerned about an issue is often an effective incentive for a decision maker to pay attention to that issue. This holds true for nonelected policymakers as well, if perhaps not as compellingly.

The poor are a sizeable constituency. Unfortunately, the resource has not been converted into effective political action. In line with their diminished political interest and knowledge, the poor tend to vote and otherwise participate in politics less than the rest of the public. Hence, while their potential is substantial, it tends largely to be unrealized.

Organizational Resources and External Supports

All of the major resources discussed to this point depend on mobilization and application either by or on behalf of the poor. The key to mobilization and application is organization, which is generally most effective when relatively permanent, although temporary organizations can be effective in the short run to deal with specific issues.

Despite efforts to organize the poor in their own interest during the past 15 years, critical problems remain. The relative low level of knowledge, interest, and money among the poor handicaps organizational endeavors. The fact that large numbers of poor move in and out of poverty complicates the process of identifying and organizing them. Finally, variances among the poor in terms of secondary characteristics—such as geography, age, occupational status, ethnicity, sex, marital status, parental status, or health—aggravate organizational difficulties. Causes and conditions of poverty as well as policies for redress and relief vary accordingly and are difficult to articulate coherently and uniformly.

Perhaps the most ambitious effort to develop political awareness and organization among the poor was the Community Action Programs (CAPs) that were part of the War on Poverty Program of the 1960s. Community Action Agencies (CAAs) were intended to organize the poor, principally the urban minority poor, in order to challenge the power structures of local government. The results were mixed.

Nonetheless, Community Action Programs managed to demonstrate that the poor can become organized, as have many other efforts across the U.S., ranging in scale from small, single-issue neighborhood associations to the National Welfare Rights Organization.[9] Organization is by no means the answer to poverty in this country, but it is a means by which the poor may participate more effectively in seeking solutions. Organization facilitates the application of other resources, even as it inevitably generates questions about whether leadership is representative, about which problems will be addressed, and about whose interests will be served.

Organization of the poor, though important, is unlikely to be sufficient. Unless organized interests have a narrow field of public policy all to themselves, and it is a field unlikely to generate opposition, it is useful for them to develop support beyond the confines of their own organization. Coalition building is probably crucial to enactment of successful policies in the U.S. because of the fragmentation of the political system and because of biases against change. Moreover, coalitions provide more unified political strength and action against opposition than does fragmented activity going in the same direction. Even in the absence of an explicit political alliance, however, external support substantially improves the prospects of success.

This is particularly true in the case of the poor, who are greatly outnumbered by the nonpoor in this country. The poor will generally lose any contest of numbers if the issue is framed simply as a case of the poor versus the nonpoor. Every interest requires at least the acquiescence of other segments of the community to achieve its ends. Whatever the value of such concepts as independence and the dignity which derives from being in control of one's own destiny, political or otherwise, society generates an interdependence which is both reflected and augmented by the political system. The blunt fact is that the poor are dependent on external supports, perhaps more than most.

Those supports can be developed in both the public and private sectors. In the public sector, agencies have been established whose principal function is to provide goods and services to the poor. As a result, the poor themselves may become advocates of larger expenditures on such goods and services. In both sectors, institutions and individuals thrive on identifying and studying the problems of the poor, and advocate policy accordingly.[10]

In some quarters, efforts by the nonpoor to help the poor are criticized as naive paternalism or as cynicism and crass deception by the "haves," who do not intend to share their wealth with the "have-nots." Such criticism illustrates the stake-in-the-system bias and discomfits those nonpoor who sincerely wish to aid the poor. Such people can be made to suffer guilt feelings regardless of what they do. If they try to help, they may be guilty of paternalism; if they don't, they may be guilty of insensitivity to those less fortunate than themselves. However, many reform efforts (and revolutions, for that matter) directed at improving the lot of the downtrodden have been at least initiated by members of the better-off segments of society.

As important as those external and institutionalized supports are, they do not come without substantial costs. The institutionalization of poverty interests, politically functional as it is, generates a stake in poverty as well as poverty policy; to keep the latter operating healthily, it is necessary to have continued poverty or at least the impression of continuing poverty. Moreover, even if current policy is the subject of dissatisfaction, substantial resistance to change may nonetheless emanate from institutionalized interests if that change is perceived as threatening to the status quo.

Similarly, supports derived from the private sector are often obtained at some cost to the effectiveness of policy, principally through broadening policy focus so that the benefits are provided to non-poverty interests. The food-stamp program was an accommodation to farm interests and was administered by the Department of Agriculture. Similarly, public housing and urban renewal programs were structured to allay the fears of private housing and construction interests, as well as those of local governments, with the result that a disturbing number of projects did little to improve housing for the poor, but were windfalls for more affluent housing and development interests.

Supports from the private sector may generate benefits for the poor as part of the intended benefits for a different target group in the populace. As such, legislation to benefit the elderly in general may have particular benefits for the elderly poor. Because the poor cross-cut so many segments of the society, they may find support in the efforts of those other groups. Such approaches result in piece-meal policy treatment of poverty, but they may be more politically feasible than the alternatives.

In summary, then, resources are available to the poor both in terms of self-organization and in terms of the support of external organizations. In the case of the former, some problems inhibit effective organization, but they are not insurmountable. In the case of the latter, certain costs often dilute any real impact on the needs of the poor. Whether the costs are worth the benefits is a question which itself becomes part of the political agenda.

Political Opposition

Effective realization of power resources has to be judged in the context of specific issues and situations. For that reason, little has been said with respect to political opposition. There is no overt anti-poor lobby in the U.S., although some organizations can be relied on consistently to oppose federal initiatives on behalf of the poor. They are generally informed by an ideological perspective that is antigovernment. Nonetheless, any proposal to aid the poor may be perceived as threatening to some interests and may generate opposition accordingly. The scale and intensity of such opposition is likely to be correlated with how those interests perceive their own costs.

Since the power relationship is defined in terms of one's own applied resources as compared to those of the opposition (as conditioned by the environment), those proposing and advocating policy to benefit the poor can make choices regarding the structure of proposals so that they have an impact on bases of potential support or opposition. If the opposition is likely to be broad-based or intense because of perceived costs, proponents might choose to counter by proposing benefits that will generate at least equally broad-based or intense support. Alternatively, they may choose to reduce the opposition's base by compromising, even if that means reducing the base of support as well.

The choices are not easy; even the perceptions and calculations are difficult. But there are no absolutes in politics. The political process is always in motion, somewhat unstable most of the time, and marked by high levels of uncertainty. The fluidity of the political process at least allows for opportunities to make the system more effectively responsive to the needs of the poor than it has been in the past.

SUMMARY: THE POOR AND POLITICAL POWER

First, political power is not a tangible thing which one either possesses or lacks, but a relationship which political actors maintain with other political actors, with political institutions, with the political environment, and with political processes. Indeed, in a sense, power *is* process because the relationship is dynamic and moves and changes with the events of political endeavor and political life. As the eminent theologian, Paul Tillich, once wrote: "Power is real only in its actualization, in the encounter with other bearers of power and in the ever-changing balance which is the result of these encounters." [11]

Second, the power position of the poor is uncomfortable, but not necessarily desperate. They are severely and inherently disadvantaged in terms of certain resources that are used for effective competition in the political process. They are also deficient in education and certain kinds of knowledge, in political skills, and in political participation. However, these deficiencies are not inevitable and are correctable. Moreover, the poor possess some ideological advantages in terms of widely accepted values which give legitimacy to their claims for redress and assistance.

Third, it is unlikely that the poor have the resources or favorable environmental conditions to exercise sufficient power to redress their conditions without the active assistance and support of the nonpoor. If public efforts to aid the poor are to succeed, the message is clear: poor and nonpoor must make common cause and each must welcome and assist the efforts of the other.

Finally, the complexities of political and economic systems make it unlikely that any comprehensive policy change will emerge and dramatically alter either the structures and processes of the systems or the condition of the less fortunate in our society. The systems are biased against such changes in numerous ways. But it is not simply the fault of the systems. There is not simply *one* problem of the poor with which society must cope, for the poor have *many* problems. Poverty is complex and cannot be treated without seriously considering the dynamics of the economy, the society, and the political system. While piecemeal policy approaches considered in isolation from each other may not be particularly successful in the long run, strategies based on numerous approaches at different levels of government and addressing the various needs of the poor and the causes of their poverty may be more reasonable and productive than the search for some dramatic and sweeping systematic change.

An effort which came as close to a sweeping change as any in the last decade was the Family Assistance Plan (FAP) proposed by the Nixon Administration. That plan would have constituted a major revision of current income-maintenance programs by instituting a form of guaranteed minimum income. The proposal failed to be enacted, in large measure because it was attacked by both liberal and conservative enthusiasts on the basis of competitive sets of values. Efforts by moderates to develop compromises ultimately failed; in this case, more alienation than support was generated by virtually every attempt at accommodation. That is not the way the system normally works. But the example is instructive regarding the pitfalls involved in making policies about poverty.[12]

Some Implications

The preceding themes suggest important implications which ought to be addressed. The difficulties posed by the nature of the poverty problem, the complexities of political and economic systems, and the frustrations of political struggle and uncertain results give ample opportunity to rationalize inaction and to maintain the status quo. Similarly, abundant incentives are provided to discourage the honestly concerned from initial or continuing involvement in efforts to aid the poor.

The temptations should be resisted. Involvement from many sectors of society is absolutely necessary if efforts against poverty are to succeed, but such involvement must be conditioned by awareness of political realities.

1. Good intentions are important but are sharply limited in terms of realistic potential for changing the world. People who have good intentions but operate in a state of unawareness or unreality may do more harm than good by wasting valuable, limited energy and resources in futile exercises, by unnecessarily polarizing rhetoric and debate, by inhibiting necessary compromise and reducing the quality of informed policy deliberations, by advocating and engendering change without respect for consequences, and by encouraging rapid, defeated, and cynical withdrawal when the presumed and righteous merits of their cause are not greeted with unanimous and speedy acceptance.

2. While opposition to any particular policy or policy proposal may be motivated by crass self-interest or perverse ideological perspective, not all such opposition can be assumed to be so motivated. Particularly in an area as complex as poverty, reasonable people may honorably and honestly disagree on policy matters even as they seek similar ultimate goals.

3. As a public issue, poverty must compete with many other worthy issues for limited resources of time, attention, and money. Moreover, efforts to alleviate poverty are not going to be undertaken

at any and all costs in other areas. For example, unrestricted economic activity and development might enhance employment opportunities for many poor people, but will probably not be permitted if intensified air and water pollution are the result.

4. Informed involvement is necessary to political success. Participants must know the system, how it works and how it can be worked. They must thoroughly understand their issue—its nature, its history, its condition in terms of past, existing, and proposed policy. They ought to make every reasonable effort to marshal accurate data regarding current conditions and the costs, benefits, risks, and anticipated effects (direct and indirect) of policy changes. And they must have a healthy respect for the fact that, in complex situations, common sense and intuition may be entirely inappropriate to creation of successful and effective policy.[13]

5. The vast majority of political involvement is not at world-shaker levels. Few, if any, will have the opportunity to recast society and eliminate poverty in great confrontations with political destiny. Major change can occur over time, however, through the more modest efforts of many people directed to the facets of social, economic, and political life which affect the poor. Individual participants and groups cannot do everything, so they must carve out a more limited piece of the action for themselves. Opportunities for even modest involvement exist at the national, state, or local levels of government, even with one's immediate neighborhood; opportunities for discovering needs, giving them visibility, moving them to the public agenda, proposing solutions, mobilizing support, lobbying decision makers, and monitoring implementation; opportunities for watchdogging and troubleshooting, not only on matters dealing directly with the poor, but on other public and private activities which have indirect or secondary effects on the poor; and opportunities for participating in the electoral process, which rarely results in clear and specific issue mandates, but has profound implications in terms of the policy predispositions and biases of many important decision makers.

In essence, then, greater political involvement by and on behalf of the poor is needed, but participants must understand what they are getting into. The systems and problems are difficult to manage successfully and are by no means fully understood. Political life is often frustrating, frequently depressing, and sometimes capricious, but also potentially satisfying and rewarding to those with endurance and commitment. To many Americans, political activity is dishonorable and dirty, but the political arena is also a major means by which society determines its operational values and shapes its present and future. There are no guarantees in political life, no assured outcomes for one's investments. But abstinence offers one certainty: if changes are to be made, they will be shaped and made by *others* according to *their* values and interests. The political game is often played by the self-seeking, but remaining on the sidelines of the game may be the ultimate in selfishness. Power relationships are cast by competitors and noncompetitors alike.

NOTES

1. Lasswell, Harold. *Politics: Who Gets What, When, and How.* New York: McGraw-Hill, 1936.
2. Bierce, Ambrose. *The Devil's Dictionary.* New York: Dover Publication, Inc., 1958, p. 101.
3. As used in this chapter, "poverty policy" and "anti-poverty policy" are interchangeable. While there are certain public policies which help to engender or perpetuate poverty, use of the term "poverty policy" refers here to efforts to combat poverty and its effects.
4. Lowi, Theodore. *The End of Liberalism.* New York: W. W. Norton, 1969, pp. 174-186, for a discussion of the oversalesmanship of threats and remedies in foreign policy. Chapters 7-9 on urban policy and welfare clearly show the applicability of the concept domestically.
5. See, for example, Sar A. Levitan and Robert Taggart, "The Great Society Did Succeed," *Political Science Quarterly,* Vol. 91, No. 4, (Winter, 1976-1977). Levitan and Taggart provide a more elaborate treatment in *The Promise of Greatness.* Cambridge, Massachusetts: Harvard University Press, 1976. See also Morton Paglin, "Poverty in the United States: A Reevaluation," *Policy Review* (Spring, 1979), which suggests that poverty is less severe than official figures suggest, in large measure because of the in-kind benefits provided by government. The Great Society contributed a lion's share of such benefits.
6. Ryan, William. *Blaming the Victim.* New York: Random House, 1971, for a stimulating, if overdone, examination of victim-blaming and an example of polemical system-blaming.
7. Hofstader, Richard. *Anti-Intellectualism in American Life.* New York: Random House, 1963, p. vii.
8. Palmer, John L., and Joseph A. Peckman, eds. *Welfare in Rural Areas: The North Carolina-Iowa Income Maintenance Experiment.* Washington, D.C.: The Brookings Institution, 1975; Joseph A. Pechman and P. Michael Timpane, eds. *Work Incentives and Income Guarantees.* Washington, D.C.: The Brookings Institution, 1975; and Peter H. Rossi and Katherine C. Lyall. *Reforming Public Welfare, A Critique of the Negative Income Tax Experiment.* New York: Russell Sage Foundation, 1976.

9. See, for example, Gelb, Joyce, and Alice Sardell. "Organizing the Poor: A Brief Analysis of the Politics of the Welfare Rights Movement," *Policy Studies Journal*, Vol. 3, No. 4 (Summer, 1975), pp. 346-354; and David Morris and Karl Hess. *Neighborhood Power.* Washington, D.C.: Institute for Policy Studies, 1975.

10. An interesting treatment of this theme (among others) is Henry J. Aaron. *Politics and the Professors: The Great Society in Perspective.* Washington, D.C.: The Brookings Institution, 1978.

11. Tillich, Paul. *Love, Power, and Justice.* London: Oxford University Press, 1960, p. 41.

12. Marmor, Theodore R., and Martin Rein, "Reforming 'The Welfare Mess': The Fate of the Family Assistance Plan." *Policy and Politics in America.* Allan P. Sindler, ed. Boston: Little, Brown & Co., 1973. A more extended treatment, by a highly interested participant, is Daniel P. Moynihan. *The Politics of a Guaranteed Income.* New York: Random House, 1973.

13. Forrester, Jay W. *Urban Dynamics.* Cambridge, Massachusetts: MIT Press, 1969, for a highly sophisticated and convincing treatment of the point. See also Alice M. Rivlin, *Systematic Thinking for Social Action.* Washington, D.C.: The Brookings Institution, 1971; and John G. Steward, "The Policy Process—The Limits of Knowledge in the Pursuit of Understanding: A Review Essay," *Midwest Journal of Political Science*, Vol. XIV, No. 1, (February 1970), pp. 139-157.

SUGGESTED READINGS

Banfield, Edward C. *The Unheavenly City Revisited.* Boston: Little, Brown & Co., 1974. A sharp neoconservative critique of federal urban policies, including those designed to aid the poor. He states that urban policies have been poorly conceived and designed, counterproductive in effects, futile in intent, and deceptive in terms of oversell and ignoring equally serious problems elsewhere. Highly controversial, it has evoked strong liberal responses.

Frohock, Fred M. *Public Policy: Scope and Logic.* Englewood Clifs, N.J.: Prentice-Hall, 1979. A sophisticated and extensive effort to integrate scholarly trends in public policy research and analysis with normative issues and problems of politics and public policy. Useful in that it grapples with the complexities of political issues and with their moral implications, subjects which are too often treated in mutual exclusion.

Hatfield, Mark. *Between a Rock and a Hard Place.* Waco, Texas: Word, Incorporated, 1976. An autobiographical pilgrimage by the senior U.S. Senator from Oregon, whose powerful commitments to his Christian faith have come into conflict with the realities of his obligations in political life. As a personal revelation of Hatfield's trials of conscience, the book focuses on some of the costs of political life. Useful as an antidote to many stereotypes of politics and politicians and as an affirmation of the compatibility of principle and political life, even if under some stress and strain.

Rodgers, Harrell R., Jr. *Poverty Amid Plenty: A Political and Economic Analysis.* Reading, Mass.: Addison-Wesley Publishers, 1979. An excellent, brief, critical treatment of issues and policies relating to poverty in America. Written from a liberal perspective which finds the roots of poverty in capitalism, elitism, racism, and geographic isolation, it makes an interesting treatise as a companion to Banfield. Useful descriptive data on the poor and surveys of transfer programs, health and employment policy, and welfare reform.

Walzer, Michael. *Political Action: A Practical Guide to Movement Politics.* Chicago: Quadrangle Books, 1971. A brief (125 pages), highly readable and informative how-to-do-it book for citizen activists and would-be citizen activists. For people who believe they can begin to assert some influence on their political system and its policies, it provides a good start and direction with respect both to various political activities and to problems which may arise in those endeavors.

STUDY QUESTIONS

What follows is an approach to individual and group self-education and awareness preceding more active involvement and advocacy:

1. Identify a community for study. *Community* may refer to a neighborhood, a district of a town or a city, a specific local governing unit, a region, a state, a nation, or the world. How you identify and define it will depend on your interests, resources, and ambition, but the project suggested here assumes a local scale. Analyze this community through the use of the information sought through Questions 2 and 3.

2. Using 1980 census data, supplemented by local data and previous censuses for comparison, develop a demographic profile of your community, with particular focus on identifying the poor. How many? What proportion of the population? Of what ethnic composition? Unemployment rates? Housing conditions (density, cost, and habitability)? Health conditions (sanitation, mortality, physical and mental diseases, etc.)? Age and dependency conditions? Crime rates? Alcoholism and drug use? Locations of various economic strata? Education and illiteracy?

3. For each or any of the following policy areas attempt to (1) identify relevant issues and policies in force (again with a focus on the poor, but keeping the comparative perspective in mind); (2) identify appropriate policy makers and policy deliverers; (3) identify persons and organizations which represent or otherwise speak for the interests of the poor; and (4) assess how well the poor are served by public policy and public services as compared to other segments of the community and/or as related to their needs (you may wish to consider such criteria as funding, accessibility to services, personnel commitments, and geographic allocations):

a. Education and vocational training
b. Health facilities and services (including sanitation and pollution control)
c. Public safety (police and fire) services
d. Zoning and planning
e. Recreational facilities, parks, and open spaces
f. Public housing, urban development, and housing assistance
g. Social services

Such an inquiry can be fairly simple, general, and elementary, or it may be exceedingly detailed, complex, and sophisticated. It may concentrate on local policy and services, or it may also consider state and federal activity. However you choose to structure it, it should be enlightened with respect to the nature of the poor, their circumstances, the political situation, the relevant policies and policy needs, and appropriate areas for further activity.

6

Some Biblical Perspectives on Wealth and Poverty

Walter E. Pilgrim

The biblical basis for a social ethic is more often than not derived primarily from the Old Testament. This is understandable because the Old Testament provides at least three major resources for developing a biblical social ethic. One is the central redemptive event of the Old Testament itself, the Exodus. As Yahweh's foundational act of liberation on behalf of his enslaved people, it has served as a powerful paradigm of the God who in every age seeks the liberation of the poor and oppressed.[1] A second resource is the legal traditions, which detail how the God of the Exodus desires to preserve social justice among his people.[2] Among the legislations are the Sabbath year, the Jubilee year, the poor tithe, and the "law of gleanings." In this material the refrain is repeatedly echoed, "Remember, you were once slaves and strangers in Egypt" (Exod. 22:21, 23:9, Deut. 24:18, 22). A third resource is the prophetic writings. With the eighth-century prophets, there emerges a remarkable prophetic tradition in which a basic theme is God's word of judgment against his people for their oppression and exploitation of the poor.[3] Hence social injustice forms the core of Yahweh's indictment of his people and the basis of the call to repentance.

In view of these clear and challenging resources for a social ethic in the Old Testament, it is small wonder that the New Testament is often neglected. Yet for the Christian community it is equally important that its own writings be examined as a potential resource for a social ethic based on and consistent with the new revelation in Jesus the Christ. The Old Testament provides the roots for the New Testament concern for justice and the poor. But both the radical love-ethic of Jesus and the early Christian understanding that with Jesus the New Age of righteousness has begun, evoke new impulses and motivations for a social ethic on behalf of the poor and exploited.

GOSPEL TRADITIONS ON WEALTH AND POVERTY

The synoptic Gospels, Matthew, Mark, and Luke, are primary sources for the following discussion, which presupposes the priority of Mark's Gospel and the existence of Q, a source known to both Matthew and Luke. Recent studies have emphasized the unique character of each Gospel's portrait of Jesus as each evangelist narrates the story of Jesus in a way appropriate to his own understanding and the needs of his community. Thus we could approach our topic by examining each gospel individually, beginning with Mark. However, we have chosen to approach the synoptics as a whole, seeking to show the basic unity of the Gospel traditions regarding possessions, while at the same time noting some major differences in emphases.

The Prior Claim of God

The starting point in the Gospel traditions about possessions is the recognition of the prior claim of God and his will upon human life. The goal of life is not the accumulation of material possessions but seeking the kingdom of God and its righteousness (Matt. 6:33, Luke 11:2-3, 12:31). Similarly, the evaluation of human life is not to be based on the abundance of a person's wealth, but on the possession of the kingdom (Luke 12:15, 32-34). This priority of God and his rule and a life that acknowledges God's prior claim immediately call into question any idolatrous role that possessions may play in human life.

The fact that possessions can and do function as primary values and goals, however, is clearly recognized in the Gospels. Hence the sharp call to choose between the service of God and the service of mammon. "No one can serve two masters; for either he will hate the one and love the other, or he will be devoted to one and despise the other. You cannot serve God and mammon" (Matt. 6:24, Luke 16:13). In this passage there seems to be little room, if any, to maneuver between service to God or service to wealth. The choice is one or the other, a kind of radical "either/or" so typical of Jesus' call to total discipleship (cf. Mark 8:34-38). Nevertheless, this does not necessarily lead to the conclusion that service to God means the abandonment of all one's possessions. What is at stake is the question of loyalty, service, allegiance—either to God and his will or to one's possessions.

Those who seek the rule of God as their primary value and goal are promised a life free of material anxiety, based upon confident trust in God's providential care. The admonition of Jesus, "Do not be anxious about your life, what you shall eat or what you shall drink," is based on the "how much more" of God's loving care for his creation (Matt. 6:25-30). Anxiety over basic human needs typifies the attitude of those who do not know the heavenly Father (Matt. 6:32). Yet God not only knows what things are necessary, he can also be trusted to provide them, especially to those who seek first his kingdom. What may appear here as a naive, simplistic call to faith, with little or no prudent concern for the morrow, becomes more understandable in the light of another statement of Jesus elsewhere in the tradition. This is Jesus' response to Peter's statement, "Lo, we have left everything and followed you." In response comes the promise that those who left all for Jesus' sake will receive more than enough in this life along with eternal life (Mark 10:28-30). Here the assurance of material sufficiency is linked to participation in a new community, where basic needs are met by mutual sharing and love. Thus along with the promise of God's care for those who put their trust in him exists the promise of a new fellowship in which caring and love are functioning realities.

The Radical Danger of Wealth

With respect to wealth and possessions, the Gospels reflect a position of utmost sensitivity to their potential dangers and seductive power. In general, wealth or the desire for it constitutes one of the greatest obstacles to entering the kingdom and living a life in harmony with the will of God.

This is illustrated in the first place by those traditions where wealth is cited as an insurmountable obstacle to fellowship with Jesus, for example, the rich man who asked how to attain eternal life (Mark 10:17-22 and parallels). The story concludes with the challenge to sell what he has and give it to the poor and then follow Jesus, a challenge he apparently cannot meet. The sequel to this story in each gospel applies this one man's failure to the plight of all who are rich: "How hard it will be for those who have riches to enter the kingdom of God!" (Mark 10:23). This is further strengthened by the hyperbole of the camel going through the needle's eye, the point of which is the near impossibility of the rich becoming authentic disciples. Jesus' own disciples are astonished at this hard saying, whose force is hardly mitigated by the additional saying, "With men it is impossible, but not with God" (Mark 10:27).

Other texts also stress the grave dangers that wealth poses to those who possess it. Three Lukan traditions are especially powerful. One is the parable of the rich fool, which underscores the ultimate foolishness of a life lived primarily for the accumulation of wealth (Luke 12:13-21). Likewise, the parable of the rich man and poor Lazarus shows the shocking social disparity that exists between the rich and the poor, a situation to be reversed in the coming age. In the second half of the parable the warning goes out to the five brothers to reverse their ways before it is too late (Luke 16:19-31). Finally, there are the woes against the rich in the Lukan Sermon on the Plain, which echo the prophetic judgment against the perpetrators of social injustice: "But woe to you that are rich, for you have received your consolation" (Luke 6:24-26).

But wealth is not just an obstacle to entering the kingdom; it is a constant temptation to those who are already disciples. Hence the interpretation of the parable of the sower warns disciples not to be choked by the thorns of "the cares of the world, and the delight in riches" (Mark 4:18-19, Luke 8:14). Other warnings are issued not to act like the scribes and Pharisees, "who devour widow's houses" and are "lovers of money" (Matt. 23:14, Luke 16:14). The horror story of Ananias and Sapphira is also retold by Luke as a warning to Christians (Acts 5:1-11). Thus wealth, from beginning to end, is regarded as one of the chief dangers to persons desiring to do the will of God.

What should be done with one's wealth? In a number of texts the call to discipleship is linked with the call to total abandonment of one's possessions (Mark 1:20, Luke 5:11, Mark 10:21, 28, Luke 12:33, Luke 14:33). Is this then the solution to wealth, to give it all away and to live from day to day off the charity of others? Or to adopt a life of poverty? Is it only in this way that one can remove the grave temptation that money poses?

It might seem so, not simply because of the texts just cited, but because of the life-style of Jesus himself. According to the Gospels, Jesus and his closest disciples abandoned their regular vocations and became full-time itinerant teachers and healers. They apparently lived from the gifts of others and from a common purse, as they moved from place to place with their urgent message of the in-breaking kingdom (Mark 6:8-10, Matt. 10:8-11, Matt. 8:20, Luke 9:57-58, 9:1-4, 10:1-8). Some women were regular contributors to their needs (Luke 8:1-3). However, this solution to the problem of wealth seems limited mainly to the historical Jesus and a small circle of his followers. It was necessitated by the immediate circumstances of Jesus' ministry and the eschatological urgency of his mission. It is not a style of life demanded of everyone in the Gospel tradition (Luke 19:1-10, 8:1-3). Nor is it the attitude toward possessions that emerges in Paul, Acts, or other New Testament writings. Thus the solution to the genuine dangers posed by wealth for the Christian probably lies somewhere else than in the total surrender of one's possessions and the adoption of a life of poverty.[4]

The Radical Challenge of Proper Use

While wealth constitutes a major obstacle to doing the will of God, the Gospels also recognize that possessions are both necessary and good gifts of God and that the basic question is one of their proper use.

Jesus and Possessions. Despite his life of voluntary renunciation of wealth, Jesus was no ascetic, nor did he advocate an ascetic life. This separated him from his predecessor, John the Baptist, and from other contemporary movements such as the Qumran community living along the shores of the Dead Sea (Luke 7:33-34). Jesus enjoyed the fellowship of banquets, with good food and drink (Mark 2:15, Luke 7:36, Luke 14:1, John 2:1-11). The accusation of his critics that he was "a glutton and drunkard" is evidence of his open life-style in sharing the daily life of his contemporaries, even those outside the realm of social and religious acceptance (Luke 15:1-2). Jesus knew people of wealth and associated with them (Luke 19:1-10, Matt. 8:5-13, Luke 7:1-10, Luke 7:36-50, Matt. 27:57, Mark 10:17-22). Moreover, his favorite image of the coming age was that of the eschatological feast, where joy would reign supreme and the Messiah and all the redeemed share in the heavenly feast.[5] Jesus' own ministry is depicted as a time of festivity. Thus Jesus' disciples, unlike those of the Baptist or the Pharisee, did not fast. The new wine required fresh wine skins (Mark 2:18-22). In sum, the portrait of Jesus' life in the Gospels shows one who accepted the goodness of God's creation and its abundance, including some of the things that only money can buy.[6]

Nor was Jesus oblivious to basic human needs. The Lord's Prayer includes the petition for daily bread (Matt. 6:11, Q). In the same text which sets forth the priority of the kingdom and its righteousness is the promise that the daily need for food, clothing, and shelter will be met by God himself (Luke 12:31). In the Lukan Beatitudes the future promise to the poor states specifically that their present hunger will be satisfied and their present mourning turned to laughter, a theme echoed as well in the Magnificat (Luke 6:20-21, 1:53). The life of the poor, with all their hardship and suffering, is therefore not any ascetic ideal in the Gospels, nor is it in harmony with the will of God. God intends daily bread and sufficient provision for all of life's needs for his creation, even for the wicked and ungrateful (Matt. 5:45, Luke 6:35).

Nevertheless, awareness of the goodness of God's gifts and recognition that God wills a sufficiency for all persons still does not put a blanket endorsement on the accumulation of wealth or justify one person's abundance over against another person's lack. The traditions indicating the grave dangers of wealth preclude this kind of conclusion. Although possessions are not inherently evil, and although God in fact wills enough for all his creatures, neither the ardent desire for nor the accumulation of possessions reflects his will!

The Right Use of Possessions. What then is the right attitude toward possessions? Here the weight of the Gospel traditions focuses on the proper use of one's wealth and possessions, that is, sharing them for the benefit of the poor and needy. This response flows directly out of the fundamental love-ethic of Jesus. Just as all of life is to be directed to one's neighbor out of love for God, so the use of possessions is to serve the neighbor, and particularly the one most in need.

This theme is developed in numerous ways. Already in the parable of the good Samaritan, the Samaritan's radical fulfillment of the command to "love your neighbor as yourself" is costly in terms of financial sharing (Luke 10:29-37).[7] Following normative Jewish practice prescribed in the Law, whereby a tithe and other gifts were

to be set aside for the poor, Jesus advocates the giving of alms to
the poor, only he insists that it be an act of spontaneous giving
without pretense of piety (Matt. 6:2-4). In the Lukan tradition,
the practice of almsgiving is further intensified and made part of the
normative life of the early church (Luke 11:41, 12:33, Acts 3:2, 10,
9:36, 10:2, 4, 31, 24:17). Its marks are to be generosity and liberality.

Still, these kinds of examples and exhortations to share with the
needy generally fall within the ethic of Jesus' day. Perhaps this is
also true of the ethical instructions of John the Baptist which are pre-
served only by Luke (3:10-14). Luke has the Baptist specify the
"fruits of repentance" for the crowds, tax collectors, and soldiers.
Essentially, the penitents are told to share with those in need, and
to act with honesty and justice in their vocations. None is asked to
leave his calling, not even tax collectors or soldiers. Nevertheless,
the ethic is not merely reflective of Palestinian Judaism. The call for
the crowds to share their coats contains an appeal for "solidarity
among the poor"; [8] nothing is said about cultic observances, only
justice, fairness, and compassion in human relations. Most striking
is the acceptance of tax collectors and soldiers, people "outside the
law" within the new fellowship of the baptized. There is even a
touch of social consciousness in the sharing of coats, the recognition
of exploitative taxation of the poor and of police-style extortion and
violence against citizens.

But the more radical demands typical of Jesus' love-ethic and
his call to discipleship in view of the coming kingdom are found in
other kinds of texts. The example of the poor widow who gives her
last two coins is contrasted with the gifts of the rich (Mark 12:41-
44, Luke 21:1-4). In the Sermon on the Mount, the love-ethic is
extended to one's enemies, and within this context of unconditional
love, disciples are not only forbidden to retaliate, but told to "give
your cloak to one who sues you," and "give to him who begs or
wants to borrow from you" (Matt. 5:40-42, Luke 6:27-30). This
same cutting ethic is carried through in other texts in Luke's Gospel. In one, Jesus' disciples are urged not only to love their enemies, but to do good and to lend to those who cannot or will not
repay (Luke 6:32-36). Here the counsel to lend *gratis* without
expecting anything in return serves as a prime example of those who
are "sons of the Most High," and who follow the character of a
merciful Father (Luke 6:35-36). In a second set of texts the law of
the kingdom is contrasted with the natural, self-centered law of
reciprocity. Both texts occur within the setting of table fellowship,

and in each the point is the same. The law of reciprocity says, "Invite your friends, brothers, relatives, or rich neighbors," those who will repay you and who are advantageous to you! The law of the kingdom (love-ethic) says "Invite the poor, the maimed, the lame, and the blind," those who can't repay you (Luke 14:12-14).

The point of all these texts together, then, is to apply the love-ethic of the kingdom to the use of one's possessions. The call of Jesus to follow him contains the challenge to a new way of life, which includes a reevaluation of possessions and their use. Possessions, as gifts of God, are not to be used primarily for one's own pleasure, comfort, or power. This is laying up treasures on earth (Matt. 6:19, Luke 12:21, 33). Possessions are gifts to be used for one's own basic needs and beyond that for the needs of others. The poor in particular are the special objects of the right use of wealth (see below).

The most powerful text in the Gospels on the proper use of wealth is found in the story of rich Zacchaeus, the chief tax collector of Jericho (Luke 19:1-10). This story is a response to the question posed in the previous chapter of Luke's gospel, Can the rich be saved? (18:24-30). Zacchaeus is the "yes paradigm" to this question. But the "yes" is no easy one. Zacchaeus' response to his encounter with Jesus is set forth in v. 8: he gives one-half of all his possessions to the poor; he restores fourfold to those whom he has defrauded. The promise of restitution falls at least partially within the framework of Old Testament Jewish law.[9] But the decision to share one-half with the poor is an unprecedented act, without Old Testament or rabbinic parallels. In fact, rabbinic law set a limit for charity of one-fifth of one's entire wealth and one-fifth of one's annual income. Here is a radically new standard or paradigm for the believer, based on the love-ethic of Jesus and the immediacy ("today") of salvation present in his person (Luke 19:9). This new model of sharing is not a legalistic prescription, since it is made gratefully and voluntarily in response to God's initiative and acceptance embodied in Jesus. But by the principle of "one-half to the poor," Luke intends to say that the act of giving should go beyond what any law can require; that it is much more than a token gift that requires little or no sacrifice; that in fact it represents a new orientation of one's life toward the cause of the poor, which shows itself in a total commitment of one's possessions for the poor and needy, consistent with the unconditional character of agape-love.

Luke clearly sees a further working out of the Zacchaeus paradigm of possessions in the life of the early community in Acts 2 and 4.

The Good News to the Poor

With respect to the poor, a couple of themes converge in the Gospels as convincing evidence that Jesus renews the fundamental Old Testament affirmation that God is the special defender of the poor and needy.

This can be seen first of all in the Gospels' identification of Jesus' ministry with the poor and the lowly. Throughout his ministry, the main objects of his outreach are the "lost sheep of the house of Israel" (Matt. 10:6). These include most of the people on the fringe of Palestinian society—socially, economically, ethnically, and religiously. They are variously identified as tax collectors, sinners, the sick, the crippled, prostitutes, beggars, the poor, and the multitudes (e.g., Matt. 11:2-5, Luke 7:21-22, Mark 2:15-16, Luke 7:34, Mark 10:46).[10] While not all were economically destitute (e.g., some tax collectors), most were. Their marginal lives were the result of social powerlessness and exploitation, along with religious ideas that often attributed their tragic circumstances to divine punishment for sin and so excluded them from normal social and religious fellowship. While means of providing aid were legislated in Old Testament and rabbinic law, by and large the masses of poor and destitute were too many and the discrepancies between rich and poor too great for any of those means to work effectively. Even Pharisees and other pious are indicted for "devouring widows' houses" and "neglecting the weightier matters of the law, justice and mercy and faith" (Mark 12:40, Matt. 23:23). Jesus obviously attracted the poor by his words and deeds, while at the same time causing great offense to his contemporaries through his association with and defense of the activities of the poor.

But not only is Jesus' ministry identified with the poor and needy. A basic theme of his preaching is the "good news to the poor" (Matt. 11:5, Luke 7:22). Since Jesus' ministry focused on the socially and religiously disenfranchised, the term "poor" cannot be immediately spiritualized, even though it may include the humble and penitent, that is, the poor in spirit.

Luke's Gospel, in particular, develops the theme of good news to the poor. The ministry of Jesus is set forth on the basis of the words of Isaiah 61:1-2, which announces good news to the poor and the acceptable year of the Lord (Luke 4:16-21). Moreover, the Isaiah quote is influenced by the ancient vision of the Jubilee year. According to the Jubilee year prescriptions, every fiftieth year the land was to lie fallow, the slaves to be freed, all debts to be remitted, and, most striking, all property was to be returned to its original owners (Lev. 25:10-24, Deut. 15:1-11). The intent was to preserve a community of justice, in which the poor would be the prime benefactors. While it is highly unlikely that Jesus intended to proclaim a Jubilee year in this manner, this vision of radical justice for the poor and oppressed was a part of his view of the New Age inaugurated by his words and deeds.[11] Thus the "good news to the poor" announced by the Lukan Jesus should be interpreted in concrete social and economic terms, as well as religious. The Lukan Beatitudes and Woes continue the theme (Luke 6:20-26), as does Jesus' response to the messengers of John (Luke 7:22-23), and other texts in which the poor are among the recipients of good news (Luke 14:12-24, 16:9, 19-31, Mark 12:41-44).[12]

This promise of good news to the poor has two main foci. One is the promise of a coming reversal of their present condition in the age to come. While in the present they suffer from hunger and need, in the coming age their needs will be met. Often this promise is linked to a reversal of roles with the rich (Luke 1:52-53, 6:20-21, 24-25, 16:19-31, Mark 10:31). Unlike some late Jewish apocalyptic literature, this theme is not connected with any motive of revenge in the Gospels; rather, the theme of an eschatological reversal bears the hope of ultimate justice for the poor, while at the same time it serves as a warning to the rich and a call to repentance (Luke 16:27-31).

However, there is also good news for the poor in the present. Already in his own ministry interpreted as the beginning of the New Age, Jesus gathers around him a fellowship of those who are poor, both socially and religiously. These poor not only anticipate the coming kingdom, but already begin to share in it, as they form the nucleus of a new community in which the forgiveness and love of God are at work. Already within this new community their needs are met and within it they experience something of the realities of the coming age in the radical love, acceptance, sharing, and service that are its marks (Mark 10:28-31). It is this vision of a new community which Luke takes up in Acts and makes the ongoing bearer of good news to the poor in his age.

In summary, both the identification of Jesus' own ministry with the poor and his preaching of good news to the poor reflect the way in which the Gospels reaffirm God's bias toward the poor and needy. The promise of ultimate justice in the future coupled with the emergence of a new community in the present provide the basic realities of hope for the poor.

Summary of Gospel Traditions

This completes the brief survey of the Gospel traditions on the subject of wealth and poverty. It began by placing possessions with the broader scope of Jesus' announcement of the rule of God and its prior claim of allegiance upon all human life. It then looked at those traditions which warn specifically about the radical dangers of wealth. The dangers exist in the way wealth or its pursuit so easily becomes the dominating force in human life, and makes one blind to the needs of one's neighbors. The solution to the problem of wealth is not finally its total denial, though Jesus and his closest followers lived a life relatively free of possessions. The chief challenge is to use it rightly. This involves the recognition of wealth as a gift of God for daily needs, but most importantly the sacrificial sharing of one's wealth for the sake of the poor. The example of Zacchaeus, who decided to give one-half to the poor, is the kind of radical paradigm in the Gospels that is most consistent with the love-ethic of Jesus. In his own ministry and teaching Jesus embodied good news to the poor, thereby confirming the basic biblical tradition of God's supreme love and concern for the poor and needy. Only Jesus does so with the authority of God himself and with the radical vision of one who knows the will of God as love.

THE NEW COMMUNITY AND THE POOR IN ACTS

The New Community (Acts 2:41-47, 4:32-37)

The vision of a new community in which the good news to the poor becomes a reality finds its clearest expression in Luke's description of the early church in Acts. To what degree this description corresponds to historical reality has been much debated.[13] In whatever way one answers this question, Luke's intent in preserving such a vision of the Christian community seems plain. His twice repeated description is meant to portray the image of the kind of community which is shaped by the Spirit of Jesus.

What kind of community is this? In two successive summaries Luke provides a brief and tantalizing glimpse of this Spirit-shaped

community of believers (Acts 2:41-47, Acts 4:32-37). Its basic characteristic is a sense of *koinonia,* that is, fellowship and unity (Acts
2:44, Acts 4:32). This fellowship was obviously the result of the
community's common faith and the gift of the Spirit in its midst.
But most interesting is the way this unity in the faith exhibited itself
in the economic and social life of the community. According to Luke,
the members shared all things in common (Acts 4:37, 2:44). And
this is further explained by saying that no one claimed that any of
his possessions was his own; rather, people sold their lands or houses
and brought the profit to the community, which distributed it
according to need.

Some have understood this description as a form of "Christian
communalism," or as others prefer to call it, a "love communism."
In this view the members sold all their possessions and lived a communal life-style from a common purse. However, a more cautious
reading would seem to indicate that Luke intends to describe something less than a total selling of all possessions. More likely, the
members of the community expressed their sense of oneness by
making their possessions available to the common good as needs
arose. Not all of their goods were sold at once, but the selling and
sharing was a continual process. Many, at least, still possessed their
homes (Acts 2:46, Acts 12:12). Moreover, the selling was voluntary,
not compulsory. What was distinctive about the community was
the *total willingness* of its members to share their lands and possessions for the sake of the poor among them. There was, as one com-
mentator has put it, "an abandonment of the proprietary spirit." [14]
The community in effect relinquished its right to private property
for the sake of the common good. Its members were determined to
have no poor among them (Acts 4:34). In this sense Luke can write,
"No one said that any of the things which he possessed was his own,
but they had everything in common" (Acts 4:32).

Thus, while this may not be a form of Christian communism,
strictly defined, it is clear that the principle of radical economic
sharing was practiced within the Christian community. In its "total
willingness" to make its resources available to the community, in its
determination to have no poor in its midst, and in its commitment
to share its resources according to the needs of its members, one
sees the kind of community, socially and economically, that Luke
"imaged" for his own church and for the church in every age.

This kind of community is also intended by Luke to be a model for society as well. The radical care of this community's members for one another along with their religious zeal and devotion attracted the attention of outsiders (Acts 2:47). Thus while Luke has little to say directly about concern for the poor outside the community of faith, he does point the way for a new vision of society in which concern for the poor is central.

The seriousness with which this radical vision of a new community is taken is illustrated by two antithetical examples. Joseph Barnabas exemplifies the Christian norm. A Jew of the diaspora, he sold a field he owned and offered the money to the apostles for distribution to the poor (Acts 4:36-37). The other example is the story of Ananias and Sapphira (Acts 5:1-11). Their sin was not their failure to keep back a portion of their profit from their land but their conspiring to lie. They were under no compulsion to sell, or to share all the profits (Acts 5:4). But by lying about their gift, they violated the unity of the fellowship and broke its spirit of love. The fact that Luke uses a case of possessions to illustrate the importance of fellowship points all the more to the seriousness with which he views the right use of possessions in the church.

Just and Equitable Distribution (Acts 6:1-6)

The first recorded dispute in the history of the early church occurred over money. It centered on the issue of fair distribution of funds for the poor. Obviously equitable distribution is not a new problem! According to Luke, the Hebrew-speaking widows were favored over the Greek-speaking widows in the daily distribution. It is probable that the Greek-speaking widows came from the diaspora and for a variety of reasons had settled in Jerusalem for the remainder of their lives. Already in the Jewish communities some tension existed between diaspora Jews, who knew only Greek and so were regarded as aliens in Jerusalem, and local Palestinian Jews. Each, in fact, had separate synagogues and probably did not associate freely with the other. This same tension may have been carried over into the Jewish Christian community, so that the Hellenists were discriminated against in the distribution.

The problem, at any rate, was recognized and dealt with decisively by the appointment of seven persons, all with Greek names, to supervise a just and equitable distribution. Just as there was to be no poor person among them, so was there to be no unfair distribution.

Ecumenical Care of the Poor (Acts 11:27-30, 20:33-35, 24:17)

Luke also preserves a few texts that point to the worldwide dimensions of the problem. When a global famine was foretold to the church located in Antioch of Syria, the Syrian church decided to send relief to the community in Judea. Apparently it was known that the church in Judea and Jerusalem was extremely poor and would not be able to survive without help. Of special interest is the fact that the Antiochan church was a mix of Jewish and Gentile converts (Acts 11:20ff.); hence the relief aid embodied both different races and nations and took on global dimensions. The principle at work was that wealthier Christians in one land should assist poor Christians in another. Within the Antiochan community itself, Luke stresses, the principle of sharing according to one's ability was upheld (Acts 11:29); that is, the more one has, the more that is required. But this principle should not be separated from the earlier one in Acts of possessing all things in common, which meant an unreserved willingness to share one's possessions with the needy. Both must be kept in tension to keep Luke's challenging vision of Christian sharing and concern for the poor in perspective.

Paul and Barnabas were named as the representatives to bring the relief aid to Jerusalem (Acts 11:30). Later in Acts, Luke briefly alludes to Paul's own presentation of "alms and offerings" to his nation, that is, the church in Jerusalem (Acts 24:17). The reference to the collection of Paul on his third missionary journey seems obvious (see below). Thus on two occasions in his brief history of the early church, Luke points to the sense of unity in the emerging catholic church which led it to take concrete action on behalf of the poor in a way that began to transcend its ethnic and national boundaries.

A fitting conclusion to Luke's social vision of the new community in Acts is found in the farewell speech of Luke's great hero, the missionary-apostle Paul (Acts 20:18-35). In his last will and testament before the Ephesian elders, Paul concludes his speech with a sharp defense of his motives. He claims he has coveted no one's money, but has worked to support himself and his companions, thereby providing an example "that through toil one must help the weak." To confirm this example of care for the needy, Luke has Paul quote a word of the earthly Jesus, "It is more blessed to give than to receive" (Acts 20:35). The authenticity of this saying, found only here, is not to be disputed. But it is not its historical authenticity which is Luke's point, but its content—a word from the Lord Jesus to his church, exhorting and encouraging it to a life of giving and sharing on behalf of the weak. Once again one encounters a word of good news to the poor, and a vision of a worldwide community in which the Spirit of Jesus is radically at work.

THE PAULINE LETTERS AND THE POOR

When one moves from the gospel traditions to the Pauline correspondence on the question of wealth and poverty, two things are immediately apparent. One is the relative lack of references to the subject of wealth, and the second is the virtual absence of radical sayings about the danger of wealth.[15] Nowhere is there anything like the sharp sayings of Jesus in the Gospels about wealth and its inherent dangers. Paul does include "covetousness" in his list of vices; but it is not singled out as in the Gospel tradition (Rom. 1:29, 1 Cor. 5:10-13, 6:10, Eph. 4:19, Eph. 5:5, Col. 3:5). Nor is there an attack upon the rich as such, even though the main recipients of Paul's preaching seem to be the uneducated and the poor. Nor are there any concrete descriptions of the economic life of the Pauline congregations, such as the kind of total communal sharing that Luke describes in Acts 2 and 4. Nevertheless, the authentic letters of Paul do touch on the subject of possessions in a number of significant ways.[16]

1. Basic to Paul's understanding of the Christian community is his conviction that with the death and resurrection of Christ a New Age has begun, in which all past relationships and structures are broken and new ones are brought into being. In this New Age, "there is neither Jew nor Greek, there is neither slave nor free, there is neither male nor female; you are all one in Christ Jesus" (Gal. 3:28). The basic equality in Christ, which erases all the old distinctions and creates "one new body," is not specifically applied to rich and poor; yet the principle is there so that one could add "in Christ there is neither rich nor poor." Applied to the Christian community, it would mean an end to all relationships in which one group dominates over another, or one group has distinct economic advantage over the other. In at least one instance, Paul is appalled when this principle is not carried out in the church. In Corinth, when the community gathered together, the rich ate and drank their fill, while the poor went without (1 Cor. 11:17-22). Paul writes, "Do you despise the church of God and humiliate those who have nothing?"

The perpetuation of divisions between rich and poor, in which the poor are neglected, is regarded as a clear violation of the new community brought about by the New Age in Christ.

2. Similarly, although the death and resurrection of Christ marks the beginning of the New Age, it does not mean the end of the Old Age. Christian existence for Paul is lived in tension between the two ages, the "already" and the "not yet." Translated into concrete realities, this means Christian existence is always a continual struggle between good and evil, between the new life in Christ active in love and the old life of egotism and idolatry. Here Luther's famous dictim *simul justus et peccator* ("at the same time justified and sinner") describes vividly the basic reality of present existence for the believer.

Within this conceptual framework of the Old and New Ages, Paul accepts the value and necessity of structures and systems as a way of bringing some semblance of justice and order into the Old Age (Rom. 13:1-7). Without it, the strong could rule as they will and the weak would exist at their mercy. Hence Paul counseled obedience to governing authorities who are instituted to prevent wrongdoings and to assure the payment of taxes.[17] At the same time, the present structures and systems are to be permeated by the radically transforming reality of the new life in Christ. Christians are not to conform to this age but to "be transformed by the renewal of [their] mind[s]" to do the will of God (Rom. 12:2). A new power is at work in the midst of the old world, in which what is good and acceptable and perfect is the norm under the sovereign rule of love (Rom. 12:9-21, 13:8-10, Gal. 5:6, 13-14, 6:15, 1 Cor. 13:13, 1 Cor. 14:1). This means too, that although the Christian community sees the value of structures and systems within the present age, it is not bound to any one form, but criticizes them all from the transforming perspective of the new reality in Christ. With respect to economic systems, this means that all of them, from Marxism to capitalism, stand under the radical critique of the gospel and are to be judged according to the way in which they are "servants" of justice for the greater good of humanity. For Paul, too, though Christians inevitably live under the structures and systems of the present age, there is a profound sense in which they are free of all structures and can live "as though" this age is passing away (1 Cor. 7:29-31).[18] Accordingly, even though Paul can speak of the "principalities and powers" which hold the world in bondage and hence dominate the present, he views them as defeated in principle, so that the Christian can oppose and resist their influence (Col. 1:15-16, 2:15).

3. Paul is also profoundly aware that the basic Christian preaching runs counter to the values and priorities of this age. His central message of a crucified Messiah was by and large rejected by the wise and powerful and well-born, and accepted by the lowly and despised (1 Cor. 1:26-29). Paul grounds this rejection theologically on the "offense" or "foolishness" that the message of a crucified Messiah caused for Jews and Greeks and sees the conflict rooted in God's revelation via weakness and suffering over against the human desire for power, status, and wisdom (1 Cor. 1:18-25). The powerful do not want to hear of a God who breaks their hold on the world's structures and calls them to a radically new system of values. So God chooses the foolish and the weak, the low and despised, in effect the "nothings" of this world, to shame the possessors and the powerful. And in this Paul sees a fundamental reversal of values and priorities connected with the preaching and acceptance of the Christian message. That God chooses the weak as the instrument of his presence in the world boldly affirms God's concern in Christ for all the lowly and despised. It calls also for a new system of values which reverses the old ones and their perpetuation by the strong.[19]

4. Paul points to his own life in Christ as an example for others to follow. The features that he especially commends are his willingness to adopt a life-style of simplicity, sacrifice and, if need be, suffering for the sake of Christ. Paul obviously sees his own life as an imitation of his Lord's (Phil. 3:17, 1 Cor. 11:1). Perhaps the agape-hymn of 1 Corinthians 13 bears features of the "imitation of Christ," as many have pointed out.

But what seems most significant is the way Paul contrasts his own life-style as a slave-servant of Christ with the life-style of other Christians, who want to adopt something other than a servant style of life.[20] Especially is this so in the Corinthian letters. "We are fools for Christ's sake, but you are wise in Christ. We are weak, but you are strong. You are held in honor, but we in disrepute. To the present hour we hunger and thirst, we are ill-clad and buffeted and homeless, and we labor, working with our own hands" (1 Cor. 4:10-12). What is at stake for Paul is the kind of life that is most consistent with the crucified Lord, one who came not to be served, but to serve. Paul's own life is that of a servant and that meant concretely a life of economic simplicity, along with a sacrificial concern for others and a readiness to do without (1 Cor. 4:8-13, 2 Cor. 6:3-10,

Phil. 4:11-12). This servant life-style is contrasted sharply and critically with a more triumphant view held by his opponents, in which material rewards, social position, and other benefits were sought.

Nevertheless Paul did not advocate a life of poverty. He himself worked for his own support and that of others, and he expected other Christians to do the same. Yet Christian leaders had the right to be supported by others (1 Cor. 9:14). Paul sees the value of his own work primarily as a vehicle for helping others, and as a model of the self-giving, servant life intended for all believers.

5. On one occasion Paul points to Christ himself as the example of how one should act toward the poor. This occurs in a passage where Paul is urging Christians to give generously for the care of poor Christians suffering in other parts of the world (2 Cor. 8–9). As primary motivation for their giving, Paul holds up the Christological image of "our Lord Jesus Christ who though he was rich, yet for our sake became poor, so that by his poverty you might become rich" (2 Cor. 8:9). While the images of riches and poverty move back and forth between a spiritual and a literal meaning, Paul leaves no doubt about his purpose. The self-giving of Christ himself is to be the source and motivation for the selfless giving of the Christian communities on behalf of the poor! Or to put it another way, for Paul, God's act of grace and love in Christ is the primary source and motive for sharing with one another.

6. The most explicit concern for the poor in the Pauline letters centers on the well-known collection Paul gathered at the conclusion of his missionary activity in Asia Minor and Greece. It was a well-organized effort made over a period of two years, which Paul himself carefully supervised and administrated.

Much work has been done to clarify the intention and importance of this collection for Paul.[21] Its origin grows out of the agreement between Paul and the apostolic leadership in Jerusalem, that he should go to the Gentiles and they to the Jews. This agreement was sealed with the "right hand of fellowship," and with Paul's promise that he would remember the poor in the church of Judea (Gal. 2:10, Rom. 15:26). By the collection, Paul is honoring this agreement. Yet it has even deeper theological meaning for Paul. As the leader of the Gentile wing of the church, it becomes the visible sign of the unity between Gentiles and Jews in Christ, and a giving of gratitude for the faith originating in Jerusalem (Gal. 2:1-10, Rom. 15:27).

However, beyond its theological importance, the practical reason for the collection was aid for the poor Christians in Palestine. Hence Paul does his best to make it a sizeable gift from his churches. In 2 Cor. 8–9, he sets forth four principles to guide the churches in their sharing: (1) One is generosity. He cites the example of the churches of Macedonia, who, though themselves poor and persecuted, gave according to their means and beyond (2 Cor. 8:1-5), and he urges others to be equally generous (2 Cor. 8:7, 24, 9:3, 6, 13). (2) A second is giving according to means. While Paul issues no command or set of specific amounts, he recognizes a "giving according to means," that is in proportion to one's wealth (2 Cor. 8:3, 12). The more one possesses, the more is required. (3) A third is a sense of relative equality of wealth in the Christian community. The goal is not the impoverishment of one community at the expense of another, but a relative equality in which the obvious disparities between the rich and poor are removed (2 Cor. 8:13-15). (4) A fourth is a global view. Paul exhibits a worldwide concern for the needy that breaks down the innate parochial vision of wealthier nations and communities. In this respect, he challenges the Christian community and nations with the vision of a world in which the abundance of the few works to relieve the poverty of the many.

In summary, it is evident that the Pauline letters do not deal with the subject of possessions as directly or sharply as do the synoptic Gospels or Acts. In particular, possessions are not singled out as a primary obstacle to following Christ, nor is there anything similar to the "community of sharing" described in the early chapters of Acts. This may in large measure, however, be explained by the nature of the Pauline letters, which were written to address specific issues in Paul's congregations and to clarify the significance of Christ's death and resurrection for the believing community. Nevertheless, Paul continues the fundamental love-ethic of the Gospels and provides a conceptual framework for viewing possessions within the community of faith. For him, the New Age in Christ means an end to the dominance of the strong over the weak, the possessors over the dispossessed. It means also a basic reversal of values in which the lowly and the powerless are given full recognition and worth in a new community of faith and love. The cross of Christ is the effective paradigm of the God who chooses the weak to shame the strong. Furthermore, as a prime exhibit of the new life in Christ, Paul is not afraid to set forth his own life as a model of servanthood patterned after the life of Christ himself. In one letter, he even exhibits the self-giving love of Christ, "who for our sakes became poor," as the primary model for the life together of a Christian community. Fortunately, too, Paul preserves the record of his ecumenical effort among his Gentile converts to care for the needs of the poor in Palestine, a "sacred cause" which he carried through at the cost of his life. Of course, the coming of the New Age did not mean the end of the old, hence the need for ethical imperatives, for examples of servant life-styles, and for structures and systems in the world. Yet Paul saw the gospel as a seed which continually transforms the Old Age. So also the right use of possessions is a matter of transforming their use from self to others, from the haves to have-nots, from the richer to the poorer.

TWO CONTRASTING VIEWS ON WEALTH AND POVERTY

The remainder of this survey concentrates on two writings belonging to the post-Pauline period of the New Testament.[22] Their contrasting emphases serve to illustrate how the problem of wealth and poverty received different treatments in the later churches of the New Testament era.

The Letter of James: An Uncompromising Tract Against the Rich

While the authorship and date of James are in much dispute, I agree with those who date it near the end of the first century. That it is the work of James, the brother of the Lord, is most doubtful; yet it reflects a Jewish Christian tradition of ethical teaching. Though it has been much maligned for its lack of specific Christian content and its potential conflict with Pauline teaching (James 2:14-26), it nevertheless has served a critical function in the New Testament canon as a call to practical Christian action.

James reveals himself as a staunch opponent of the rich and as a spokesman for the oppressed. Apart from Luke-Acts, he has the most to say on the rich and poor in the New Testament. He defines religion as concrete deeds of love for the poor and the needy (1:27, 2:14, 17). By this standard the rich fail miserably, which he is quick to point out. He regards the rich, both those within and without the Christian community, as chiefly exploiters of the poor.

Three passages in particular echo James' prophetic-like judgments against the rich.

In 1:9-10, James refers to the coming exaltation of the poor and above all to the coming humiliation of the rich. What does he mean?

Since the sense of the entire passage is strongly judgemental toward the rich, it is best to interpret the boasting ironically, that is to say, the rich man has had his day and the only thing he can boast of is his coming sure humiliation. Thus the announced reversal of conditions between the rich and the poor appears to point to the imminent eschatological reversal, when God will exalt the lowly and humble the rich and mighty.[23] The fate of the rich is assured; their pursuit of wealth will come to nought.

In James 2:1-9, the author makes an eloquent plea for equal treatment of the poor in the Christian assembly. His plea is based on his observation of what in fact has happened in Christian assemblies. Contrary to what ought to exist, the rich have been given preferential treatment and the poor maltreated. In effect, the church acts no different than the world. Two arguments are pursued against those who favor the rich. On the one hand, God himself has chosen the poor to inherit the kingdom (cf. Luke 6:20, 1 Cor. 1:26ff); on the other, it is the rich who oppress the poor, dragging them into court and so blaspheming against Christ (James 2:6-7). Thus to favor the rich is not only foolish, given the fact that many Christians are poor, but, most significantly, it goes against the way God acts. God sides with the poor against their exploiters. So the congregation is strongly admonished to fulfill the "royal law" ("love your neighbor as yourself") and to avoid the sin of partiality (2:8-9).

It is evident that the author considers the rich to be enemies of the Christian community and abusers of the poor. They are seeking entrance into the church and are being received with open arms. But the author is wary of their presence, to say the least, and sees a fundamental conflict between their wealth and Christian values. For his part, God has cast his lot with the poor.

James 5:1-6 contains the severest condemnation of the rich, a passage which echoes the prophetic language of woe and judgment (Isa. 10:1-4, 13:6). The author announces the coming judgment upon the rich. There is no call to repentance, only the stated certainty of their coming miseries at the last day. A few of the sins of the rich are carefully spelled out. They have held back the wages of the laborers and harvesters by fraudulent means (v. 4); they have themselves lived in affluent luxury (v. 5); and they have somehow harmed the faithful believers ("the righteous") who are helpless to resist their oppression and injustice (v. 6).

It is obvious that a long history of exploitation lies behind these stinging words.[24] They are a cry of outrage against the structures of injustice. Only now they are intensified by the expectation of the end. Are they addressed to people within the community known to James or to persons outside, that is, to Chritsians or non-Christians? Opinions are divided. James may intend to prevent the wealthy from entering his community, since he regards their wealth as ill-gotten and synonymous with exploitation, and fears the importation into his community of values contrary to those of justice, equality, and sharing. Therefore he condemns "the whole world of the rich" and sees their coming doom!

Or James may be issuing a warning to wealthy Christians within his community about the incompatibility of their wealth and the Christian way of life. As a friend of the poor, he wants to make sure that the community will continue to identify with the poor and oppressed, and not give preferential treatment to the rich or allow the values of affluence to creep in.

This, then, is the rigorous and uncompromising attitude of James toward the rich. His sympathies belong wholeheartedly with the poor and needy, the age-old victims of exploitation and oppression. If there is any hope for the rich, it can lie only with an end to their oppression, an abandonment of their trust in wealth and the adoption of a life-style radically different from their present affluence, a life-style that identifies closely with the poor whom they have so long exploited. Admittedly, James does not really take up this possibility in his eagerness to expose their sins.

The Letter of 1 Timothy: A Compromise with Wealth

While James represents a radical noncompromise with the rich, 1 Timothy represents something closer to a realistic compromise on the subject of possessions. 1 Timothy belongs to the so-called pastoral epistles, which the majority of scholars attribute to the post-Pauline period, near the end of the first century A.D. There is still a lively awareness of the danger of possessions to the faithful Christian life. For example, the author clearly describes the potential temptations of wealth which, if unchecked, lead to ruin, and he states rather bluntly that the love of money is the root of all evils (1 Tim. 6:9-10). Moreover, he rehearses personal experiences of tragedies due to the craving of money (1 Tim. 6:10). He also advocates a life-style reminiscent of the teaching of Jesus. Christians are to be content with the basics of food and clothing. "We brought nothing into the world, and we cannot take anything out of it" (vv. 7-8). Simplicity and contentment are the chief virtues. Consistent with this is the warning not to be greedy or lovers of money (1 Tim. 3:3, 1 Tim. 3:8, Titus 1:7), a word enjoined on all members of the community (2 Tim. 3:2, Titus 3.1).

Yet 1 Timothy has no radical critique of wealth itself and no radical concern for the poor, such as in the Gospels and James. People seem to be settling down in the world to live a sane, sober, and godly life (Titus 2:11-12). The danger of riches appears to be applicable only for a few, and not nearly the temptation that, for example, false teaching is. God's friendship for the poor is scarcely echoed; in fact, slaves are exhorted to regard their masters with honor and serve them faithfully (1 Tim. 6:1-2).

This sense of accommodation to the structures and systems of the world is reflected further in the words addressed to the rich (1 Tim. 6:17-19). Their presence in the community is not challenged, as in James, nor are their riches *per se* questioned. The challenge to these wealthy members is twofold: they must guard against pride and the temptation to idolatry and give freely of their possessions for others. Then the rich can be saved and can participate in the life of the Christian community.

While not as radical as James or many of the Gospel traditions and more willing to compromise with the reality of social and economic distinctions among persons in the community, the author of Timothy still seeks to affirm basic Christian values toward wealth. What he will not compromise is the idolatry of wealth and the fact that those who have possessions are called to use them more equitably and more liberally for the good of the poor and needy. Only by struggling toward greater justice for the poor is there evidence that Christians have not sold out to the structures and gods of the present age.

SUMMING UP

The purpose of this chapter has been to demonstrate the various ways in which the New Testament writers treat the subject of wealth and poverty. Rooted deep in the traditions of the Old Testament and Judaism, with their profound concern for a just treatment of the poor, the authors of the New Testament reflect a similar concern, some more and some less.

There are at least two areas of broad agreement among the writers regarding possessions. The first is the grave danger that wealth poses to the faithful Christian life and to human beings in general. It is clearly recognized that the desire for or accumulation of wealth represents a major temptation to idolatry and greed, a temptation selfish human beings find difficult to resist. The teaching of Jesus particularly underscored this danger, though it is reflected by the other documents as well. One can therefore agree with the author who states that the love of money lies at the bottom of a vast reservoir of human injustice and oppression. The second area of agreement is that the primary purpose of wealth, beyond the provision of daily needs, is to benefit those most in need, especially the poor and weak. The theme of God's love and care for the poor runs like a golden thread throughout both testaments. Accordingly, those who possess more are urged to share with those who have less. Again, the teaching of Jesus, with its challenging love-ethic, contains the strongest invitation to and demand for sacrificial sharing. But the same insistence continues throughout the New Testament.

Within these two fundamental themes, one encounters a variety of responses and directives. In some sources the dangers and challenge of possessions are posed more urgently and explicitly than in others. This is especially true of the synoptic Gospels, Acts, and the letter of James. But in others, such as the Pauline letters and 1 Timothy, there is a lessened intensity on these issues, perhaps even the beginnings of what one might call a compromise on wealth.

This raises the inevitable question: What should be the normative teaching for contemporary Christians? Should it be the most radical sayings, in which the love-ethic reaches out for an unconditional kind of willingness to share with the needy, perhaps modeled after the communal sharing depicted in Acts? Or should it be the less demanding exhortations to share liberally and to be content with one's wages? [25]

Human beings generally choose the less demanding way and seek the most compromise. To counter this, there is the constant need for a renewed hearing of both the potential temptations inherent in wealth and the call to unlimited sharing with those in greatest need. And this necessity is all the greater, as society becomes more affluent. Accordingly, the Zacchaeus paradigm of "one-half to the poor" in Luke's Gospel, or the uncompromising disapproval of the wealthy in James may be the New Testament voices Christians should most urgently hear for this time and place.

Yet Christians live in two worlds, biblically speaking, the old and the new, and the old is always with them. To ask for the impossible runs the risk of losing credibility. Even the sharpest demands to share one's wealth in unlimited manner with the poor cannot be heard uncritically, lest they deny reality or compound problems. Moreover, Protestants at least have not regarded the strongest gospel demands as the private preserve of a few super-saints, but have applied them equally to the whole community of faith. Hence a Christian realism seems best, which keeps in tension both the vision and the reality in such a way as to allow the Spirit of God to transform more fully human lives and human communities.

Finally, in light of the New Testament teachings on wealth and poverty, what steps can and should be taken by the Christian community to ensure that the poor are not forgotten and that wealth is distributed far more equitably? While other chapters will explore this question more fully in its various ethical, social, and political dimensions, a few simple proposals based directly on the New Testament sources are offered here.

1. Within Christian communities themselves, poverty should be eliminated, and each individual community should see itself as a working model of caring, sharing, and serving together. The paradigm for this is the new community of believers in Acts. While the church has often been a model to the world throughout Christian history, especially in its care of the sick, it has not fared well in modeling communities in which possessions are more equitably shared than in the surrounding culture. This task should begin with real urgency.

2. Outside the specific communities of faith, both the churches as institutions and individual Christians need to work more effectively to help restructure social and economic systems so that they are weighted more favorably toward the poor, and there are sufficient social means to ensure that the basic needs of the poor are met and that a relatively just social order exists. This complex task is necessary on both a national and global scale. The love-ethic of Jesus must be understood anew in a way that moves beyond the individual care for our neighbor to a genuine wrestling with the demonic powers and systems that perpetuate suffering and injustice, at home and abroad.

While the goal of such efforts is not the perfection of the kingdom, or a strict egalitarianism, it is the formation of human societies where there is the least possible gap between the rich and the poor, and where the rich and powerful are faced with the necessity to share their abundance and power more equitably with the poor and suffering. At least to rich Christians today the gospel challenge is to act in accordance with the "good news to the poor," which translates into a love-ethic of sacrificial sharing and service, patterned after the life, death, and resurrection of the one "who for our sake became poor."

NOTES

1. This is especially true today in the liberation theologies of Third World churches. For example, see Gustavo Gutierrez. *A Theology of Liberation.* Maryknoll, N.Y.: Orbis, 1973, pp. 155-159.
2. The three major legal traditions in the Old Testament are found in Exod. 20:22–23:33 (The Book of the Covenant), Deut. 5–28 (Deuteronomic law code) and Lev. 17–26 (Holiness Code).
3. See a recent popular study by James Limburg. *The Prophets and the Powerless.* Atlanta: John Knox, 1977.
4. Yet the example of Jesus and his disciples who "left all for his sake" is not to be forgotten as a sign of the cost of discipleship. Perhaps that is the same kind of witness that a vow of poverty or other radical forms of communal sharing can make within the whole Christian community. Cf. the stance of pacifism in the church.
5. Many parables reflect this imagery (Matt. 22:1-10/Luke 14:16-24, Luke 15:11-24, Matt. 8:11/Luke 16:29); also the eschatological expectation at the Last Supper (Mark 10:25/1 Cor. 11:26).
6. So Martin Hengel. *Property and Riches in the New Testament.* Philadelphia: Fortress, 1974, p. 20.
7. The Samaritan uses his costly oil and wine, pays for the inn plus two extra denarii (1 denarius = 1 day's wage for a laborer). Jeremias, *Rediscovering the Parables,* Fortress, p. 160.
8. The crowds probably represent the poor *am haaretz,* "the people of the land," who were looked down upon by the pious for their laxity toward the law. Most of the poor owned only one undergarment; if two, the second was saved for the Sabbath. Here, the second is shared.
9. Only full restitution plus 20% was required by Jewish Law (Lev. 5:20-26), except for cattle theft, where fourfold restitution was legislated (Exod. 21:37, 22:1).
10. Joachim Jeremias. *New Testament Theology,* Vol. 1. New York: Scribners, 1971, pp. 109-113. Even shepherds belonged to the despised classes (cf. Jeremias. *Jerusalem in the Time of Jesus.* Philadelphia: Fortress, p. 306). Priests belonged to the poorest class as did the *am haaretz* (masses) and the *anawim* (a movement of the "pious poor" in Palestine).
11. For the view that Jesus did proclaim the Jubilee year at the beginning of his public ministry, see John Yoder. *The Politics of Jesus.* Grand Rapids: Eerdmann's, 1972, esp. pp. 34-40.
12. Readers should carefully note the difference between the Lukan and Matthean Beatitudes. In Matthew, there is a strong spiritualizing tendency (5:3 "poor in spirit," 5:6 "hunger and thirst for righteous-

ness"). In Luke, there is no such tendency. The contrasting Woes, in fact, speak concretely against the rich and the filled. Luke consistently has the social dimensions in mind when he speaks of the poor.

13. See Ernst Haenchen. *The Acts of the Apostles.* Philadelphia: Westminister, 1971, pp. 230-234. For more moderate conclusions, cf. F. F. Bruce. *Commentary on Acts.* London: Tyndale Press, 1952.

14. Ronald Sider. *Rich Christians in an Age of Hunger.* Downer's Grove, Ill.: Intervarsity Press, 1977, pp. 98-101. He further writes of the "total economic liability for" and the "total economic availability to" the poor in the early community.

15. See the fine article by Nils Dahl. "Paul and Possessions," *Studies in Paul.* Minneapolis: Augsburg, 1977, p. 22.

16. Among most commentators, the authentic letters include Romans, 1-2 Corinthians, 1-2 Thessalonians, Galatians, Philippians, Colossians, and Philemon (a few question 2 Thessalonians and Colossians); Ephesians is doubtful; the Pastorals (1-2 Timothy, Titus) belong to the post-Pauline generation, although they reflect genuine Pauline traditions at certain points.

17. Romans 13:1-7 has been a much abused text in Christian history, often used to justify unqualified obedience to the state. Even apart from other New Testament texts which view the state as an enemy of the faith (Revelation), Paul's whole argument is built upon the assumption that the state is acting to uphold the good. He does not deal at all with the question of an essentially unjust state.

18. Though Paul develops this thought within the framework of an imminent expectation of the end (1 Cor. 7:29, 31), it is not limited to this framework since the New Age is already a present, though unfulfilled reality.

19. According to 1 Corinthians 1:26-28 it would seem that the Pauline congregations were basically lower-class. However, N. Dahl, *Studies,* p. 27, e.g., argues that we know little about the social composition of the Pauline churches, and he doubts that as a whole, they belonged to the proletariat. There were slaves and slave owners, most persons appear to be economically independent, many are probably small craftsmen and shopkeepers, a few at least are wealthy and own houses in which Christians worship (Rom. 16:23, 3-5, Col. 4:15, Philemon).

20. Greek *doulos* means "slave" or "servant."

21. See Keith Nickle. *The Collection.* Naperville, Ill.: Allenson, 1966.

22. Another example that could have been used is 1 John, with its strong emphasis on practical love for the brethren (3:17-18, 4:7-12, 20-21).

23. So Martin Dibelius. *James.* Philadelphia: Fortress, p. 84. This theme echoes Luke 1:52-53, 6:20-23, 16:19-31.

24. Dibelius, *James,* pp. 39-45, identifies the author as a spokesman for the *anawin,* a tradition of the "pious poor" that stretches all the way back to the exile period.

25. For further reflections on this topic, consult R. Stivers, "Deciding

on Christian Life Styles," *Christian Century*, December 17, 1980. Also Walter Pilgrim, *Good News to the Poor: A Study of Wealth and Poverty in Luke-Acts.* Minneapolis: Augsburg, 1981.

SUGGESTED READINGS

Barclay, William. *The Letters to the Corinthians.* Daily Study Bible Series. Philadelphia: Westminster Press, 1956.

Bruce, F. F. *The Acts of the Apostles.* London: Tyndale Press, 1952.

Cassidy, Richard. *Jesus, Politics and Society: A Study of Luke's Gospel.* Maryknoll, N.Y.: Orbis, 1978.

Conzelman, Hans. *I Corinthians.* Hermeneia series. Trans. by J. Leitch. Philadelphia: Fortress Press, 1975.

Dahl, Nils. "Paul and Possessions," *Studies in Paul.* Minneapolis: Augsburg, 1977.

de Santa Ana, Julio. *Good News to the Poor. The Challenge of the Poor in the History of the Church.* Trans. H. Whittle. Geneva: World Council of Churches, 1977.

Dibelius, Martin. *James.* Hermeneia series. Rev. by H. Greeven, trans. by M. Williams. Philadelphia: Fortress Press, 1976.

Gutierrez, Gustavo. *A Theology of Liberation.* Maryknoll, N.Y.: Orbis, 1973.

Haenchen, Ernst. *The Acts of the Apostles: A Commentary.* Philadelphia: Westminster Press, 1971.

Hengel, Martin. *Property and Riches in the Early Church.* Philadelphia: Fortress Press, 1974.

Jeremias, Joachim. *Rediscovering the Parables.* New York: Charles Scribner's Sons, 1966.

Jeremias, Joachim. *Jerusalem in the Time of Jesus.* Philadelphia: Fortress Press, 1969.

Jeremias, Joachim. *New Testament Theology.* Vol. I. New York: Charles Scribner's Sons, 1971.

Limburg, James. *The Prophets and the Powerless.* Atlanta: John Knox Press, 1977.

Pilgrim, Walter. *Good News to the Poor: A Study of Wealth and Poverty in Luke-Acts.* Minneapolis: Augsburg, 1981.

Sider, Ronald. *Rich Christians in an Age of Hunger: A Biblical Study.* Downers Grove, Ill.: Inter-Varsity Press, 1977.

Stivers, Robert. "Deciding on Christian Life Styles," *Christian Century*, December 17, 1980.

Yoder, John Howard. *The Politics of Jesus*. Grand Rapids, Mich.: Eerdmanns, 1972.

STUDY QUESTIONS

1. In the discussion of the gospel traditions, the Zacchaeus paradigm of "one-half to the poor" was held up as the paradigm for Christians most consistent with the radical love-ethic of Jesus and its call for sacrificial sharing on behalf of the poor and needy. How do you respond to this paradigm? How might it be used in a Christian community?

2. If God's love and care for the poor is a golden thread that runs through both Testaments, how do we account for its relative neglect as a central element in contemporary Christian preaching, teaching, and practice? Can "abundant wealth" be reconciled with this theme?

3. How might congregations respond to the suggestion that Christian communities should eliminate poverty among its members, and become living models of more equitable sharing of possessions?

4. What concrete steps might be taken by individuals or groups to put Jesus' love-ethic into practice against unjust social structures and practices that favor the rich and harm the poor? Identify structures and practices that need to be challenged from the perspective of the love-ethic.

5. We have noted that the New Testament contains both radical and less radical teachings on possessions and their dangers. What are the implications of this for making ethical decisions? How does one counter the human tendency to take the least challenging and change-necessitating route? On what basics regarding possessions is the New Testament in essential agreement?

6. How does the early communities' practice of full economic sharing bear on the question of economic systems? Is there a Christian "economic system"? What should be the criteria for judging the relative merits of different economic systems from a New Testament perspective? (See p. 180.)

7

Poverty, Distribution, and Christian Ethics

Robert L. Stivers

Communities—church, local, or national—may be linked to houses. They come in a variety of shapes, sizes, and colors, have different foundations, and usually are surrounded by walls called borders or qualifications for membership. American Christians, reflecting their larger society, have found the split-level design especially to their liking.[1]

On the one hand, Americans profess to live on a single level. Equality is the name given to this level, and it is supported by strong beams resting on a solid foundation of religious and philosophical ideas. Some of these beams have labels: "All are created in the image of God and are equal in God's eyes"; "all are one in Christ"; "equality of opportunity"; "one person, one vote"; and "equality before the law." There are, of course, problems on this level. Just as reality never attains the ideal, actual equality does not match what is professed. Nevertheless, at least in terms of political freedoms, America does not come off too badly in comparison with other nations.

On the other hand, Americans live on split-levels in their economic arrangements. The upper level is called wealth and high incomes and is inhabited by a few fortunate individuals. The lower level is called poverty and holds about 12% of the nation's people. The majority is somewhere on the ladder between the levels trying either to hit the jackpot which will boost them up or to avoid the disaster which will push them down.

For those who claim to be Christian and are committed to basic equality, the difficulties with this split-level arrangement are several.

First, grinding poverty is dehumanizing and a threat to the community. In spite of the unprecedented abundance of the split-level economy, many on the lower level lead marginal lives without the means to meet basic necessities. The living conditions on the lower level may be better than in other houses in other countries, but they are still impoverished and in comparison to conditions on the upper level, demeaning to the spirit. Extremes of poverty and wealth also make community building all but impossible.

Second, the split-level economy poses the basic problem of justice. If justice is fairness or treating equals equally, then there are ethical problems with the economic structures Americans have built, no matter how productive they are.

Third, there is the matter of tradeoffs. Some claim that Americans as a whole gain from inequality. Inequality, they argue, is a result of providing incentives and preserving certain freedoms. Reward and freedom to act are essential to productive efficiency, which improves conditions even on the lower level.[2] Justice, they imply, must be sacrificed to a degree for the overall good of the community. A debate between efficiency and freedom on the one hand and justice and care for the poor on the other has grown out of these claims. Are there tradeoffs between efficiency and justice, freedom and equality? If so, has too much justice and equality been traded off for efficiency and the freedom of a few?

These difficulties raise ethical questions for Christians. The concern of Jesus Christ for the poor, for community, and for social justice calls for a response. Papering over these difficulties with the diligent pursuit of the jackpot or everyday economic concerns is not an appropriate response.

To build a more adequate response or combination of responses requires familiarity with present structures. The process of familiarization will begin with a review of the facts about the split-level structure and then proceed to an exploration of Christian ethical foundations, to a measuring of the split-level system against the ethical insights, and finally to some conclusions on the construction of a more adequate response.

THE SHAPE OF THE HOUSE

To discern the shape of the structure, several relevant questions must be posed:

1. What is the condition of America's poor?
2. What are the causes of poverty and wealth?
3. What are the values and beliefs which influence the distribution of income and wealth and taken-for-granted understandings about wealth and poverty?
4. Are there tradeoffs between equality and efficiency and equality and freedom, and if so, how problematic are they?

The preceding chapters have addressed many of these questions. A brief review and some comments are necessary, however, to set the basis for ethical analysis.

1. Condition of the Poor

Since World War II, conditions have improved for poor and rich alike. Until recently the percentage of persons below the officially established poverty line has steadily decreased. Real incomes have more than doubled. Even so, economic insecurity has stripped families and individuals of their resources, and child abuse, divorce, and even suicide increased as a consequence. Wages for some are insufficient to cover basic family needs. Welfare for the poor and food stamps help to avoid the worst physical consequences of poverty, but the welfare system does not cover all basic necessities, is often demeaning, and has side-effects which promote dependency and continuing poverty. For those not receiving assistance, life can be desperate indeed. The so-called "culture of poverty" continually breeds a new generation of poor without the capacity to live productive lives.

2. Causes of Poverty and Wealth

Poverty is a large, complex topic. It causes are many. Some are obvious, for example, racial and sexual discrimination, lack of skills and abilities, inadequate wages in seasonal and low-paying jobs, insufficient education, unemployment, inadequate retirement benefits, and personal crises, such as illness. Less obvious are the causes attributable to the "culture of poverty," to the side-effects of the welfare system, to the lack of power to influence national and local legislation, and to unemployment caused by structural changes in the economy.

Few of these causes of poverty can be blamed solely on individuals. Almost all involve a social dimension. This is not to say that poverty is beyond the ability of individuals to influence. Some choose poverty. Others do not take the initiative to upgrade their skills. Still others resign themselves prematurely to their condition. Nonetheless, poverty is a result of both social and individual factors, and both must be taken into account.

In contrast to life on the bottom level of poverty, life on the top level of riches has been good in material terms and remains so. Statistics on wealth and income reveal great inequalities, greater for wealth than for income. They also reveal the persistence of substantial inequality in both categories through the decades and a very high concentration of certain forms of wealth, such as holdings in property, stocks, bonds, and other marketable securities.

To determine why inequality exists, one must probe the determinants of wealth, high incomes, and poverty. Economist Arthur Okun in his highly regarded book, *Equality and Efficiency*, has detailed many of these determinants.[3] Individuals accumulate wealth through saving earned income and from gifts, bequests, and inheritances. Educational levels, good fortune, family wealth and connections, and, as with poverty, skills and abilities have an important bearing on both income and wealth differentials. High lifetime income is especially important for wealth. While the poor find it extremely difficult, if not impossible, to save or to accumulate financial resources, the very wealthy manage to save approximately one-third of their incomes.

Dividends, interest, rent, and other property income are the sources for about one-fifth of total income and accrue primarily to top wealth holders.[4] One-tenth of all income, for rich and poor alike, comes from transfer payments, which include unemployment benefits, welfare for the poor, and Social Security. These payments, according to Okun, are the "equalizer" and accrue mostly to those with low incomes. Without them, inequality would be considerably worse.

Okun is, of course, correct about the "equalizer" but has revealed only half of the picture. Counting only direct disbursements as transfer payments overlooks the so-called "welfare program for the rich." This alternate welfare program (generally referred to as tax expenditures) does not consist of disbursements to individuals. Rather, transfers are made indirectly through intermediaries or through tax write-offs. According to sociologists Jonathan Turner and Charles Starnes, this alternative program includes: 1) government purchases in the economic market, (2) government price supports, (3) government market regulation, and (4) government tax expenditures.[5]

The fourth is especially significant. Turner and Starnes estimate that in 1975 $65-$77 billion were bestowed on individuals and large corporations by way of federal tax codes alone, through tax exclusions, tax deductions, tax credits, special tax rates, and tax sheltering. The inclusion of these in the tax code means reduced taxes for those able to take advantage of them. The effect on the budgetary balance between income and disbursements and on the income of privileged recipients is exactly the same as that which occurs when welfare payments are made. A dollar not paid in taxes contributes both to government deficits and to personal income just as much as a dollar paid to the poor. The overall effect of these so-called tax expenditures is a severe reduction of progressiveness in the tax system at higher levels of income.

Over two-thirds of total income comes from wages and salaries.[6] The causes of differentials in such income are numerous. First, differences may be the result of voluntary choices made by individuals. Some people may seize upon opportunities for overtime work or take second jobs, while others will elect leisure or simply work less than normal. Second, the status of a job or occupation plays a role. In general, the higher the status, the higher the pay, although this does not hold true for some occupations. The unequal distribution of transfer payments, including the welfare program for the rich, is a third means by which income differences are perpetuated. Transfer payments have opposite effects at the extreme ends of the scale, for they contribute to inequality through concessions to the rich and to equality through direct payments to the poor.

A fourth, more general reason for differences in income is related to the idiosyncrasies of families and individuals. The wealth, educational attainment, work habits, and general attitudes of parents play an important role in the level of their children's income. Intelligence, however difficult to measure, and specialized abilities are still other factors.

Luck or chance is a fifth factor, while age, size of community, and geographical region can be combined to form a sixth. Finally, racial and sexual discrimination deny equal opportunity to minorities and women, resulting in a significant decrease in their earnings. Together these seven factors account for the bulk of the differences in the distribution of income.

3. Values and Beliefs

While economic and political structures are powerful in their own right, they do not function independently of values and beliefs. Values and beliefs interact with and modify the shape of structures and provide the foundation which justifies them. Current values and beliefs are products of a long historical process involving complex and little-understood social movements.

Values may be understood as the general and abstract conceptions held by the people of a society that provide their standards and criteria for judging desirable or ethical behavior.[7] Put more succinctly, values and beliefs are general criteria for evaluation and action.

Beliefs are less general and abstract than values. While values transcend specifics, beliefs are tied to actual people, events, groups, and situations.[8] Thus, beliefs are the specific conceptions held by the people of a society that constitute their understanding about the nature of reality and their feelings about what should be going on in their lives.

Values and beliefs are related to each other and together form systems which are more or less integrated and consistent. These systems evolve and are influenced by the factors which influence social systems in general. Of particular importance in the industrialized countries is the influence of economic factors. It is largely their influence which has given American values and beliefs their particular cast.

The significance of values and beliefs for the present incidence of poverty and for the distribution of income and wealth cannot be minimized. They are instruments of power, tools used in the competition to divide economic surpluses. In the hands of those who have won victories in the competition and choose to exercise the power which wealth and income convey, values and beliefs are subtle instruments of social control. They allow for a decreased reliance on force by making the victors appear legitimate and existing arrangements appear natural.

But values and beliefs are not the sole prerogative of those in power. They can be used also by the "have-nots," since value and belief systems are never completely consistent and integrated. Also, competing systems are usually available. Marxism, for example, has been used by those not in power to counter capitalism. Christian ideas about freedom are being used as a support for liberation movements in several parts of the world.

In the United States, as elsewhere, the dominant values and beliefs generally favor existing arrangements. They make the differences in wealth and income appear equitable and natural, and give the impression that the rich are deserving, the poor undeserving, and economic activity highly praiseworthy. Sociologist Robin Williams has isolated 13 elements of the American value system.[9] For purposes of the present discussion, ten of those are relevant: (1) efficiency, (2) practicality, (3) achievement, (4) materialism, (5) progress, (6) freedom, (7) individualism, (8) equality, (9) morality, and (10) humanitarianism.

Why do these values and not others appear on this list? A materialist would answer that they are dominant values because they reflect and support existing productive arrangements. Six of the ten enhance the present process of production in a society which prizes productive activity: efficiency, practicality, achievement, progress, materialism, and individualism. The other four also contribute through special interpretations.

German sociologist Max Weber, writing early in this century, was not satisfied with the explanations of the materialists. He argued that values develop as a result of a complex interaction of ideas, social structures, and material forces. His investigation of the relation between capitalism and the Protestant Reformation attempted to show how certain ideas held by the reformers contributed to the development of capitalism.[10]

For example, Weber held that the Christian doctrine of election, especially in its Calvinist form, was instrumental for the development of values and beliefs concerning work. According to Weber, among the most important of Calvinist beliefs was the sovereignty of God. God was thought to be all-powerful, all-knowing, all-loving, and in control of the destiny of everything. Coupled with this exalted view of God was a dim view of human beings, at least by way of contrast to God. Humans were and are totally depraved, and their only hope is salvation through the gracious gift of God, which they do not deserve.

In contrast to the present, in which a secular milieu has largely replaced the religious, individual salvation was a burning issue for the Calvinist. Unfortunately, there was no sure way to tell if one were saved. It all depended on God, who alone elected some for salvation and others for damnation. All was not lost in the calculation of individual election, however. The believer did know that a good tree bears good fruit and a bad tree, bad fruit. One way to identify the damned was by their evil ways. Thus, if the believer attempted in all he or she did to serve God, the matter was at least open. There was the possibility that one's righteousness was a result of God's helping hand. One's good works might indicate election.

To relieve the anxiety created by doubt about salvation and damnation, the Calvinist divines urged their parishioners to assume that they had been elected and to go about their activities, whatever they might be, with a singleness of purpose—the service of God. This the Calvinists did, giving fantastic energy to their endeavors while at the same time avoiding consumption and worldly pursuits. A daily diet of hard work and the avoidance of consumption were, of course, the precise prescription for the development of capital and fit neatly the requirements of the budding capitalistic economic system.

At the same time that these religious ideas were gaining favor, Europe was experiencing the emergence of a new social class, the bourgeoisie, whose power base lay in the urban areas and in the new industries beginning to appear there. For this group of people, hard work and saving were essential to the survival of their enterprises and the advancement of their social status. It was this class of people which by and large picked up and espoused the new religious beliefs, having found them to be complementary to their own secular needs and their struggle with the feudal aristocracy for social position.

The story is much longer and more complex, but suffice it to say that the combination of hard work and saving and the income and wealth which frequently resulted from it came to be viewed as God's will and reward to the elect. Conversely, poverty came to be seen as God's punishment of the damned. As the societies of Westeern Europe and America became increasingly industrial and secular, the divine element in the belief system dropped out. But while God dropped out, the values and beliefs persisted. Even today they persist. On the one hand, Americans value hard work and the things that complement hard work, such as efficiency, practicality, achievement, and progress. On the other hand, many Americans still regard poverty as a sign of some kind of condemnation. They will not accept welfare under any circumstances, and they attack programs designed to help the poor as mere "gifts" to the lazy and undeserving.

The significance of this brief excursion into the history of ideas lies in what it reveals about values and beliefs. They are not carved in stone or dropped from heaven. They develop over time and are influenced by a vast number of variables, some religious, most not. Values and beliefs develop, as it were, lives of their own and persist with remarkable power, even when underlying philosophical and religious systems change.

As for specifically American values and beliefs, their connection with Christian understandings has all but been eliminated in spite of the historical association. The idea system associated with industrialization—namely, scientific materialism—has generally replaced Christianity at the foundational level. To put it differently, God has been dropped from the system as economic and material considerations have proved themselves far stronger among Americans. Christianity has little influence on the shape of things.

A few examples will illustrate how the ten values mentioned above affect the lives of the poor and buttress the existing distribution of income and wealth. The value of freedom has been interpreted primarily to mean freedom from governmental restraints. As a result, political freedom as opposed to freedom from the miseries of poverty has been stressed and *laissez-faire* attitudes have predominated. Freedom as absence of restraint has also been allied with individualism. The combination translates into belief in the free play of individual competition and assumes that the outcomes of the competition are equitable.

Conveniently, at least for the victors, inequality of opportunity and the increasing dominance of large organizations over individuals are overlooked. These realities notwithstanding, the American interpretation of freedom and individualism has led to a general acceptance of the end product, reluctance to interfere, and a glossing over of the many advantages given to the rich in the struggle.

The values of efficiency, practicality, achievement, and individualism are part and parcel of the work ethic, whose origins in Protestantism have been noted. The work ethic, still alive and well in spite of premature death notices and certain concessions to consumption, rewards the victors in the competitive struggle and stigmatizes the poor. That many rewards come not as a result of hard work and achievement and that poverty is often not a consequence of laziness or unwillingness to work are again conveniently overlooked. The end result is that the rich are thought to be hard workers, justly rewarded with income and wealth, while the poor are regarded as lazy and shiftless, justly condemned to poverty.

The attacks on the poor which result from these beliefs are a further convenience to the rich. They create a diversion which attracts attention away from the advantages given to the rich. These advantages are also built on the values of efficiency, materialism, and progress. Efficiency and growth, of course, are very important economic consideration in industrial societies. Unless industry can develop methods to produce more with the same amounts of raw materials, to attract investment capital, and to grow, rising material standards and employment become problems. The promotion of efficiency and growth are thus among the most justifiable reasons for tolerating unequal outcomes. But it is also an ideological weapon, especially in materially-oriented societies. The notion of promoting efficiency and growth becomes a potent tool to pry loose rewards above and beyond those actually required to maintain efficiency.

Not all American values and beliefs result in greater inequality. Working in the other direction are the values of equality, humanitarianism, and morality. Actually, the value of equality is somewhat ambiguous. It serves to increase inequality, if interpreted merely to mean equality of opportunity or equality before the law. For many Americans, however, it also means some measure of equal outcomes and some proportionality of reward and contribution.

Humanitarianism and an emphasis on morality work to create compassion for the less fortunate and to accept social justice. Without these values and the derived belief that society is responsible for meeting basic needs, the plight of the poor would be much worse and the distribution of income and wealth more uneven.

4. Efficiency and Equality—The Problem of Tradeoffs

The case for efficiency in the tradeoff between efficiency and equality rests on the argument that increased equality will reduce incentives to work and to invest and will entail heavy administrative costs. Given a system which relies primarily on the market to determine outcomes, which permits the politically and economically powerful to dominate the market, and which places great emphasis on material growth and efficiency, the case is plausible. Tradeoffs do exist in this context. They are also present in nonmarket societies and may even be endemic to the human situation.

The nature of the tradeoffs and the "leaky bucket" effect, that is, the disappearance of money when transferred from rich to poor, have been described in other chapters. Two things should be noted, however. Equality and efficiency are not always at odds. The elimination of racial and sexual discrimination, for example, would contribute to efficiency and equality.

In addition, the placing of efficiency and equality on the same footing is problematic for Christians. Efficiency is at best a secondary value. Its importance stems from the good it produces, in this case, increased material well-being. While important to Christians, material well-being beyond sufficiency is not a critical concern of the Bible. In contrast, concerns about the equality of persons before God, the establishment of close-knit and sharing communities, and social justice in behalf of the poor are critical. Thus, equality is a presumption in the tradeoff. This does not mean equality always takes precedence. A destitute, but economically egalitarian, society is in no way desirable. Rather, it means that the burden of proof is placed on efficiency except under those conditions where poverty is general in a community. Or, put in slightly different terms, significant gains for efficiency must be demonstrated before inequalities are ethically justifiable.

A tradeoff between equality and freedom is also present when freedom is defined as the absence of governmental restraint and when economic freedoms such as freedom from grinding poverty are ignored. The tradeoff comes when governments transfer money from rich to poor. The freedom of the rich to consume or invest is said to be restricted, and no doubt it is, for most people give up wealth and income only reluctantly.

Unlike efficiency and like equality, freedom is a critical norm in Christianity. Neither freedom nor equality takes precedence. But if the notion of economic freedom is allowed, that is, freedom from poverty and from the domination of the economically powerful, then the question is not so much a matter of trading off freedom for equality as it is a matter of trading off freedoms. In fact, the amount of freedom in a society may actually be increased by restricting the few a great deal and freeing the many a little.

THE RELIGIOUS FOUNDATIONS

The shape of most houses can be deduced from their foundations. The split-level house which characterizes the United States does in fact reflect the social values and beliefs of Americans. For American Christians who are serious about their faith, this presents a dilemma. Christians claim their foundations lie in the Bible and the traditions of the church. The dilemma is evident when Christians try to fit the split-level American structure onto biblical foundations.

Goals

The four cornerstones of the biblical tradition concerning poverty and distribution were put in place in the preceding chapter. The first stone is a clear understanding about goals. In the Christian view the goal of human life is the kingdom of God, not possessions, efficiency, or high growth rates. This does not mean economic considerations are irrelevant. Both those who live within the kingdom of God and those outside of it need food, clothing, and shelter. These are provided by economic systems, not faith. To seek the kingdom of God and to love the neighbor, which are two primary dimensions of living in the kingdom, necessitate among other things attending to and participating in the marketplace.

But while economic concerns are relevant to life in the kingdom, they are secondary matters. They are means, not ends. The purpose of economic systems is to improve human life and to provide the material conditions in which human communities may flourish. That economic concerns and possessions tend to become ends in themselves and to push the kingdom out of sight and mind is recognized in the Bible. The Bible calls this the worship of mammon and finds it incompatible with the worship of God. The warnings about the impossibility of serving both God and mammon at the same time and about the dangers of possessions have a special ring of authenticity in a society which finds so much of its identity wrapped up in the marketplace and consumer goods. For Christians in particular, the warnings should cause uneasiness and soul-searching.

Concern for the Poor and for Social Justice

The second of the four cornerstones and perhaps the most important is the biblical concern for the poor. This concern is found in both testaments. In Exodus it is the liberation of the oppressed slaves in Egypt. For the prophets it is simple social justice. In Luke it is a special identity with the poor and the promise of good news to them. For Paul it is sharing. In spite of the differences between the present age and the biblical age, this concern remains primary for Christians. On the personal level it calls for love and sharing, on the social level for justice.

Justice is rooted in the very being of God. It is part of God's infinite love and the human response of faith. In simplest terms it means fairness, treating equals equally and unequals unequally. For the biblical writers, however, the poor are not only the special objects of love but also are described as unequal when they should be equal. The Bible is biased in favor of the poor but without making any claim that poverty leads to salvation or even human moral superiority.

Justice is also the working out of love on the social level. Love presupposes a relatively intimate relation of one person to another, a closeness and sharing which take into account special needs and circumstances. Such love is impossible on the social level. One cannot love and personally share with millions of people. Governments are incapable of loving welfare clients or the wealthy. One can insist, however, that the government should treat people fairly. Hence, justice in Christian perspective is a love of others writ large on the social level, again with special interest in the unfortunate others.

In accord with conventional philosophical understandings, justice may be broken down into two regulative principles, liberty and equality, which serve as critical standards for legal and distributive systems. These regulative principles get their authority not only from the principle of justice itself but also directly from the Bible. Liberty is an assumption of Christian freedom and a necessary condition of living in love. The notion of equality stems from several sources, notably the understanding of persons as being made in the image of God (Gen. 1-3) and the affirmation of the oneness of all people in Christ (Gal. 3:27-28).

The use of these two regulative principles is easily understood. They are standards at which people are expected to aim, and they imply the conditions that would hold in a perfect world. Clearly the United States is not a perfect world and is unlikely to become one any time soon. Coercion and inequality abound. Concessions must be made in order to live at all. But coercion, inequality, and concessions are not the standards to be aimed for. They should be allowed only in situations where a greater good can be achieved by their use or a greater evil incurred by their nonuse. For Christians, therefore, the moral assumption is in favor of liberty and equality. The burden of proof is on those who would coerce or depart from equality. Thus, the principle of equality prescribes that inequalities of income and wealth are not justified until relevant grounds for them are established, and relevancy is to be established on the basis of Christian values and beliefs.

The mention of relevancy points to two additional subprinciples.

The first is relevancy itself, which establishes a procedure to determine on Christian ethical grounds the acceptance of proposals calling for coercion and departures from equality. Efficiency, for instance, has been offered as an acceptable reason for departing from equality on the grounds that it contributes to overall material well-being. Since material well-being, especially of the poor, is a Christian concern, this is an acceptable or relevant departure, provided the proposed efficiency does in fact contribute to overall material well-being and alleviates the condition of the poor.

The second subprinciple is proportionality. If a person deserves a reward, the reward should be roughly proportional to what is deserved. Thus, if one assembly-line worker puts in twice as much time as another worker at the same hourly wage, it is fair to pay him twice as much, nothing more or less. His pay should be proportional to the time he gives. Applied to the present discussion, this principle asserts that the amount of coercion or inequality allowable should be roughly proportional to the good that is provided. Thus, if efficiency is relevant, and tax concessions are granted to stimulate efficiency, the concessions should not be unlimited but be tailored proportionally to the efficiency that will result.

In summary, social justice in Christian perspective is the social equivalent of love and implies special concern for the poor and a rough calculation of freedom and equality. In the absence of other considerations the ethical thrust should be to relieve the worst conditions of poverty, powerlessness, and exploitation; to support programs that help the poor achieve productive, useful, and sharing lives; to avoid coercion; and to narrow inequalities.

Community

The third cornerstone is the Christian understanding of community. As the preceding chapter has shown, the emphasis on community in the New Testament is critical. The essence of community or, in the case of the New Testament, the church, is *koinonia*, which is the spirit of fellowship and unity in Jesus Christ. *Koinonia* is the glue of the church and makes possible closer-knit communities. The ideals are established in the opening chapters of the book of Acts and include sharing through work and gifts, fellowship, and unity in Christ, ideals which Paul confirms in Romans 12 and in his call to the Greek churches to share with the poor Jerusalem community. For some Christians, in particular the early community in Jerusalem, the ideal also included the holding of possessions in common.

To translate these ideals into a statement about the wider community is problematic. Some Christians have mistakenly tried to separate their life of faith within the church from their lives as citizens under the state. They have misunderstood the concept of the two kingdoms of God and made it difficult to apply Christian ethical standards to the affairs of the state. Correctly understood, this concept underscores the fact that God rules in both modes. On the one hand, as Creator, God is at work through the human powers of reason, coercion, law and justice, and the agencies of the family, the state, and other social institutions. On the other hand, as Redeemer and Sanctifier, God works through the gospel, by which all human beings are graciously invited to the joy and freedom of the forgiving love in Christ. God is at work among all human beings through law and gospel, both in the church and in the state. Christians respond in faith and seek God's will in the church as well as in the state. And while the close-knit fellowship which should and sometimes does characterize actual churches is impossible to realize in states, it does set the direction. From the Christian perspective actual churches and actual states should be working toward sharing, fellowship, unity, and, following the example of the Jerusalem community, a greater sharing of material goods.

The Christian understanding of community thus gives further warrant to efforts which narrow the gap between rich and poor, move toward greater social justice, and relieve the worst conditions of poverty. It also calls the churches themselves to bring their own fellowships closer into line with the New Testament ideal.[11]

Living Between the Ages

The fourth and final cornerstone comes from biblical theology. It arises from the tension between the way things are and the way they ought to be in the kingdom of God. This tension appears in the first pages of the Bible. People are made in the image of God (Gen. 1) but starting with Adam, fall into sin (Gen. 3). It reappears again and again in the history of Israel as the Israelites wrestle with the obligations of the covenant, comparing their own situation to the responsibilities set forth by Yahweh.

In Jesus' message the tension appears in his teaching that the kingdom of God is at hand. Later Christians reformulated this slightly to say that the kingdom had been inaugurated in the life, death, and resurrection of Jesus Christ, but that its fulfillment awaited his second coming. "Here, but yet to come," repeats the tension. The tension also turns up in other teachings of Jesus. In Matthew 10:16, for example, Jesus advises his disciples to be sheep among the wolves and to have the wisdom of the serpent and the innocence of the dove.

For Christians, this tension is found preeminently in the cross and resurrection. The cross is reality at its worst. The cross points to the depth of human sin. It points as well to the limitations of individuals and groups and to the need for structures and order to keep sin in bounds. Furthermore, the message of the cross says emphatically and convincingly that living in times short of the kingdom of God involves dealing with the realities of sin and death, including one's own.

Yet the cross is not the last word in Christianity. It is followed by the victorious new word of the resurrection. The resurrection points to God at work in the human situation, overcoming sin and death. It points as well to the possibility of "new creations" in the lives of individuals and groups and to the creative potential of love and justice. It teaches Christians that while they still live in the age of sin and death, God's love has broken in, there is hope, and their efforts in response to God's love are not in vain. As a result, Christians are invited to deal with a partly open future where even small responses can make a difference. The cross and resurrection together teach Christians to be realistic and hopeful and to have the wisdom of the serpent and the innocence of the dove.

Finally, the tension is highlighted by Paul's sense that Christians live between the ages. They live in the Old Age of sin, death, injustice, and limits. They are called to live according to the New Age, inaugurated by Jesus Christ and made present by the Holy Spirit. Insofar as they live in the Old Age, they give limited support to systems which perform minimal economic tasks and preserve some openness, however imperfect. They also recognize the need for concessions to provide incentives whose side effects widen the gap between rich and poor and threaten democratic procedures and human rights. Building and maintaining functional economic and political systems is no easy task to be borne lightly with talk of instant revolution.

Nevertheless, Christians do not live according to the Old Age but according to the New Age. More equitable economic and political systems are the true direction. Equality takes precedence over efficiency. The freedom to change structures outweighs the need merely to preserve.

MEASURING UP

At first glance, American economic and political systems seem to be doing a fairly good job. Order is being maintained. Political freedom is extensive. The economic tasks of allocation and distribution are being performed. Indeed the economic system itself has been very effective in raising many people above subsistence levels. This in itself is a tremendous gain in human well-being.

If one considers only these things and compares the United States to other nations (some of whom are doing better, others worse), a mildly favorable verdict can be rendered. It is only when surface phenomena give way to more thorough investigation and Christian principles become the standard of comparison that cracks appear in the facade of the American political and economic house. Mild affirmation must therefore be followed by a more critical assessment.

Condition of the Poor

Measured against the strong biblical concern for the poor, for sharing, for social justice, and for community, the existing economic and political system falls short. The presence of real suffering from poverty in the world's richest nation betrays a lack of concern. The dominance of individualism and of economic values and beliefs exposes the low priority placed on these biblical concerns. Divisions caused by extremes of poverty and wealth thwart efforts to build community. This assessment is compounded when the American response to world poverty is considered. The United States does not have the capacity to eliminate world poverty, but it certainly can go a long way to improve the amount and quality of aid it gives and to eliminate abuses which contribute to the plight of the poor. The insufficiency of the response is one of the most telling arguments against the legitimacy of American power.

Not to be overlooked is the state of affairs in the churches themselves. The churches reflect the larger society more than their own heritage. If Christians were serious about their foundations, care for the poor, sharing, and cohesive communities would be matters of greater importance to local congregations.

Justice and Tradeoffs

The basic ethical principle of justice raises several questions. Are the differentials in wealth, income, and power justified by the overall good that results from them? If one concedes that productivity is enhanced by a degree of inequality, is the present degree out of proportion to the enhanced productivity?

To begin the process of measuring up, it is well to recall the groundwork provided in the preceding section on religious foundations. For Christians, the starting point in assessing a just distribution is equality. Equality takes precedence over strictly economic criteria. In more refined terms, the first question is whether on the basis of Christian criteria, existing and proposed inequalities are relevant departures from equality.

To get at this question, it is necessary to review the factors contributing to the existing distribution and to measure them against Christian ethical criteria. First are the causes of poverty, a few of which are relevant grounds for departure. The tradition of asceticism in Christianity makes voluntary poverty a virtue. For a variety of reasons, including the decision to be ascetic, some individuals are poor by voluntary choice. The inequality which results from a decision for ascetism is justifiable in that the decision is the free choice of individuals and groups trying to live out new life-styles. More complex is the choice of homemaking over a wage-paying job. Insofar as this decision is freely made, inequalities are to be expected and are justifiable. Nevertheless, homemaking contributes significantly to the community. The choice for it should not be the occasion for a life of grinding poverty. The community should compensate for it at least to the point where basic needs are met.

Poverty by voluntary choice makes only a small contribution to overall poverty. However, a much larger contribution is made by causes over which individuals have little control and for which they are not responsible. Many causes are socially based and can be overcome only with extraordinary initiative, talent, and luck. Discrimination, both racial and sexual, is the most obvious and, in Christian terms, denies the basic equality of persons. Overwhelming personal crises, unemployment due to changes in the economy, birth into the so-called culture of poverty, and low-paying jobs all have social roots beyond control of the individual. Lack of skills and abilities, insufficient education, and inadequate retirement benefits are similar in nature though perhaps more amenable to control. Departures from equality which result from social causes beyond individual control are not supportable. They represent a failure of community responsibility, the neglect of justice, and a violation of concern for the poor.

Turning to the causes of income and wealth differentials, much the same conclusion can be reached. Wealth is a result of savings from lifetime income, gifts, bequests, and inheritances. Many people justify gifts, bequests, and inheritances as relevant departures from equality on the grounds of social custom or the preservation of family wealth. Such justifications and the inequality which results are difficult to support on Christian grounds. Appeal to custom has little to do with Christianity. Worse, the appeal to family promotes a group selfishness foreign to the other-centeredness of Christianity. Good fortune, family connections, and status as causes of both high income and wealth are similarly not supportable.

Partially supportable are differentials caused by harder work, rewards for educational achievement, higher intelligence, community size and location, and decisions to hold more than one job. These are unsupportable insofar as they are matters beyond individual control—as they all are to a degree—but, insofar as they promote efficiency and productivity, they are justifiable for the material good they help to realize. Incentives to take risks, to work hard, to increase production, and to take responsibility are necessary in the Old Age of sin. Almost all existing communities find it necessary to reward certain behaviors in order to provide the minimal cooperation and work required for community maintenance. In other words, the good of the community and material productivity are supportable grounds for some degree of inequality. Efficiency and work are derivative goods necessitating limited tradeoffs with equality.

Despite this, a word of caution is in order. The existing differentials in wealth, income, and power cannot be justified on the grounds of efficiency alone. The presence of so many other insupportable factors means that the actual distribution is skewed far more than can be justified on efficiency grounds. Moreover, the dominance of economic factors in American values and beliefs leads to an overstatement of the justifications offered on the basis of efficiency and work. Americans, who are willing to give reward to the producers of economic growth and productivity, neglect criteria of need and equality and too easily accept claims and justifications for special privileges. If it is justifiable to trade equality off for efficiency, Americans are indeed more than generous.

Nor do the problems with the tradeoff stop here. If powerful groups claim special privileges, it is axiomatic that their claims and rewards will be out of proportion to the duties and responsibilities they undertake. The principle of proportionality is seldom observed in the United States, even though the graduated income tax pays lip service to it. But if the graduated income tax pays lip service, tax loopholes and the regressiveness of other taxes make a mockery of proportionality.

Not only is the principle of proportionality largely ignored, but so also is the principle of relevancy. The actual distribution is a result of market forces mitigated by transfer payments. Little effort is made to justify departures from equality. Justice has been and continues to be a balance of power between groups seeking special privileges and rewards. The burden of proof is reversed. It now rests on those who would limit special privilege. The biblical concern for the poor and for the community and the American value of humanitarianism which recognizes need as a criterion have been overwhelmed by the market cast of society.

The conclusion that maldistribution characterizes the American split-level house is inescapable. This is an ethical judgment, not a statistical one. Statistical tables detailing who gets what cannot determine maldistribution. But it can be judged by ethical criteria. Maldistribution is a distribution of income and wealth in which:

1. Relevant ethical criteria for departures from equality are of little significance;
2. Irrelevant criteria dominate and are allowed to widen the distribution markedly;
3. No conscious effort is made to determine proportionality;
4. The question of relevancy is largely ignored;
5. Little effort is made to correct inequalities through a progressive tax system;
6. The burden of establishing proof is shifted to those who would have greater equality;
7. Poverty exists in the midst of plenty and the poor are neglected; and,
8. Racial and sexual discrimination are important sources of inequalities.

When a significant number of these factors are present in the actual distribution of income and wealth, maldistribution exists and justice is violated. The available evidence and analysis of the actual distribution support the conclusion that maldistribution exists in the United States.

As for the tradeoff between freedom and equality, little needs to be added to the previous discussion. From a Christian ethical perspective, the economic freedom of the poor is just as important as the political freedom of the rich to consume and invest according to private desire. Transferring the income and wealth of society from rich to poor may actually increase freedom.

TOWARD A SINGLE LEVEL

From a Christian perspective, the ethical challenge to Americans is to reduce poverty and narrow income and wealth differentials. Whether or not this is the best thing to do when economic and political considerations are weighed in the balance is a debatable point. Personally, this writer thinks it is. The challenge is to reduce and narrow income and wealth differentials, not to eliminate and remove them. This may seem to be a compromise of what Christians mean by freedom, equality, community, and radical sharing. Some would argue that the ideal should be the objective, not something less. But here a distinction is needed between the ideal and more realistic objectives. The ideal is not realizable short of the kingdom of God. This does not mean it is irrelevant. Ideals have power. They push and pull human behavior to higher levels of ethical realization. However, human sin has power too, and human actions almost always fall somewhere between the extremes of the ideal and of self-centeredness. Realistic objectives are those which help to move actions away from the pole of self-centeredness toward the ideal. In terms of the present discussion, the realistic objectives are to reduce poverty and to narrow the wealth and income differentials, and to do so in a way which preserves democratic processes.

To work out a blueprint for action is, however, another matter. For this writer, a highly progressive tax system coupled with confiscatory inheritance taxes on big estates, the elimination of most tax concessions, and a negative income tax designed to preserve incentives as much as possible make the most sense. Programs for job training, upgrading skills, raising levels of education, and eliminating racial and sexual discrimination would also be appropriate.

Standing in the way of such programs is the ubiquitous problem of power. Political power is just as poorly distributed as income and wealth. This power distribution is buttressed by a way of thinking that values the virtues of the wealthy. The combination of power, ideology, and a few sound arguments based on economic theory tends to forecast inertia in the foreseeable future. The prospect for the poor and for a greater approximation of justice is not good. The situation will probably not change until the powerless are empowered.

Inevitably this raises the question of total change. Should American capitalism and the inequalities it spawns be overthrown and some other economic and political system be substituted, presumably a form of democratic socialism? Such a solution may appeal to idealists, but its prospects in the United States are even dimmer than the combination of programs cited above. Furthermore, the violence generated by such a radical change would probably outweigh the good produced.

In the final analysis, the best prospects for the reduction of poverty and the narrowing of income and wealth differentials probably rest with gradual change in incremental stages, abetted by an increasing awareness of current injustices. Where such increasing awareness will come from is difficult to predict, but high rates of inflation and shortages of energy and other resources seem the most likely stimuli. The economic pie will not continue to grow, and more people will become aware that the rewards and costs of American society are not justly distributed.[12] One would be foolish not to admit, however, the ugly possibility that matters could also go in the opposite direction, as the more powerful try to preserve their affluence at the expense of the less powerful.

The Christian community itself should also be a focus of attention. Stratification inside is just as bad as outside and the churches often neglect even their own poor. Christians can hardly expect the larger society to change when their own house is in such bad order.

Finally, a word must be said about the Spirit of Christ. Christians do not work alone on behalf of the poor and for greater justice. The Spirit of Jesus Christ is with them. And while the Spirit cannot be controlled, the ultimate hope for the reduction of poverty and the realization of greater justice rests on God's presence among us. Because the presence of the Spirit is assured, the possibility of improvement is very real.

NOTES

1. Okun, Arthur. *Equality and Efficiency: The Big Tradeoff*. Washington, D.C.: The Brookings Institution, 1975. Okun uses the image of the split-level house very effectively in this excellent essay.
2. In Chapter IV, Stanley Brue defines *efficiency* in two ways. First, it is a generic term "to describe the optimal production of products and services and the corresponding optimal generation of national income." The term *productivity* is often used as a shorter term for this longer definition. Many economists, however, feel that the real trade-

off being pointed to with the term *efficiency* is not so much the one between productivity and equality as the one between total or economic growth and equality. Thus, Brue adds a second definition of efficiency, namely, economic growth. He then lumps these two definitions together in his preferred understanding: "the 'efficiency' goal might be better described as the 'employment, production and growth' goal." In what follows, the term *efficiency* will follow Brue's preferred understanding.

3. Okun, Chapter 3.
4. *Ibid.*, p. 67.
5. Turner, Jonathan H., and Charles E. Starnes. *Inequality: Privilege and Poverty in America.* Pacific Palisades, Calif.: Goodyear Publishing Company, 1967, Chapter 6.
6. Okun, p. 67.
7. Turner and Starnes, *Inequality*, p. 66.
8. *Ibid.*
9. Williams, Robin M. Jr. *American Society: A Sociological Interpretation.* Second ed., rev. New York: Alfred A. Knopf, 1967, pp. 437-500.
10. Weber, Max. *The Protestant Ethic and the Spirit of Capitalism.* Trans. by Talcot Parsons. New York: Charles Scribner's Sons, 1958.
11. Throughout this chapter, a limited priority has been given to the community over the individual. By community is meant not just the church, but also families, local organizations, national societies, and global efforts to unite people. The basis for this priority has been the Christian emphasis on the community of believers as opposed to individual believers in isolation. This emphasis implies that individuals find fulfillment and receive grace primarily in communities and that community is the basic unit for human life. To be clear, speaking of priority does not mean that the individual is to be swallowed up by the community or that recent gains for individual liberty should be negated. The individual must, of course, be protected by such things as bills of rights and church constitutions.

This priority has further implications for the distribution of the social product, at least as far as Christians are concerned. In the discussion of the welfare program for the rich, alternatively known as tax expenditures, income was assumed to be a grant to the individual by the society of a share of the social product. With this assumption it was then legitimate to talk about tax expenditures as social giveaways even though nothing actually was given away.

This was a big assumption that should not be accepted without examination. Many Americans will find it hard to accept, educated as they have been into a highly individualistic way of thinking. For those who believe the individual takes priority over the society, personal income is an earned right or something that belongs to the individual before any social considerations. To this view thinking in terms of tax expenditures is illegitimate since income belongs to the individual and is not something granted by the society.

The question is, who owns property? At the most fundamental level the Christian answer is clear. No one owns property. Property belongs to God and human beings are merely sojourners and stewards. According to Leviticus 23:23, for example, "the land shall not be sold in perpetuity, for the land is mine; for you are strangers and sojourners with me." This is also implied in Genesis 1:26-28, where human beings are given dominion over the earth and commanded to care for it as good stewards. Thus, property is a trust from God to be organized in ways which enhance all created life. As for more specific guidance on how this trust is to be organized in terms of human ownership, the Bible and the tradition are not of one voice. Both individual and communal ownership are possibilities, and the decision between them is a pragmatic one.

Without getting into the complicated and often emotional debate over communal versus private ownership, what is being maintained in this chapter is the limited priority of the community. This limited priority is derived theologically from the Christian emphasis on community and from Genesis 1:26-28, where God gives dominion to "man," which means that dominion is given to all men and women *together*. In other words, the community is the holder of the trust even though in its wisdom it may delegate this responsibility to individuals. Philosophically this priority rests on common-sense reasoning that there would be no product to appropriate individually unless men and women were associated in a common effort. Hence all that is produced is truly social with individual appropriation being merely a matter of convenience, practicality, and protection of the individual.

One further question is, Who speaks for or represents the community on matters of property and ownership? The answer is by no means clear, especially in a highly pluralistic society such as the United States. For better or worse, however, it is the government within the bounds of law which is the only practical representatives of the multiplicity of communities.

It would be well for Americans of an individualistic bent to appropriate a little more of their Christian heritage. Individualism has proceeded beyond what is healthy. Americans neglect community and the psychological consequences are devastating to those who in crisis find themselves without communal resources. In the face of these consequences, worries about communism and socialism seem ludicrous. The problem is not too much, but too little and the wrong kinds of community.

12. Stivers, Robert L. *The Sustainable Society.* Philadelphia: Westminster, 1976, Chapters 5-9.

SUGGESTED READINGS

Hengel, Martin. *Property and Riches in the Early Church.* Philadelphia: Fortress Press, 1974. This is one of the best scholarly efforts to uncover the attitude of the early church on such subjects as property, wealth, poverty, asceticism, and community. Less than 100 pages in length, it can be read without expert knowledge.

Limburg, James. *The Prophets and the Powerless*. Richmond: John Knox Press, 1977. Limburg sets forth the prophetic message concerning the misuse of wealth, the demand for justice, and care and compassion for the powerless. This is a short and readable book for all audiences.

Miller, Herman P. *Rich Man, Poor Man*. Through the presentation of statistics on wealth and income, Miller draws the map of American distribution. There are surprises in those statistics which few are aware of.

Niebuhr, Reinhold. *Moral Man and Immoral Society*. New York: Scribners, 1932. This is a classic in social ethics. Although written fifty years ago, its analysis of the hypocrisy of individuals and nations is up-to-date. For more knowledgeable readers, Niebuhr in this volume sets a basic Christian stance of realism and hope.

Okun, Arthur. *Equality and Efficiency: The Big Trade-off*. Washington, D.C.: The Brookings Institute, 1975. Okun uses the image of the split-level house in this brief and readable volume. He also develops the trade-offs implicit in distribution questions and outlines the sources of income and wealth differentials.

Turner, Jonathan H. and Charles E. Starnes. *Inequality: Privilege and Power in America*. Goodyear Publishing Company, 1976. This is without doubt one of the most revealing essays on the subjects of poverty, wealth, and distribution. The institutional, ideological, and political foundations of maldistribution are presented here in readable fashion.

STUDY QUESTIONS

1. How do values influence the definition given to poverty? In studying this question use information from the other chapters in the book in conjunction with the discussion presented in Chapter 7.

2. Inventory your own beliefs and values about the rights and responsibilities that human beings have. How do these beliefs and values influence the form that political and economic systems should take? How do your beliefs and values compare to other people you associate with and with the views expressed in Chapter 7?

3. Examine what was said by various political groups and the Moral Majority in the election campaign of 1980. Assess how those statements tell you their ideas about poverty and the distribution of wealth. Were their ideas based on accurate information?

4. How can groups that you belong to be used to create changes in the distribution of wealth in America? In examining this question, create a list of the groups you belong to and outline what these groups think about poverty and a more equitable distribution of wealth in the United States

192 Poverty, Distribution, and Christian Ethics

and the world. If you don't know what those groups think about these issues, decide how you can learn what they think and then seek the information.

5. Compare the arguments presented in Chapter 7 about elimination of poverty and achieving greater equity in the distribution of wealth to the policies and programs by socialist countries, countries that have adopted a welfare state, and the U.S., as discussed in Chapter 8.

8

International Approaches to Poverty and Income Distribution

John A. Schiller and Arturo Biblarz

Solutions to poverty often are considered within the context of economic or political systems. The most commonly discussed systems in our time are capitalism and socialism. Some propose that poverty is inherent in capitalism, that it is only by destroying capitalist societies that poverty will finally be overcome. Others propose that socialist countries are inherently incapable of reaching the levels of productivity that are necessary to assure their populations an adequate standard of living. Therefore, some form of poverty will always exist in socialist societies. Whether or not there is any truth in these two claims, it seems proper to view these claims as oversimplifications. Furthermore, each makes certain assumptions about the nature of human beings never made explicit in the argument.

The social causes and solutions of poverty are not only economic and political but also involve value orientations and family systems, as well as the interaction among all of these factors. In addition, the stage of development in which a specific society is at a particular point in time will have an influence on the incidence and nature of poverty in that society.

This chapter, too, will be guilty of oversimplification. Seven different countries will be examined to assess their policies as they relate to poverty. Discussion will be restricted to their political-economic policies and realities; it is in these areas that most work has been done by other scholars. But even here, analysis is hindered by inadequate information. The reader should keep the limitations of our approach in mind.

Since political-economic issues are to be discussed, general clarification of some commonly used terms is essential. These terms are capitalism, socialism, communism, and the welfare state.

Too often Americans live under the erroneous belief that the United States has a free-market economy. This is not the case. There is governmental control and planning that regulates, influences, and supports the economic system at national and international levels. American economists call it a modified free-market economy. Keeping this in mind, *capitalism* can be defined as an economic system in which the means of production and distribution of goods and services are primarily owned by individuals or groups of individuals, rather than by the state or by the society as a whole. Furthermore, the means of production and distribution are not owned and controlled by the people who work in them, with the exception of some small businesses. Finally, in capitalist societies one of the primary commitments of government is to preserve, protect, and enhance this kind of private ownership and control.

The theoretical basis of this system is that through the process of supply and demand, consumers will inform producers of their needs, and producers will place their resources in those areas where consumer needs are sufficiently great to permit producers the realization of an adequate profit. Planning, therefore, is not centralized, except to the extent that producers are centralized and except in emergency situations. When emergencies do arise, government may encourage and attempt to regulate planning until the crisis is overcome. One example can be seen in the present energy crisis in the United States.

The second concept that needs clarification is the *welfare state*. This term is often used synonymously with socialism, but this creates confusion. Many welfare states are predominantly capitalistic, and socialist states do not necessarily include all the human-service programs characteristic of the welfare state.

A *welfare state* can be defined as a society whose government is committed to providing a minimum of goods, housing, clothing, education, and health care to all of its members, whether or not they are employed. In effect, the government attempts to create a level below which no person will fall, and leaves it up to private individuals or groups to decide whether or not they will rise above that level, and how far they will rise. In order to provide these and other government services, taxes tend to be very high and often act as a disincentive for people who would like to improve their own economic position.

Additionally, many welfare states have governments that, from time to time, are dominated by socialist parties; the philosophy of these parties is one of the major factors contributing to the existence and maintenance of the welfare state. Furthermore, the socialist character of these parties is expressed in conviction that public ownership of the means of production and distribution is a goal to be obtained, although they generally oppose any sudden or violent transition. When they are in power, they attempt to strengthen the welfare policies that already exist and to continue any former attempts to increase government control and planning of the economy. To the extent that they succeed, they create in their nations increasingly mixed economies; some amount of governmental control and planning exists alongside a preponderance of private control and the operation of traditional market forces.

The last two concepts to be discussed are *socialism* and *communism*. These are frequently used interchangeably. Here again, it may be useful to make some clear distinctions. Marx was one of the first to propose that the changes that he felt to be necessary in order to overcome the problems of capitalism, including the problem of poverty, would occur in two stages. One of these stages, Marx theorized, would be sudden and dramatic, while the other would be gradual and relatively smooth. The first stage, for theoretical purposes, can be called socialism. It was expected to involve seizure of political power by a political organization representing the workers, appropriation of the means of production and distribution from the hands of private capitalists and their control by the new government, and the establishment of a series of reforms that would insure the complete transformation of society. None of these proposed reforms, however, involved the elimination of inequality, including income inequality. As Marx said, at this stage,

> the worker gets back exactly what he gave—his labour. Here equal right is still a bourgeois right—the quality that exists is that an equal standard is used, labour. But this equal right is an unequal right for unequal labour. It recognizes no class differences, because everyone is only a worker, like everyone else, but it tacitly recognizes

unequal individual endowment and thus productive capacity as natural privileges. It is therefore a right in inequality in its content, like every right—Thus with an equal output, and hence an equal share in the social consumption fund, one will in fact receive more than another, one will be richer than another and so on.[1]

Inequality, therefore, would continue to exist, but the inequality would be between individuals rather than between groups; people who work harder and better would receive more, those working less would receive less. The motto for this stage was, "To each according to his work." A society such as this, where all people worked (except those too sick or disabled), and where government directly represented the people, would then slowly transform all social institutions as well as the cultural and personal values of its members until the ethics of economic individualism and competition would be transformed into the ethics of economic collectivism and cooperation.

At this stage it was expected that people would voluntarily work wherever they were needed and do whatever was required and in return they would take from society whatever they required. As Lenin put it,

> From each according to his ability, to each according to his need, i.e., when people have become accustomed to observing the fundamental rules of social life and their labour is so productive that they will voluntarily work according to their ability. The narrow horizon of bourgeois right will have been left behind. There will be no need for society to make an exact calculation of the quantity of products to be distributed to each of its members, each will take freely according to his need.[2]

Thus, inequality would still be present, but an inequality based only on each person's needs, existing in the context where all persons would have equal opportunity for the satisfaction of their differing requirements. This last stage of socialism, which we will call "theoretical communism," has never occurred in any known human society. Whether or not such a society is possible is an issue that need not concern us here. For our purposes, it is enough to propose that most existing Marxist societies are more properly considered *socialist*, or societies that are attempting, or have attempted, to reach the first stage described by Marx. Thus, we can compare the achievements of these societies and their recent historical changes with the theoretical ideals on which they were founded.

To summarize, we are dealing with three types of political-economic system: capitalism, the welfare state, and socialism; communism is a strictly theoretical, nonexistent system. The other three types can be said to exist, but none of them in a pure form; each has some features that belong to the others. Each represents an attempt to create an equitable and just society, where individuals and groups can exist and thrive. Capitalism, on the one hand, emphasizes the significance of individual effort at the expense of community concerns; socialism, on the other hand, emphasizes the total collectivity at the expense of any given individual. With these ideas in mind, we can now examine some concrete examples.

SOCIALISTIC STATES

Union of Soviet Socialist Republics

As was pointed out above, communism at its present stage has as its goal to provide social services and economic rewards according to the kind of work and the amount of work done. It has not yet achieved that point in society where economic and social benefits are given according to an individual's need.

The development of the present economic and social policies of the Soviet Union can be divided into three periods. The first period was the pre-Stalin period. During that time the state gained control of the economy. During the Stalinist era, collectivization of the peasantry into state farms and collective farms was completed. It was also during the Stalinist era that the intelligentsia and the political administrative and party leadership were given special financial rewards. During the post-Stalinist era there has been a more aggressive effort to raise the standard of living of the peasants, who up to that time had been living in poverty, to increase the standard of living of every Soviet citizen, and to create a more egalitarian social structure.[3] However, the overriding goal in all of these years has been to increase the productivity of the country. This overriding concern, with its accompanying economic and social policies, has not produced an egalitarian society nor has it eliminated poverty.

A closer examination of the social stratification system will shed further light on the consequences of Soviet political and economic policy. The first objective of the revolution was to alter the worker's relation to the means of production. This follows from Marxian ideology which holds that class is a consequence of the relationship of the worker to the means of production. By placing the means of production into the hands of the proletariat—in other words, the state—that class distinction is eliminated. In that process rural workers were separated into two kinds of work settings, state farms and collective farms. Persons working on state farms were classified among those workers who had achieved the socialist relation to the means of production. Persons working in collectives were considered second-class citizens. For many years the wages of collective workers were less than agricultural workers on state farms; state farm workers had the benefit of the same social services and pensions that urban workers had, whereas, collective farm workers were left out. Urban workers and state farm workers constituted the major category of workers in the system. A second group developed under Stalin, constituting the intelligentsia and political administrators, neither of whom was related to the means of material production. This group had the most favorable economic position. The group at the bottom of the economic ladder were the farm workers on collective farms.

Soviet sociologists today report a stratification system of eight to ten sociooccupational groups based on complexity and responsibility of work performed, amount of education acquired, income received, and life-style.[4] Western sociologists point out, however, that this classification does not include the upper levels of political power in the state administrative structure, professional, executive, and economic management.

The U.S.S.R. has employed a planned economy in the development and distribution of economic resources. It has carefully controlled production and prices according to goals established for the kinds of consumer goods desired. One way to assess the result of this program is to note that in 1972, the average monthly wage of Soviet workers was 130.3 rubles (about $159.90) which was less than two-thirds of the amount necessary to maintain a family of four at minimum living standards. Income distribution for workers in the Soviet Union is shown in Table I.[5] To this report of income must be added hidden income through the underground market, preferential housing and preferential shopping places for the political and administrative elite.

TABLE I

Distribution of Wages and Salaries in the Soviet Union in 1966

Wages and Salaries (rubles per month)	Percent of Workers
30 to 39	2
40 to 49	9

50 to 59	9
60 to 69	12
70 to 79	10
80 to 99	18
100 to 119	14
120 to 139	10
140 to 159	5
160 to 199	10
200 to 300	2

Mervyn Matthews has provided data on the wages paid in the Soviet Union for the various kinds of occupations under the rubric of "manual worker." Table II shows that, though Khrushchev sought to produce a more egalitarian society, there was still a wide divergence in wages paid to workers in 1967. Matthews concludes "that by the mid-sixties, a third or more of the Soviet working class could be thought of as 'poor' by accepted Soviet standards." [6] Occupations listed in Table II do not include the Soviet elite. It is difficult to get precise information about the income received by the intelligentsia.° This group makes up about 13 percent of the population. It consists of persons engaged in mental, intellectual labor in the most demanding managerial governmental and party positions, the elite, "the uppermost tip of the Soviet labour force; here we have the people who, in their working hours, really control the Soviet Union." [7] Their income includes salaries, bonuses, fringe benefits, and privileges—their total income is not ascertainable but is much higher than the incomes reported in Table I.

TABLE II

**Average Monthly Wages in the Soviet Economy
for Selected Occupations, 1967**

Work Category	Average Wage (Rubles)
Science and supporting enterprises	122.0
Construction (building and repair personnel)	118.1
Transport, all types	115.0

° More recent detailed analysis of income distribution for Soviet society is not readily available to Western researchers. As late as 1980, W. O. Connor, a specialist on Soviet social stratification still had to rely on data from the mid-sixties: Walter O. Connor, *Socialism, Politics and Equality: Hierarchy and Change in Eastern Europe and the U.S.S.R.* New York: Columbia University Press, 1980.

State and economic apparatus, administration officers of cooperative and public organizations	112.5
Industry (production personnel)	111.7
Education (schools, colleges, cultural institutions)	96.5
Credit and insurance institutions	93.0
State farms and subordinate agricultural enterprises	84.1
Trade, catering, supplies	82.5
Health services	82.4
Housing and communal services	78.6
Office workers, cashiers	45-60
Unskilled laborers	50-60
Shoemaker, seamstress, laundress	46-55
Ship assistant (junior)	55

Adapted from Matthews, Mervyn. *Class and Society in Soviet Russia.* New York: Walker and Company, 1972, pp. 88-89.

The priority of economic growth and development is also reflected in the policy and programs of income maintenance. These are structured and determined so as not to interfere with or hinder the incentive to work. (This is much the same attitude as expressed in the United States but for different ideological reasons.) Therefore, social programs do not include unemployment compensation or financial support for the unemployed who are able to work. And it also affects the amount of support provided for those less able to work but of working age or for those in retirement who have not worked as much or not at all. Soviet ideology employs the sanction of loyalty to the collective and the state. Every Soviet citizen has a right to a job, so theoretically there should not be any unemployment. Frictional unemployment, of which there is quite a bit, is ignored. (See Chapter 1 for a discussion of frictional unemployment.)

Soviet income-maintenance programs include sick benefits; old age, disability and survivors pension; sickness and maternity benefits; work injury and family allowances.[8] However, there are some inequities in these various programs. Not all programs cover all people equally. The major discrepancy in the social-insurance program is the differential benefits paid urban workers in contrast to agricultural workers, especially workers on collective farms. For example, collective farm workers do not receive partial disability pensions, have a lower sickness benefit, and receive 25 rubles a month less in minimum pensions than do agricultural workers on state farms.[9]

Pension benefits vary among urban occupations and are based on earnings and length of employment. For some occupations, pension benefits are paid at the 100 percent level, and workers are permitted to continue to work after retirement at age sixty, while receiving their full pension. A weakness in the pension system is that after retirement, there is no adjustment of the pension payment to compensate for the increase in the cost of living.[10]

Craig R. Whitney reported in the *New York Times* that many elderly people live impoverished lives because of inadequate pensions. He reports that official Soviet statistics say that it takes 50 rubles a month for a person to provide food, clothing, and housing. The legal minimum pension payment is 45 rubles and the maximum is 120 rubles. Pension payments average 45 to 50 percent of the worker's last monthly pay. Minimum pensions for collective farm workers, first included under a pension program in 1964, are 28 rubles per month. There are millions not entitled to pensions, who get even less than the minimum. As of 1970, of the 36.2 million men of retirement age, 23.7 million were receiving pensions. Approximately one-third of the retired men and women in the Soviet Union are not receiving pensions.[11] Social service programs are designed to encourage women to work and to encourage large families.

Retirement benefits are inversely related to earnings. If your earnings are such that you get less than the minimum pension, you get 100 percent of your earnings. If your income is more than 100 rubles per month, you get 50 percent of your earnings. Women, unless they are also in the labor force, suffer most from pension allotments as survivors. The female survivor is paid only one-third of the pension award. This forces women to get into the labor market to assure a better retirement income. Jack Mimhoff and Lynn Turgen conclude that "it must be charged against the Soviets and the East Europeans that their pursuit of increased production has made a mockery out of society's pledge to provide income security to all in need." [12]

People's Republic of China

Our second example of a socialist state program to alleviate poverty is one developed by the People's Republic of China. It is generally conceded by every authority on China that the masses of Chinese are living better today than prior to the revolution of 1949. People are healthier, the country is cleaner, the standard of living has been raised, and more people are working for a living. But that does not mean that poverty has been eliminated. George Taber estimates that if China is able to maintain an annual growth rate of six percent, it will be A.D. 2000 before it achieves a per capita income of $1000, which is the presently accepted international poverty level.[13] In spite of that, the revolution has achieved some interesting and remarkable successes. But at the same time, some problems are developing that the present system has not yet been able to overcome.

During the first years of the revolution which began in 1949, land was redistributed to the peasants and then transferred to collectives. Banking was nationalized. Private enterprise was replaced with state monopolies. A balanced budget became economic policy. A comprehensive program of sanitation, health, and education was begun.

During the first nine years of the revolution, China leaned heavily on Russia's method of operation. By 1958, however, the country discarded the Russian pattern and determined to make the great leap forward to a more advanced stage of socialism. Ideology overtook realism. Chinese leaders pushed vigorously the ideology that was to have pulled its citizens together into a true collectivist society in which personal reward would be replaced by the good and goal of the larger society.

During the next 15 to 20 years, Chinese leadership vacillated between pure collectivist policy that eliminated all private property and personal incentives on the one hand, and some private property and limited personal incentives on the other hand. During the last several years, the ideology of Mao Tse-tung has given way to a more pragmatic economic policy which combines centralized economic planning, market forces, and local community initiative, profit, and planning. This has resulted in increasing the number of private plots of ground for agricultural workers, providing wage incentives, bonuses, and fringe benefits, and speeding up industrial development in whatever way possible.

China is still an agricultural country. Eighty percent of its people live in the country. The effort during 1958 to 1960 to bring industry to the countryside by having a "steel mill in every backyard" did not succeed. Large-scale modern steel plants proved to be more efficient and productive. China is still, however, a labor-intensive economy. High birth rates have contributed to a rapidly growing population. In 1949 China's population was estimated at 540 million. Today it is 977 million. Population growth has led the Chinese to encourage retirement at 60 for men and 55 for women and to encourage birth control in an effort to reach zero population growth by A.D. 2000. (Its growth rate was 30 per 1000 in 1950, 12 per 1000 by the late 1970s.) Housing is at a premium, and three-generation families living in the same household is commonplace. This is due partly to the income difference between younger workers and retired persons. If several generations of families did not share households, they would not be able to live on the salaries younger workers make.[14]

An assessment of economic consequences is hampered by a lack of accurate data. Limited information about income variation among the provinces and between urban and rural workers, as well as contradictions among experts, compound the problem.[15]

There is a difference in income among various groups of people in China. A semiskilled worker with 20 years of experience in the factory gets 62 yuan a month (1 yuan equals 60¢). A manager in that same plant gets 180 yuan per month. Women receive the same pay as men. Workers in agricultural communes receive 45 yuan a month.[16]

There is a greater disparity, however, between persons who have retired and younger workers. This is especially true in the cities. A husband and wife, if both have worked for 20 years, will receive a total pension of 155 yuan a month, while their 25-year-old son, a textile worker, earns 41 yuan a month.[17] This has begun to create some discontent among the younger people in China. The ideology of the revolution and the long history of veneration of elders have certainly reduced the potential conflict that such an income differential could create. But one additional reason for this retirement policy is the need to create jobs for younger workers. Peking, for example, has developed a unique system by which a person who is retiring is permitted to bring into the factory his son or daughter as a replacement. It is estimated that 80 percent of the workers in some factories get their jobs in this way.[18] Many of those children live with their parents and share incomes. In fact, many young people up to age 35 are paid such a low salary that they must depend upon pooled family incomes to exist.

Retirement for commune or agricultural workers is financially unfavorable. Just as wages for commune workers are much lower, so is their retirement income. Whereas the retirement income for a husband-wife who have worked in the factory is 155 yuan per month, a husband and wife who have worked in the commune receive 50 yuan per month. The difference is justified by the argument that the rural couple can provide for most of the necessities of life by farming their family plot of ground.

Though salaries for younger workers are quite low, a series of services are provided by the government. They include social insurance, sickness and maternity benefits, work injury and family allowances. Other kinds of services are the responsibility of the factory where the person works. Persons working in communes do not receive all of the benefits that urban workers receive. Nor are the rates as high for those benefits that rural workers receive.

The government assumes there is no unemployment in China. In fact, communist ideology in China, as in the Soviet Union, holds that if a person does not work, neither shall that person eat. Loyalty to the society demands that one work, so there must not be any unemployment. Therefore, the government has no program of support for persons who are in poverty because of unemployment. Yet Professor Davis Friedman, who studied employment in China during the summer of 1979, reports that there are 20 million unemployed persons in China.[19]

China is aware of the low income of its people and has followed a rigorous economic policy of controlling inflation, pricing nonessential items high, keeping them scarce, so that people spend money only on essentials. As a result, Chinese people have a savings rate of 25 percent, which is four times that of the people in the United States.

Communist ideology has built upon the tradition and solidarity of Chinese culture to foster an attitude that submerges the interests of the individual to the interests of the group, that assumes progress is being made and that there will be eventual success in bringing all of its people to a much higher standard of living. Though progress has been made in behalf of the masses since 1949, egalitarianism has not been achieved, and many people are still in need. The present trend is moving toward an increase in the inequities that exist because of an increase in the use of the incentive and bonus system and the differences between rural and urban pay scales. Some of the inequities are tolerated because of the supportive culture of the extended family. The desire to succeed, and the willingness to practice pragmatism while placing ideology on the back burner, may or may not thwart the ultimate goals of the revolution.

Tanzania

Tanzania provides us with an example of a country that deliberately moved to implement economic democracy. It did it, however, by purchasing foreign enterprises rather than by confiscating them, as some countries have done. This move to economic democracy reversed the policy of centralized planning and reliance on national corporate development, which was highly dependent on production of consumer goods imported from other nations and production development through foreign corporate efforts. What caused such a reversal?

The existing pattern of centralized planning and dependence on foreign goods and large private businesses had created a rapidly growing economy. But at the same time, the gap between the rich and the poor was growing at an increasing rate. Of the 80 percent of the population that was rural, a small group was becoming a wealthy landowner class. At the same time, the unequal access to public services (health, education, pure water, etc.) was on the increase.

Following President Nyerere's rural safari in 1966, Tanzania developed the Arusha Declaration of 1967 and the Mwongozo Guidelines of 1971. These two actions set the country firmly in the direction of achieving the following: 1) to assure everyone the necessary income to buy the basic necessities of life, 2) to provide everyone with the necessary human services, 3) to develop the necessary structures and capital resources to produce their own consumer goods and services, 4) to assure adequate employment and wages so that people could purchase essential consumer goods, and, 5) to assure citizen participation at the lowest levels in economic and governmental planning and implementation of programs.[20]

The last objective was the most distinctive. It established regional, district, and village units for policy and administrative decision making and planning. Independent citizen economic enterprises were established with strong worker councils in which workers constituted 40 percent of the boards of directors. Villages and collectives, at the district and local levels, became the vehicles through which these new economic processes and structures were to be implemented.

To begin the process, several other significant actions were taken for the country as a whole. Persons graduating from advanced educational programs had to engage in a period of national service with a reduction in salary during that national service. Persons working in salaried positions had salary cuts ranging from five to twenty percent. Yearly wage increases were limited to a maximum of five percent per year. Party, government and civil service leaders were no longer permitted to serve on boards of directors or have ownership in the private sector dominated by foreign capital. Tanzania was attempting to correct a danger that Mahbub Al Hag warns about in developing countries; namely, that growth with justice, growth with a more equal distribution of income, will not be assured just because there is an increase in the gross national product. He notes that production and growth plans must include distribution and employment policies.[21]

What were the results of such actions? The wage differences in Tanzania were reduced from a ratio of fifty to one in 1969 to nine to one in 1974. The growth of the economy was maintained at a five to seven percent rate. Purchasing power was increased in many parts of the country so that consumer goods produced within the country increased fourfold. For example, in 1971 the textile industry was producing a surplus, but by 1974 it had to increase its production by employing four shifts of workers, and imports of textile products increased threefold.[22]

Though accurate figures are not available, it seems that unemployment is minimal. Since, however, 80 percent of Tanzania is rural and dependent on agricultural or rural employment, it is difficult to assess the actual employment situation. Greater equalization of income has been achieved. The widening gap between the rich and the poor that developed in the 1960s has been reversed. Differences between the various villages and districts within the country do exist and seem to be more of a problem than inequalities within each village or district. The rural standard of living is still about 50 percent of that of urban households. Discontent exists among salaried workers, who are primarily in governmental and administrative public positions, because their salaries have been reduced and increases controlled, while efforts are made to increase the purchasing power of the wage earners in the city and country.

An additional effort at increasing the purchasing power of the lower-income groups has been attempted through a progressive taxing policy. The lowest incomes are taxed at a 12.5 percent rate, highest incomes are taxed at an 80 percent rate. The minimum wage is not subject to an income tax. Sales taxes have been eliminated from unprocessed foods, thus favoring the rural population, which is poorest. There is a 10 percent sales tax on consumer goods and 10 percent sales tax on luxuries, which increases the tax paid by those whose purchasing power is greatest.

Tanzania is struggling to find the proper balance between central governmental and economic planning while at the same time creating structures for local, district, and regional democratic decision making. This process is influenced, however, by a strong extended family. The experiment is still too young to determine what the ultimate result of economic democracy will be. Present indications are that economic self-determination at the grass roots level has begun. Local production and consumption of essential products has increased. The buying power of the masses has been increased, and greater equity of income distribution is being accomplished.

THE WELFARE STATE

According to the definition of the welfare state given above, Sweden and Israel can be considered welfare states. Each has certain unique characteristics that require separate discussion.

Sweden

Marquis Childs describes the primary character of Sweden's economic and social policies in this manner: "If anything does typify the Swedish economy, it is surely the mixture of an extremely modest degree of social ownership and a soaring ambition with regard to social influence over the course of economic events. This combination of private ownership and social control over the economy can, in fact, be said to constitute the foundation of the Swedish variation on the theme of the mixed economy." [23]

Sweden's present economic, political, and social policies have had a unique history and environment. Several factors have contributed to this development: 1) Sweden enjoys a communal way of life that has its origins some centuries ago, in the influence of the Lutheran church; 2) its people have been, and still are, quite homogeneous; 3) the country has been very self-sufficient for many years; 4) it has had a long history of organizing itself in a democratic way to attack problems or issues confronting it; 5) since the 1930s, partnership between socialist and agrarian political groups and between labor and industry have characterized the approach to economic and social issues; 6) there has been a comprehensive and well-organized labor movement that included both blue-collar and white-collar workers; 7) disputes between labor and industry have been settled through a nonpolitical tribunal or labor court; 8) a strong cooperative movement developed that influenced the economic and political policies of the country; 9) economic and political policies assured tax laws that encouraged rapid reinvestment by industries; and 10) a philosophy that could not accept the inherent goodness of human beings or the natural development of human progress. They were convinced that the solution of human problems would require much planning and effort.[24]

Sweden's social and economic policies developed out of a complex set of forces and circumstances. As a result, Sweden has more social programs than any other country in the world. The purpose of these social programs, together with economic and taxing policies, is to assure everyone an adequate income and support for the contingencies of life. Based on the comparative analysis of social services programs of the countries done by Thursz and Vigilante, it is safe to conclude that the government of Sweden has provided its people with the largest number of services, the greatest level of support, and the highest standard of living of any country in the world.[25]

In order to accomplish this level of support and standard of living, Sweden has enacted a proportional income tax collected by counties and local authorities, a progressive income tax at the state level, a property tax collected by the state, a value-added tax which replaced the sales tax, and special taxes on certain consumable goods—gasoline, alcoholic beverages, and tobacco. As of 1971, 48 percent of the wage earner's salary was paid to the government in taxes. Families with the lowest income pay taxes amounting to 73 percent of their income. Up until the last several years, unemployment rates were only two to three percent.

In the last several years, however, Sweden has begun to experience some difficulties. Its high standard of living has reduced its ability to be competitive in the world market. As a result, for example, it has had to subsidize its automobile market and provide a large number of jobs through government-created programs. Thus, it is not at all certain that internal economic planning can assure that everyone will be able to live adequately at the standard of living attained to date without the support of international trade.

How has Sweden's progress and its programs influenced the distribution of income among its wage earners? Gwartner and Stroup report the results of a comparative study done by the World Bank in 1975. It shows that there is little difference in the income distribution among the developed countries of the world. For example, the income distribution of the United States and Sweden is almost identical, as is demonstrated in Table III.

TABLE III

Distribution of Income Among Developed Countries

Percentage of Income Received by

Country (year)	Bottom 20 Percent	Second Quintile	Third Quintile	Fourth Quintile	Top 20 Percent
Japan (1971)	4	11	16	23	46
England (1968)	6	13	18	24	39
Sweden (1970)	5	10	18	25	43
United States (1971)	5	11	16	23	45
West Germany (1970)	6	11	15	23	45

Table III was adapted from James D. Gwartner and Richard Stroup, eds. *Microeconomics: Private and Public Choice*, Second ed. New York: Academic Press, 1980, p. 328.

Even with all of the services provided by the government, four to six percent of the population need special economic support from the government because they are not being provided for through the various social insurance programs. There are some working families in larger urban centers who experience poverty because of low incomes and high rent.[26]

Esther Adams reports that there has not been an adequate discussion of poverty by the government. In 1965 the government established a Low Income Commission, but that commission created such controversy that it was disbanded. Assuming that people earning less than 50 percent of the median income in 1971 are poor, she estimates there were 1,810,192 poor persons in Sweden out of a population of 8,127,396.[27]

Excessive taxation of professional people and other people at the top of the wage scale reached a crisis stage in 1975. Several instances of high salaried professionals having to pay 100 percent of their entire income in taxes led the Social Democrats to change the law so that professionals would not have to pay taxes equivalent to their total income. The development of a barter system to avoid paying taxes on income is further evidence of the rebellion to excessive tax rates and inflation in Sweden.

It is true that, in spite of some of its people being poor, Sweden has been more successful than most countries in the world in assuring all of its citizens adequate resources through government services and wages to take care of the basic necessities and contingencies of life.

Israel

Harold L. Wilensky calls Israel a welfare state. He defines the essence of the welfare state as "government protected minimum standards of income, nutrition, health, housing, and education, assured to every citizen as a political right, not as charity." [28] Several historical forces and contemporary events in Palestine have contributed to the present political, social, and economic policies operating in Israel today.

Jewish religious tradition fostered an obligation to provide for the needy, not as an act of charity, but as a principle of righteousness. Zionism brought a large number of Jews to Palestine from all parts of the world who were given financial support from many of the countries from which they emigrated. Outside financial support has continued to support the economic system in Israel. Among immigrants since the 1900s were Jewish intellectuals committed to socialism who settled in rural areas and developed an ideology implemented in the *kibbutz* but which also had its influence in the Labour Party, the labor movement, and official governmental policies and programs. The General Federation of Labour *(Histadrut)* has had a profound influence on social services, taxing policies, and economic policies of the government.

The strong socialist labor movement and the Marxist ideology of Jewish immigrants developed a particular form of welfare state in Israel. As a result, though there was a commitment to welfare legislation, government control of economic forces, and a goal of reducing inequality as much as possible, there was also a commitment to a democratic process of reform and a willingness to let private enterprise exist and prosper.

After 1948, Israel sought to bring together under one governmental structure communal groups, agricultural communities, diverse immigrant communities, a strong labor party, and a private enterprise system that was developing while rapid urbanization and industrialization were taking place. The existence of poverty and its alleviation was influenced by all of these forces.

The General Federation of Labour was able to unionize 85 percent of all wage and salaried workers. It developed a strong insurance program for medical services and retirement benefits. It administered and controlled all monies paid into those programs and the payment of benefits to its members. At the same time, the Labour Party was instrumental in getting the government to establish social-service legislation to be implemented by the Ministry Services, housing policies, a progressive tax policy, family allowances, and unemployment benefits.

While progressive tax rates were implemented, a progressive principle regulated the insurance rates so that low-income groups paid a minimal premium. Family allowance benefits increased with the number of children in the family so that the allowance for the ninth child was 18 times greater than the allowance for the first child.[29]

As conditions in Israel have changed, there has been a countervailing influence that has modified the socialistic ideology of the immigrants and the socialism of the Labour Party. Rapid industrialization and urbanization, a wartime economy, and the necessity to maintain strong economic growth to absorb large numbers of immigrants have deradicalized some of their socialistic ideology. In recent years, according to Rivka Bar-Yosef, British socialism has had a major impact on developments in Israel.[30]

Though there was a strong egalitarian ideology, pay scales within and among occupations and among regions have contributed to some degree of inequality. Only about three percent of Israel's population live in *kibbutz* communities. And even there, industrialization and technology have had an adverse impact upon the original intent of egalitarianism.[31]

It is somewhat difficult to draw precise conclusions about the number of persons living in poverty. Even the government has had difficulty defining poverty. Its Committee on Income Distribution, as reported by Bar-Yosef, "did not regard as its function to determine what is the poverty line since the definition of poverty is—a value judgment on the part of society influenced by various economic and social factors." [32]

One can draw some inferences about the success of the government's efforts at a more equitable distribution of income through progressive tax policies and income transfer programs. Prior to taxes and income transfers, the Gini coefficient of income distribution was 0.428. After taxes and income transfers, the Gini coefficient was 0.349, an 18.6 percent reduction. And yet the Gini coefficient of income distribution is not that much different from that of the United States, which averages about 0.39.

Persons in Israel who have retired and who are not part of the Histadrut and its National Insurance Institute get only 30 percent of their previous salary as a pension. Persons belonging to the Histadrut receive an additional pension from the National Insurance Institute, which then gives them a pension equal to 70 percent of their previous salary. Habib argues that there is a strong correlation between poverty and family size, noting that the poverty rate which is six percent among families with one to two children, 14 percent among families with three children, 25.6 percent among families with four to five children, climbs to 52.9 percent among families with six or more children. There is job discrimination against certain immigrants that also contributes to the incidence of poverty. The Sephardim, immigrants from Asia Minor and North Africa, and the Moroccans are given the lowest-paying jobs and the less desirable dwelling places. They are overrepresented among the poor.[33]

Greenberg and Nadler conclude that low salaries, large families, high taxes and staggering inflation are pushing many wage earners into debt and into poverty. They must depend on supplementary maintenance.[34]

External financial support sheds further light on the success or failure of the economic and political policies of Israel to eliminate poverty and narrow the gap between the poor and those at the top of the income ladder. Prior to 1973, 70 percent of the state's budgetary deficit was offset by money that flowed into Israel from other countries. Part came through restitution and reparation payments for Nazi damages. The United Israel Appeal brought contributions from 55 different countries. Loans and development bonds from other countries accounted for about 30 percent of their unearned capital.

Social services are also dependent on funds from outside of Israel. David Macarov estimates that 35 percent of all welfare expenditures come from philanthropic sources, much of which comes from outside the country. Contributors include Quakers, Lutherans, Mennonites, B'nai B'rith, American Joint Distribution Committee, Women's International Zionist Organization, and the Jewish Agency for Palestine, which is the executive body for all world Zionist organizations.[35]

One must conclude, therefore, that Israel's limited success to reduce poverty and to create greater income equality is somewhat dependent on the contribution of resources external to its own economic and political system and policies. Another contributing factor is its war economy which has contributed to a low employment rate of one to two percent over the last 30 years. A negative factor has been a rapid rate of inflation reaching over 100 percent this past year.

United Kingdom

The United Kingdom, like Sweden and Israel, seeks to provide a basic income and basic human services to its citizens, in addition to narrowing the gap between the rich and the poor, through governmental services and economic planning. The Thatcher government, like the Reagan administration in the U. S., is trying to change this policy.

England, like Sweden and Israel, has a progressive income tax and an income transfer program. But unlike them, its pension program is not keeping up with inflation. Present flat pension rates are below what Parliament has set as a basic minimum income. Nor has England been as successful in keeping working families out of poverty. Kincaid reports a 100 percent increase in the working poor from 1966 to 1970.[36] This increase is due in part to a weaker union movement and Labour Party than in Israel or Sweden. Only 40 percent of British workers belong to the union. Nor does Britain have a minimum wage law. Based on a 1968-69 survey, Peter Townsend in a 1980 report estimates 14,000,000 British people live in poverty.[37]

Rising unemployment rates, rising inflation, slow economic growth (three percent per year), and an imbalance of imports and exports are having a negative influence upon the country's efforts to reduce income inequality. As in the case of Israel and Sweden, part of the success of a nation's programs and policies to reduce poverty and redistribute income is dependent on the international arena.

MODIFIED FREE-MARKET ECONOMY

The United States

Preceding chapters have provided a detailed analysis of poverty, income distribution, and the consequences of income inequality for the United States. However, several comparisons should be made to note differences between the United States, which is not a welfare state, and Sweden and Israel. And though the policies and programs of the Reagan administration have not yet been finalized or adopted by Congress, some possible implications can be noted.

The U.S. economy operates with less governmental control than welfare-state economies. Reagan policy would lessen that control. When economic planning and control occur, the time span is much shorter, and both industry and government cooperate to a limited extent. Americans live under one kind of social-service policy and program at the federal level and under any one of fifty different social service programs and policies at the state level. This diversity will be increased under President Reagan's policy of increasing block grants to the states and reducing categorical grants. To a great extent, state voluntarism shapes the services and financial support that individuals receive. Under Reagan's policy of block grants, states will have increased power to establish benefit levels, eligibility criteria, and work requirements.

Tax policies show the same pattern of variation. Some states have a more progressive tax program than others. The federal income tax is less progressive than that of Israel or Sweden. And though the United States has a wide range of income transfer programs, none are as inclusive as those in England, Israel, or Sweden. Nor do its transfer programs provide adequate amounts of financial support for retirement or for the exigencies of family life. The United States is the only western country without a universal health-insurance program or a family policy.

As was noted in earlier chapters, single-parent families with children make up the highest percent of families living in poverty. These families depend, of necessity, upon Aid to Familes with Dependent Children (AFDC). Inflation has had a detrimental effect on these families. Proposed Reagan policy and programs will increase the hurt to these mothers and their children.

Inflation hurt AFDC recipients even though the average monthly benefits rose from $171 in 1969 to $272 in 1980. In constant dollars, the benefit declined by 56 percent.[38] AFDC benefits are caught in a trap because they are not "indexed." Moynihan conclusively shows, in contrast to advocates of Reagan's policy, that the war on poverty is being lost.

Researchers at the University of Chicago have made estimates of the effect on poverty of Reagan's proposed budget cuts in Medicaid, federally-funded jobs, food stamps, and AFDC. They conclude that "in some cases, the combined impact of the administrative budget proposal will reduce the income level of the poor to less than 50 percent of the poverty standard." The response of the administration's Office of Management and Budget is that they have "no great challenge to the figures." [39]

The union movement is not as strong nor as inclusive in the U.S. as it is in other western countries. Therefore, a larger proportion of salaried and wage-earning Americans do not have the support of unions to bargain for wage increases to keep up with the cost of living and inflation. As a result, some people who work full-time nonetheless live in poverty. Reagan policymakers do not have a strategy for the working poor other than the force of a free-market economy. And if American policy does not attempt any controls to prevent poverty among persons working full-time, then it is reasonable to assume that international economics will create more poverty in the U.S.

American political philosophy emphasizes individual responsibility and minimizes communal responsibility, as noted in Chapter 1. As a result, Americans tend to blame individuals for whatever unfavorable economic conditions they must endure. Other Western countries often place the blame for adverse conditions on the political and economic institutions of society.

SOME OBSERVATIONS

From this brief overview of seven countries certain general observations can be made. Every society examined has been seeking solutions to poverty. Irrespective of the specific political-economic system, each nation has made some progress toward a more equitable distribution of resources. None of the countries has been able to reach equity. Nor have they reached an egalitarian stage. Processes at work in all countries could lead one to speculate that equalitarianism will not be accomplished.

Several factors are common to each of the systems examined. Nations are not able to solve the problems of poverty, or a more equitable distribution of resources, or the raising of the standard of living in isolation from other countries of the world. International economic and political forces influence what can or cannot be done in a country. Sweden's effort to raise the standard of living and eliminate poverty is being threatened by international competition in the economic market. Israel has been highly dependent on a war economy and a flow of humanitarian dollars into the country. China is being influenced by its need to industrialize its urban areas to maintain a gross national product that will support a higher standard of living and increase employment. This requires economic intercourse with other nations. The Soviet Union is dependent on the importation of agricultural products and certain technology to maintain the economic growth required to assure the resources needed to provide a more equitable income.

When employing a socialist political-economic policy, countries primarily dependent on an agricultural economy are able to establish a more equitable distribution of resources and raise the standard of living of the masses in a shorter period of time. It seems inevitable, however, that industrialization quickly develops. As industrialization develops and more surplus is created, differential reward systems develop, and a wider range of income distribution occurs. A more diverse number of elite groups slowly come into being. Gerhard Lenski's theory of stratification seems to be demonstrated; namely, as surplus develops, the class structure is more fully developed and accentuated.[40]

Industrialization and specialization is accompanied by a greater number of rungs in the economic and occupational ladder. This creates the potential for relative deprivation. Individuals feel far more sharply the inadequacies of their own rewards as they see many others benefiting from the range of reward opportunities available. Each country reviewed in this chapter is experiencing this kind of deprivation among its people.

Though it has not been examined in detail in this chapter, family systems have an important influence on the nature of the political-economic system. Tanzania depended heavily on the solidarity of the extended family structure to develop its collective communities. China would have more conflict over the wage differential between the retired workers and the younger members of the family, had the respect for elders in the family and clan not been a part of that cultural heritage.

But it is also true that the immediate or nuclear family influences and encourages the differential reward system as surpluses develop in a society. Parents want to do the best they can for their children. The spouse wants to get ahead in order to gain benefits for family and posterity. It was this function of the family as an institution that led to the reinstatement of inheritance taxes in the Soviet Union in 1937, which was a major factor in changing the course of the revolution. There seems to be an inherent desire to gain security and prestige for the nuclear family, apart from the community, that will benefit one's offspring.

Finally, it seems ironic that in every society examined there is an ideology or belief system that holds high the virtue of being poor. Poor, in this instance, is not interpreted as being destitute.

Marx wrote, "The more the material world gains in value, the more the human world loses in value. One is directly related to the other." Mohammed prayed, "O Lord, grant that I live poor and die

poor." Both the Jewish writings of the Old Testament and the sayings of Jesus warn against the dangers of wealth and praise those
who have little.[41] And yet the followers of Marxian ideology, Jewish
tradition, Islamic religion, and the Christian faith have created
political-economic systems in which wealth is unequally distributed,
many are poor, relatively speaking, and too many live in poverty.
One cannot help but ask, "Why?" Is it perhaps in the nature of
human beings when in community, that systems they create prevent
the achievement of the ideal set for the community? And yet a common goal in each of the societies examined was to alleviate poverty.
Human societies need to operate from a value system stated by
Alphonse Gratry: "Poverty is neither destitution nor indigence. It is
everyday life won by labour. It is something sacred, to be respected,
to be prized, to be sought after." [42] Albert Tevoedjre has expressed
it this way: "I look on [poverty] as something useful, a lever in the
machinery of development as a sheet-anchor in a world in which
one must constantly rethink the way to fulfillment. . . . Poverty
looked on in this way, not as a fatality calling for resignation, but as
a positive value to be chosen freely, is a challenge to all the people
of the world." [43]

NOTES

1. Adoratsky, V., ed. *Karl Marx: Selected Works.* Vol. II. New York:
   International Publishers, 1933, pp. 563-564.
2. *Ibid.,* p. 566, fn. 1.
3. Yanovitch, Murray. *Social and Economic Inequality in the Soviet
   Union: Six Studies.* White Plains, New York: M. E. Sharpe, Publisher,
   1972, Chap. 1.
4. *Ibid.*
5. Schnitzer, Martin C., and James W. Nordyke, eds. *Comparative Economic Systems,* Second ed. Cincinnati: South-Western Publishing Co.,
   1977, pp. 425-426.
6. Matthews, Mervyn. *Class and Society in Soviet Russia.* New York:
   Walker and Company, 1972, p. 89.
7. *Ibid.,* p. 143.
8. United States Department of Health and Human Services. *Social
   Security Programs Throughout the World, 1979.* Washington, D.C.:
   Social Security Administration, Office of Policy, Office of Research
   and Statistics, Research Report No. 54, Rev. May, 1980.
9. Minkoff, Jack, and Lynn Turgson. "Income Maintenance in the
   Soviet Union in Eastern and Western Perspective," in *Equity, Income, and Policy: Comparative Studies in Three Worlds of Development,* ed. by Irving Louis Horowitz. New York: Praeger, 1977,
   pp. 179-182.

218   *International Approaches*

10. *Ibid.*
11. Whitney, Craig. "Pensions in the Soviet Union Leaving Many Elderly Impoverished," in *New York Times*, Nov. 11, 1978, pp. 1, 18.
12. Minkoff and Turgson, p. 200.
13. Taber, George. "Chinese Social Policy Today," in *The Journal of the Institute for Socioeconomic Studies*, Vol. IV, No. 2, Summer, 1979, p. 10.
14. Schnitzer, Marian C., and James W. Nordyke. Chap. 18. Ding Chen. "The Economic Development of China" in *Scientific American*, September, 1980, Vol. 243, No. 3, pp. 152-165.
15. Taber, p. 6.
16. *Ibid.*, p. 3.
17. *Ibid.*, p. 9.
18. Butterfield, Fox. "China's Elderly Find Good Life in Retirement" in *The New York Times*, July 29, 1979, pp. 1, 13.
19. *Ibid.*, p. 13.
20. Green, Reginald H. "Income Distribution and the Eradication of Poverty in Tanzania," in *Equity, Income and Policy: Comparative Studies in Three Worlds of Development*, ed. by Irving Louis Horowitz. New York: Praeger, 1977, p. 214.
21. Haq, Mahub Ul. *The Poverty Curtain: Choices for the Third World.* New York: Columbia University Press, 1976, Chap. 5.
22. Green, pp. 213-277.
23. Childs, Marquis W. *Sweden: The Middle Way on Trial.* New Haven: Yale University Press, 1980, p. 167.
24. *Ibid.*
25. U.S. Department of Health and Human Services and Ake Elmer, "Sweden's Model System of Social Services Administration" in *Meeting Human Needs: An Overview of Nine Countries*, ed. by Daniel Thursz and Joseph L. Vigilante. Beverly Hills, Calif.: Sage Publications, 1975, pp. 196-218.
26. Adams, Esther, "Social Welfare Programs in Sweden," in *Collected Papers on Poverty Issues*, ed. by Doris Yokelson. New York: Hudson Institute, June, 1975, pp. 261-291.
27. *Ibid.*, p. 263.
28. Wilensky, Harold L. The Welfare State and Equity. Berkeley: University of California Press, 1975, p. 1.
29. Marcarov, David. "Israel's Social Services: Historical Roots and Current Situation" in *Meeting Human Needs: An Overview of Nine Countries*, ed. by Daniel Thursz and Joseph L. Vigilante, Beverly Hills, Calif.: Sage Publications, 1975, pp. 130-153.
30. Bar-Yosef, Rivka. "Egalitarianism, Participation, and Policy-Making in Israel," in *Equity, Income, and Policy: Comparative Studies in Three Worlds of Development.* New York: Praeger, 1977, pp. 106-145.
31. *Ibid.*
32. *Ibid.*, p. 123.
33. Greenberg, Harold I., and Samuel Nadler. *Poverty in Israel: Eco-*

nomic Realities and the Promise of Social Justice. New York: Praeger, 1977.
34. *Ibid.*
35. Macarov.
36. Kincaid, J. C. *Poverty and Equality in Britain: A Study of Social Security and Taxation.* Baltimore: Penguin Books, 1973.
37. Townsend, Peter. *Poverty in the United Kingdom: A Survey of Household Resources and Standards of Living.* Berkeley: University of California Press, 1980.
38. Moynihan, Daniel Patrick. "Children and Welfare Reform" in the *Journal of the Institute for Socioeconomic Studies,* Vol. VI, No. 1, Spring, 1981, pp. 1-20.
39. *Ibid.,* pp. 20 and 181.
40. Lenski, Gerhard. *Power and Privilege: A Theory of Social Stratification.* New York: McGraw-Hill, 1966.
41. Tevoedjre, Albert. *Poverty: Wealth of Mankind.* Oxford: Pergamon Press, 1978, Chap. 1.
42. From sources by Alphonse Gratry quoted by Albert Tevoedjre in *Poverty: Wealth of Mankind.*
43. Tevoedjre, p. 10.

SUGGESTED READINGS

Greenberg, Harold I. and Samuel Nadler. *Poverty in Israel: Economic Realities and the Promise of Social Justice.* New York: Praeger, 1977. An excellent analysis of the economic and political development of Israel. It provides a rather complete description of present economic conditions and of the social services provided for Israel's citizens.

Haq, Mahbub Ul. *The Poverty Curtain: Choices for the Third World.* New York: Columbia University Press, 1976. The author writes from having experienced development programs in Pakistan as well as working in the western world with economic and political agencies that were developing strategies to help the developing countries. He has changed his opinion on strategies to be used in the developing countries and outlines what the new strategies should be.

Horowitz, Irving Louis, ed. *Equity, Income and Policy: Comparative Studies in Three Worlds of Development.* New York: Praeger, 1977. A series of thorough articles by specialists on different countries of the world, including Russia, Israel, Sweden, China, Tanzania, and the United States. Policies intended to create greater equity are examined. Not the easiest book to read but very informative and thorough.

Tevoedjre, Albert. *Poverty: Wealth of Mankind.* Oxford: Pergamon Press, 1978. The author is the director of the International Institute for Labour Studies at the Hague. He advocates looking at poverty as a positive value. Third World countries are urged by him not to fall into the trap of western values. An exciting, stimulating, and rewarding little book.

Taussig, A. Dale. *Poverty in a Dual Economy.* New York: St. Martins Press, 1975. In a perceptive way, Taussig examines the consequences of an economy that maintains the nonpoor in a way of life that is impossible for the poor. He compares the consequences of experiencing such a dual economy in a developing country in contrast to a developed country.

STUDY QUESTIONS

1. Review the problems that are common to the programs of each of the countries examined in Chapter 8. Analyze those problems and draw some conclusions that may provide guidance in seeking a solution to the unequal distribution of wealth in a society.

2. Some argue that poverty develops because the systems human beings create to regulate the distribution of resources contain the seeds of eventual inequality. Others argue that the greed of human beings is the cause of inequity. On the basis of the analysis in Chapter 8, develop a case for both positions.

3. Using the definition that "values are criteria used to make choices," develop a value system for society that would result in an economic system that would assure a more equitable distribution of resources. (This is not an easy task but a very fruitful endeavor as a learning experience.)

4. Use the material provided in Chapter 4 and Chapter 8 to assess the possible success or failure of the political and economic policies of Sweden.

5. In Chapter 7, ethical questions of justice and equity were examined. Using the arguments presented by Robert Stivers, assess the programs of the countries discussed in Chapter 8 and determine which program is most successful in meeting the criteria he established.

6. Using the definitions of capitalism, socialism, welfare state, and communism, decide how much each of the countries discussed demonstrates the characteristics of these political-economic types.